SOCIETY FOR NEW TESTAMENT STUDIES
MONOGRAPH SERIES

GENERAL EDITOR
MATTHEW BLACK, D.D., F.B.A.

10

ISRAEL IN THE APOSTOLIC CHURCH

ISRAEL IN THE APOSTOLIC CHURCH

BY

PETER RICHARDSON

CAMBRIDGE
AT THE UNIVERSITY PRESS
1969

Published by the Syndics of the Cambridge University Press
Bentley House, 200 Euston Road, London N.W. 1
American Branch: 32 East 57th Street, New York, N.Y. 10022

© Cambridge University Press 1969

Library of Congress Catalogue Card Number: 74-79055

Standard Book Number: 521 07592 0

Printed in Great Britain
at the University Printing House, Cambridge
(Brooke Crutchley, University Printer)

CONTENTS

CONTENTS

PREFACE

The publication of dissertations is always attended by serious difficulties, which the present work cannot claim to have avoided. It has been revised in the hope of making a technical piece of research more readable, but the basic form of the original has been retained. Parts have been rewritten, some of the detail has been removed and other larger portions of it revised and brought up to date.

The work was originally presented to Cambridge University in 1965 in fulfilment of the requirements for the degree of Doctor of Philosophy. Since then much has been written impinging on the subject, the most important of which has been read and has now found its way into the footnotes.

In the preparation of the manuscript for publication I was greatly assisted by the Rev. Alex Zeidman of the Scott Mission, Toronto, and by Mr Herbert Simmonds. To them much of the credit must go for what degree of accuracy and exactness the book maintains, though of course the responsibility for the errors that will have crept in rests solely upon me.

I would like publicly to express my debt to the Rev. Professor C. F. D. Moule of Clare College, Cambridge, for his encouragement at every stage of the work; his interest has been a source of joy. I am also indebted to the Rev. Principal J. Stanley Glen of Knox College, Toronto, for my first taste of the excitement of New Testament study, and to the Rev. Dr William Fitch of Knox Presbyterian Church, Toronto, for the demonstration of the challenge of applying scholarship to the consistent weekly exposition of the scriptures of the Old and New Testaments. I have learned from the example of all of these men how love for Jesus Christ results in a commitment to the Word of God and respect for it. None of them will agree with all that I have said, but, if the volume has any dedication, it is to these mentors in the study and application of the Bible.

G. P. R.

Toronto, Canada
1969

INTRODUCTION

The heart of this book, as a glance at the Table of Contents will make clear, is the chapter on Paul. The reason for this is the obvious one that we have in these epistles good information about developments over a period spanning parts of three decades within early Christianity. Paul's letters always form one focus for investigation into life and thought of the early Church.

In order to prepare for this extended analysis of Paul's letters, the book opens with a general statement of the problems connected with the Christian take-over of the name 'Israel'. Since this is the subject of considerable discussion a starting-point has been taken on the interpretation of which there would be little dispute. This fixed point is found in Justin Martyr. The historical phenomena of the period to A.D. 160 are also discussed in order to discover what part these external factors might have had upon the relationship between Jew and Christian.

A more positive assessment follows of the development of the Christian awareness of the need to appropriate Jewish titles and privileges. The first stage in this development is Jesus. The Pauline material is considered at length and the post-Pauline developments are examined sketchily to show how these relax the fundamental tension which exists between Jesus' and Paul's attitude to the problems posed by Israel's unbelief. An attempt is made to show how far each had progressed towards an identification of the Church with Israel. The concluding synthesis describes and accounts for two important facts: first, that the name 'Israel' is applied to the Church at all, and second, that it was only applied at a late date. The position adopted here is that 'Israel' is never specifically applied to the Church until Justin equates the two in his *Dialogue with Trypho*. In the New Testament, and in the Apostolic Fathers, there are many, and growing, indications of the need for this identification, but it is not made openly until *c*. A.D. 160.

Three Appendices are included which more fully document the approach suggested on the *Apology* of Aristides, Paul's use of λαός, and the attitude of the sects of Judaism to 'Israel'.

The method adopted in footnotes is to cite in the first instance the full bibliographical information, and thereafter to use an obvious abbreviation of the title. In some cases the title of an article is omitted when the context makes plain the subject the author is discussing. Series of commentaries are cited by author's name, series, edition, and date. Fuller information is given under the list of abbreviations.

Biblical and other references are given in the usual abbreviations. Generally quotations or allusions are my own translation unless specifically acknowledged. All references to the Greek Old Testament are given in the Septuagint numbering, including those for the *Psalms of Solomon*.

TEXTS AND ABBREVIATIONS

Standard Texts:

NT   *Novum Testamentum Graece cum apparatu critico*, ed. E. Nestle revised by E. Nestle and K. Aland (Stuttgart, 1963, 25th edition).

OT (BH, MT)   *Biblica Hebraica*, ed. R. Kittel, P. Kahle with A. Alt and O. Eissfeldt (Stuttgart, 1945, 5th edition).

LXX   *Septuaginta*, 2 vols., ed. A. Rahlfs (Stuttgart, no date, 6th edition).

Qumran   *Discoveries in the Judean Desert*, 1 ff. ed. D. Barthélemy, J. T. Milik (Oxford, 1955 ff.). Other texts noted where relevant.

Standard Works:

Bauer/A–G   *A Greek–English Lexicon of the NT and other Early Christian Literature* by W. Bauer, translated and adapted by W. F. Arndt and F. W. Gingrich (Cambridge, 1957).

Bl–D/Funk   *A Greek Grammar of the NT and other Early Christian Literature* by F. Blass and A. Debrunner, translation and revision of the 9th–10th German Edition by R. W. Funk (Cambridge, 1961).

Liddell–Scott   *A Greek–English Lexicon* compiled by H. G. Liddell and R. Scott, revised and augmented by H. S. Jones (Oxford, 1940).

Moule, *Idiom*   *An Idiom-Book of NT Greek*, C. F. D. Moule (Cambridge, 1960, second edition).

Moulton   *A Grammar of NT Greek*, I, *Prolegomena*, J. H. Moulton (Edinburgh, 1908, 3rd edition).

Moulton/Howard   *A Grammar of NT Greek*, II, *Accidence and Word Formation*, J. H. Moulton and W. F. Howard (Edinburgh, 1929).

Moulton/Turner   *A Grammar of NT Greek*, III, *Syntax*, J. H. Moulton and Nigel Turner (Edinburgh, 1963).

MM	*The Vocabulary of the Greek Testament illustrated from the Papyri and other non-literary sources*, J. H. Moulton and G. Milligan (London, 1914–29).
RAC	*Reallexikon für Antike und Christentum, Sachwörterbuch zur Auseinandersetzung des Christentums mit der antiken Welt*, ed. T. Klauser (Stuttgart, 1950 ff.).
RGG	*Die Religion in Geschichte und Gegenwart, Handwörterbuch für Theologie und Religionswissenschaft*, ed. K. Galling (Tübingen, 1957 ff., third edition).
StrBill	*Kommentar zum neuen Testament aus Talmud und Midrasch*, H. L. Strack and P. Billerbeck, 5 vols. in 6 (München, 1922 ff.).
TWNT	*Theologisches Wörterbuch zum NT*, ed. G. Kittel, G. Friedrich (Stuttgart, 1933 ff.).
TDNT	*Theological Dictionary of the NT*, ed. G. Kittel, translated from the preceding by G. W. Bromiley (Grand Rapids, Michigan, 1964 ff.).

Commentaries (in citing commentaries where the name is obvious from the context only the series name and date is given):

BNTC	*Black's NT Commentaries* (London).
CGT	*Cambridge Greek Testament* (Cambridge).
CGTC	*Cambridge Greek Testament Commentaries* (Cambridge).
CNT	*Commentaire du nouveau testament* (Neuchâtel).
Ellicott	Commentaries by Bishop C. J. Ellicott, usually entitled *A Critical and Grammatical Commentary on...* (London).
EtBib	*Études Bibliques* (Paris).
HNT	*Handbuch zum neuen Testament* (Tübingen).
HTK	*Herders theologischer Kommentar zum neuen Testament* (Freiburg).
ICC	*International Critical Commentary* (Edinburgh).
KEK	*Kritisch-exegetischer Kommentar über das neue Testament*, begründet von H. A. W. Meyer (Göttingen).
McM	Commentaries published by MacMillan's of London, not strictly a series but all following the same format and originally intended to form a

	complete set by Lightfoot, Hort and Westcott. Later, others were asked to fill in the missing volumes, with some duplication.
MNTC	*The Moffatt New Testament Commentary* (London).
NCB	*New Clarendon Bible* (Oxford).
NLC = *NICNT*	*New London Commentary* (London), the English version of the American series, *New International Commentary on the NT* (Grand Rapids, Michigan).
NTD	*Das neue Testament deutsch* (Göttingen).
RNT	*Regensburger neues Testament* (Regensburg).
ThHNT	*Theologische Handkommentar zum neuen Testament* (Leipzig).
TNTC	*Tyndale NT Commentary* (London).
WC	*Westminster Commentaries* (London).

CHAPTER I

THE CHURCH AND ISRAEL

THE HISTORICAL PROBLEM

The word 'Israel' is applied to the Christian Church for the first time by Justin Martyr *c.* A.D. 160. It is a symptom of the developing take-over by Christians of the prerogatives and privileges of Jews. Initially there is hesitancy about this transposition: but a growing recognition of the necessity to appropriate titles and attributes ensures a complete transfer. The date A.D. 160 corresponds roughly with the beginning of a new attitude to Judaism. Prior to this time there is a measure of continuity between the Church and Israel: they are able to talk together, in some places to worship together, to expect and receive converts from one to the other; but after the mid-second century these possibilities seem to disappear and discontinuity becomes more radical.

The break did not happen suddenly. It is clear that the appropriation of 'Israel' as a designation for the Church is not itself the motivation for a change in attitude, but is the sign of something far more profound. Justin's *Dialogue with Trypho*, in which this transposition is effected at last, is not itself the great divide. In the creative step in which the equation is made explicit—'Church' = 'true Israel'—Justin gives accurate expression to a long-standing tendency to increase the degree to which Christianity views itself as the heir of all which Israel once possessed. Justin also witnesses to the fact that in A.D. 160 there is still a sensitivity to the close relationship which obtains between Christianity and Judaism: Justin and Trypho can talk reasonably, without malice, and to a large extent from common ground.

If the complete transposition from Israel to Christianity is not effected until such a date, what are the factors which work towards it? Is it possible to isolate a point, or a principle, or an historical factor which inevitably determines the way in which the later argument would develop? While acknowledging the radical nature of the life, death and resurrection of Jesus Christ, it is necessary to recognize that his disciples, even after his death, are still within the bounds of Judaism. Ensuing developments create a *de facto* break between Jews and Christians from place to place but, theologically, the break remains an inference within the NT and not an explicit requirement. Can we pinpoint the earliest steps away from Judaism by the early Church, which set the pace for the later developments? Can we find in Jesus' words and in the Evangelists' reports of those words traces of the break? Can we find in Paul's writings a new step on the way to separation? What part does Judaism play? What are the principles which determine the course later reflection on the problem of the relationship between Jew and Christian takes?

Such an examination has some hope of success. Even if it must rely upon inference and, to some extent, speculation, it is a quest that should not be avoided. The 'parting of the roads'[1] is of great importance for the history of both Christianity and Judaism. Misunderstanding of it colours the Church's attitude to Judaism and contributes to anti-Semitism. None the less, the parting is two-sided. Each engages in controversy with the other, and each addresses an informed apologetic to the other. But the evidence which we have seems also to speak of a Christian concern for Judaism, and especially of the desire to show Jews the truth of Jesus Christ.

In the earliest period there is a theological necessity, from the Christian side, to retain close communication with Jews. Only slowly does this need give way, in the face of the *de facto* break, to the other solution of actively asserting Christianity's right to all those things which it finds valuable in Judaism. It transposes what it can, transforms other things, and leaves behind what has no value. This shift from an actual to a theoretical state of affairs is very important, but so close are the NT authors to their own situation that it goes unrecognized by them. It is not until after the close of the NT period that consistent consideration is directed towards this theoretical side. We shall attempt to trace this shift, and to describe and discuss the factors

[1] The title of a book edited by F. J. Foakes Jackson (London, 1912), being 'Studies in the Development of Judaism and Early Christianity' by members of Jesus College, Cambridge. Unfortunately only one essay, by Ephraim Levine, deals with the 'breach'.

which are at work in it. The centre of interest is in the name
'Israel'. It is the most crucial prerogative pertaining to the
people of God, and for that reason it later provides the most
powerful apologetic device.[1] We shall also consider other aspects
of Jewish life and practice and the degree to which Christians
assert their right to them.

THE SOCIOLOGICAL PROBLEM

The relationships between Jew and Christian present a borderline situation; like all boundary cases, this confrontation between
similar yet different groups poses the greatest problems and
creates the most violent upheavals. In our own day the relations
between Communist China and Communist Russia are a close
parallel. A large measure of agreement is coupled with a small,
but significant and growing area of disagreement, creating the
tension that ends in rupture. A few ecclesiastical examples are
the Anglican/Methodist difficulties in the eighteenth century,
the Exclusive/Open Brethren break in the early nineteenth
century, and the Presbyterian splintering in the mid-nineteenth
century in Scotland.[2] Such events are often marked by great
bitterness and opposition.

When one examines the NT records, it is evident that the
early difficulty in the proclamation of the faith is the transition
to a Gentile mission. In fact the Jewish mission is the one which
questions the accepted presuppositions more thoroughly. When
one is thrown up against fellows rather than opposites, one is
driven to the most searching re-examination of the basic tenets.
It is often easier to be a missionary to pagans than to neighbours.

Amos, Ezekiel, John the Baptist, and Jesus: each faces his
nation with a boundary-line problem. Each comes in the first
instance with a creative message from God for his own people,
setting apart those who respond to the challenge as a slightly
different group—a sect. Each creates a new boundary-line or

[1] One could also say the same things of the OT scriptures. There is the
same importance, apologetic value, and reluctance to be explicit about their
exclusive transfer to Christians.

[2] A similar observation has been made concerning the Jewish non-
conformist sects of the first century in their relationship to the ortho-praxis
of the Pharisees, by Matthew Black, *The Scrolls and Christian Origins* (London,
1961), p. 166.

I-2

shifts the old one. The degree to which the developing group becomes self-contained affects the speed with which the boundary-line is transformed into a wall of separation. With the OT prophets this never really happened. Even in the NT this is not a straight-line development where the same changes take place everywhere at the same time; there are local variations of time and emphasis. Generally, similar solutions to the tensions created by the boundary are adopted. There are two approaches to the inevitable dissolution of the tension: erasure of the boundary-line by giving up the distinctiveness of the new; or erection of a dividing wall so that the new might be emphasized in isolation and the old let go. In the latter case the wall may be erected from the other side too, of course, by the explicit rejection of everything new. Our problem is to examine this tension, not only between the two sides of the border, but also between the two approaches to the dissolution of the tension.

THE THEOLOGICAL PROBLEM

Theological issues are raised by such considerations. One cannot speak of the historical factors at work impelling one or the other solution, without at the same time recognizing the underlying theological issues which must have been in the minds of those who influence the direction events take. The central issue, theologically, is the relationship of the Church to Israel after the work of Christ is finished. In any attempt to define the problem more exactly consideration must first be given to questions raised by such a seemingly simple assertion. In order to do this, it is necessary to start back in the time before Christ.

In the prophetic writings the doctrines of election and of the remnant begin to be used to distinguish what is and is not Israel. The criterion of birth remains a factor, but faithfulness to the covenant of God is stressed increasingly. At the same time there is an incipient universalizing of Judaism, so that there is a dual possibility: a narrowing of the category 'Israel' within Judaism, and an opening up of the same designation to some from outside. There is a distinction between these two tendencies, however: the one is based on ritual and ethical standards and is present and observable; the other is an eschatological conception.

The exclusivist tendency is complicated by the distinction between Northern and Southern Kingdoms—between Israel and Judah—where a nationalistic criterion for this limitation is substituted for one which is based on purity of heart. Both Judah and Ephraim lay claim to God's favour. Each national entity tends to absolutize itself in an almost sectarian way, though Hosea and Ezekiel clearly show that in very different contexts the sense of unity has not been lost altogether: there is an eschatological possibility that God will overcome the present separation.

Sectarian tendencies increase in the inter-testamental period.[1] Polemical and apologetic considerations lead groups to posit such a discontinuity between themselves and the rest of Israel that they move towards an identification of their own sect with 'Israel'. Antagonism often leads to the assumption that those not with them are no longer a part of Israel. This tendency exercises a widespread influence.

Against this background, John the Baptist appears in Palestinian Judaism. His relation to Qumran, while important, is incidental to this analysis. What is important is the purpose and significance of his baptism. One theory holds that it is basically a proselyte baptism which has for its presupposition that all Jews have forfeited their right to be Israelites, have become as Gentiles, and therefore have to be readmitted.[2] This may overstate the case, and need not be pressed, but certainly his baptism implied

[1] See Appendix C: cf. W. Förster, *Palestinian Judaism in New Testament Times* (Edinburgh, 1964), pp. 187 ff.

[2] See R. Eisler, *The Messiah Jesus and John the Baptist* (London, 1931), pp. 267–70; W. H. Brownlee, in *The Scrolls and the New Testament*, ed. K. Stendahl (London, 1958), pp. 33–53, esp. p. 37; cf. also A. Oepke, art. βάπτω etc., *TDNT*, I, 529–46, esp. p. 537. C. H. H. Scobie, *John the Baptist* (London, 1964), criticizes this view but not convincingly, and he finally arrives at a point not far removed from Brownlee, cf. pp. 99 f., 101 with 114. G. R. Beasley-Murray, *Baptism in the New Testament* (London, 1962), adopts a mediating position, e.g. pp. 18, 31, 41 f. (although he rejects the identification of proselyte baptism with John's baptism); both he and W. R. Farmer (art. *Interpreters' Dictionary of the Bible*, Nashville, 1962, *s.v.*) emphasize the eschatological nature of the act. Cf. also P. Vielhauer, art. 'Johannes', *RGG*, III, cols. 804 ff.; H. H. Rowley, *HUCA*, xv (1940), 313 ff. On the origin of proselyte baptism, see T. F. Torrance, *NTS*, I (1954–5), 150–4; *per contra*, T. M. Taylor, *NTS*, II (1955–6), 193–8.

a large degree of discontinuity between those who sought it and those who rejected it. Whether these formed, in John's teaching, the true Israel as over against Judaism we shall probably never know, but we can say with reasonable assurance that there is a quite sharp discontinuity on the one hand, with at least a latent possibility of the universalizing of God's fellowship on genuinely equal terms on the other. John is a marginal case, part of both old and new.

This is the background for an assessment of the measure of continuity and discontinuity between Jew and Israelite. It becomes a more acute problem with Jesus' Incarnation, life, death and Resurrection, and with the fulfilment of the old which he claims for his life and work. Can there be any continuity between the previous entity and its continuation after the Easter events? If the answer is affirmative, what are the relationships between the various groups involved: the people of God before Christ, the people of God after Christ, Judaism, Israel, the Church? We cannot simply draw a diagram so that all comes to a focus in Jesus, and when the lines broaden out on this side introduce completely new categories or thoroughly transpose the old ones. In this interpretation, at the one moment when Christ is alone on the cross, he and he alone is 'Israel'.[1] The conclusion drawn from this is that 'Israel' then comes to be applied to those who follow Christ after the event. There can be no continuity between Israel B.C. and A.D. because, in this scheme, the continuation loses all significance. There would, therefore, be no need even to look at the post-Easter relationships. This we reject; for, while there is theological truth to the assertion, it obscures history hopelessly.

Another position might be described, beginning from the observation that parts of the NT testify to a continuation of a group after Easter called 'Israel' which is distinct from the Christian Church. If so, there is a valid continuity between 'Israel' before and after Christ. This we suggest is the new situation which accounts for many of the problems faced in the NT. Jesus' coming has not obliterated all distinctions. We suggest as a preliminary hypothesis that some of the NT pre-

---

[1] This can be found from Justin to Barth, but it is nowhere said in the NT, although perhaps inferred in a non-schematic form in a passage such as John 15: 1 ff.

supposes a distinction between Jew and Israel outside Christianity. Together with the failure of the NT to assert that Jesus is himself 'Israel', this is evidence against a schematic view, which holds that the Church is the continuation of 'Israel' B.C., and that any other physical continuation is not the People of God. The issue at stake is the degree to which the Church fulfils and supersedes what Israel is. It must be affirmed that the Church is both continuous and discontinuous with Israel B.C. There is also discontinuity between the Church and Israel A.D. In spite of the many attributes, characteristics, privileges and prerogatives of the latter which are applied to the former, the Church is not called Israel in the NT. The continuity between Israel and the Church is partial; and the discontinuity between Israel B.C. and its continuation A.D. is partial. The two sides of the problem must be retained: What is the continuity and discontinuity between Israel B.C. and A.D.; and between Israel and the Church?

In the same way that there are historical relationships before Christ bearing upon the main theological problem, so there are practical relationships after Christ which elucidate the central problem and provide the only background against which it can be understood. There are four groups to be considered, connected with four dissimilar words that play a large part in the investigation: Jew, Israel, Gentile, Church. Some combinations of these are important for us.

(*a*) We shall have to determine whether there is a distinction between Jew and Israel after the Resurrection. We have maintained the theoretical possibility, but we must investigate whether the distinction is submerged or retained.

(*b*) The relationship of the Gentile to Jew-Israel (to blur the categories) is relevant as a means of explaining the reaction of the earliest Church to universalizing tendencies and the problem of mission.

(*c*) What then is the attitude of the Church to Gentile mission? Later it is assumed that only Gentiles will respond, but in the earliest period this is balanced by the Church's close tie to Judaism-Israel.

(*d*) We must investigate carefully how the Church interprets itself *vis-à-vis* the Jew who was not convinced of the Messianic claims of Jesus.

(*e*) And finally, we must determine the relationship of the Church to Israel.

This last constitutes the real borderline case, and thus demands caution. Its importance lies in the fact that it poses in an historical setting the question discussed above in a theological setting. Most of our data for establishing the theological conclusion will have to be developed from the historical analysis.

(*f*) An appended relationship is that between Christians of a Gentile origin and those of a Jewish origin. It is a microcosm of the larger issues noted above. In the light of the claim by some that 'Israel' describes Jewish Christians alone, it might indeed suggest that there is a serious exclusivist limitation to the kind of continuity that obtains.

There is one further preliminary observation: the conditions were not static. The historical and practical situations presuppose shifting relationships in which one stage of development may not obtain elsewhere. Whether the theological awareness lagged behind or went ahead of the actual situation is not always clear; probably it more often lagged. Furthermore, there must have been considerable tension between various factions in the early Church, so that there was not a single normative view of the relationship of the Church to Israel. From a necessarily analytical approach a synthesis will be attempted on a different level. What factors were at work moulding these opinions and creating these fluctuations, and finally developing a monolithic view of the Church/Israel relationship?

CHAPTER II

THE CHURCH FATHERS TO A.D. 160

JUSTIN AND THE TRUE ISRAEL

In his *Dialogue with Trypho* Justin asks Trypho and his friends:
'What is the force (δύναμις) of the name, Israel?'[1] This also is
the question asked here, but not in an etymological sense like
Justin's.[2] The other side of the question is: What does 'Israel'
signify in relation to the Church? There is no doubt about the
answer given in the dialogue: Ἰσραηλιτικὸν γὰρ τὸ ἀληθινόν,
πνευματικόν, καὶ Ἰούδα γένος καὶ Ἰακὼβ καὶ Ἰσαὰκ καὶ
Ἀβραάμ...ἡμεῖς ἐσμεν.[3] The transference from Israel to the
Church is complete; but, and this is the point we wish to make,
Justin's dialogue with Trypho is the first time in Christian
literature that such an explicit claim has been made.

One of the obvious marks of this transference is the increased
emphasis on newness and finality. This comes in the opening
paragraphs of the first main section, e.g. 11.2 f.: 'For in fact
I have read, Trypho, that there is to be both a final Law and a
Disposition (τελευταῖος νόμος καὶ διαθήκη) that is superior to
all others (κυριωτάτη πασῶν), which must now be observed by
all those who lay claim to the inheritance of God. For the law
given at Horeb is already antiquated (παλαιός) and belongs to
you alone, but that other belongs to all men absolutely. And a
Law set over against a law has made the one before it to cease.'[4]
Something of this same force is evident in the concern for
'twoness', as in 12.3: 'A second circumcision is now neces-

---

[1] 125.1: for translation and numbering, see A. Lukyn Williams (London,
1930), *Translations of Christian Literature*, Series 1; for text see J. C. T. Otto,
Iustini Philosophi et Martyris Opera (Jena, 1876, 3rd edition).
[2] The answer is given christologically (125.3): 'a man overcoming
power'.
[3] 11.5; much of 10–29 is concerned with this same question, and the
contrast: failure among you, acceptance among us, is present in much of the
dialogue; note especially 14.1; 29.1, 2; 55.3; 63.5; 87.5; 116.3; and see
below.
[4] Cf. also e.g. 11.4; 24.1; 33.1; 43.1.

sary',[1] which carries with it an implication which comes to the surface clearly in 63.5—we are to leave the old behind and 'forget even the old customs of our fathers'.

As well as a general transference (82.1: 'what was of old in your nation has been transferred (μετετέθη) to us'), specific items become the property of Christians. In the same passage, the gifts of prophecy are mentioned, and a little later it is said that scripture is now misinterpreted by Jews (82.3; the example follows in 83, cf. 84.4; 55.3) because they are Christian scriptures, not Jewish (29.2: 'your scriptures, or rather not yours but ours, for we obey them'). So also, Christian sacrifices are better (29.1; 117.1) because they are now the high-priestly race (116.3). This is because they have believed and Jews have not (14.1). Specific typological transferences are made also: the flour offering becomes the bread of the Eucharist (41.1); sacrifices generally become bread and wine (41.3); circumcision becomes a spiritual circumcision (41.4); the seventh day is superseded by the eighth (41: 4); the twelve bells on the priest's robe are now the Twelve Apostles (42.1). Generally the principle is: 'all the other things...appointed by Moses [are] types, and figures, and announcements...' (42.4).

Justin deals at length with the hardness of the Jews and their rejection of the good news offered by the Messiah,[2] as well as noting at numerous points the active opposition of the Jews to the progress of the gospel.[3] The corollary to this is an unparalleled emphasis on the Gentiles as the heirs of these promises (particularly 109 ff.), whose 'otherness' is so stressed that a Gentile exclusiveness almost replaces the former Jewish exclusiveness.[4] Along with this he implies that to accept Christianity means the abandonment of one's Jewishness (cf. 64.5).

In asserting that Christianity is the true Israel (and Jacob), Justin maintains that Christ himself is Israel and Jacob. 'Israel

---

[1] On this 'need' cf. 19.3, 5; on 'second' cf. 113.6; 114.4; and 135.6: 'two seeds of Judah, two races, two houses of Jacob'.

[2] See 12.2; 18.2; 27.4; 33.1; 44.1; 46.5.

[3] Note the Synagogue Ban (16.4; 38.1; 96.2; 137.2) and the messengers who denounce the Christian heresy to the world (17.1; 108.2; 117.3).

[4] Cf. especially 119 ff.; e.g. 119.3: ἡμεῖς λαὸς ἕτερος...ἡμεῖς δὲ οὐ μόνον λαὸς ἀλλὰ καὶ λαὸς ἅγιός ἐσμεν, and 119.4: τοῦτο γάρ ἐστιν ἐκεῖνο τὸ ἔθνος, and 122.6. This same theme is found in the *First Apology*, 52–3.

and Jacob' is a catchphrase,[1] but it is not completely clear whether the equation Christ = Israel + Jacob, or Christians = Israel + Jacob is the primary one in his exegesis. In any event, the result is that the Church is now Israel, so that after the exposition the question which comes to Trypho's mind is: 'Are you Israel, and does He say all this about you?' (123.7), to which the answer is returned: 'so also we...are...both called and in fact are Jacob and Israel and Judah and Joseph and David, and true children of God' (καὶ θεοῦ τέκνα ἀληθινὰ καλούμεθα καί ἐσμεν, 123.9).[2] A little later he says again: 'As therefore he (quoting Isa. 43: 15) calls Christ Israel and Jacob, so also we, quarried from the bowels of Christ, are the true race of Israel' ('Ισραηλιτικὸν τὸ ἀληθινόν ἐσμεν γένος: 135.3). Christians are a *genos* which has superseded the Jewish race, and

---

[1] So W. Bousset, in his chapter on Justin in *Jüdischchristlicher Schulbetrieb in Alexandria und Rom: literarische Untersuchungen zu Philo und Clemens von Alexandria, Justin und Irenaüs* (Göttingen, 1915), *FRLANT*, neue Folge, 6 Heft, pp. 294 f., referring to chapters 121–3; and later, pp. 296 f.: 'Mit Kap 130 lenkt Justin dann sichtlich zum Jakob = Israel-Thema zurück...Der λαός, so deduziert Justin, ist nicht das empirische Israel, es sind Abraham, Isaak und Jakob und alle Gott Wohlgefälligen im Volk des alten Bundes, aber nicht dieses Volk selbst...Das empirische Israel...kann unmöglich das wahre Jakob und Israel sein (131–133)!...Christus ist Israel...Christus is Jakob und Israel...Das Thema ist: die Christen, das neue Gottesvolk, das wahre Jakob und Israel (Juda).'

[2] On chapter 123 see P. Prigent, *Justin et l'Ancien Testament: l'argumentation scripturaire du traité de Justin contre toutes les hérésies comme source principale du dialogue avec Tryphon et de la première apologie* (Paris, 1964), p. 298: 'Le lecteur reste étonné: Pourquoi, dans ce développement sur le nom d'Israël comme appellation des chrétiens, Justin ne dit-il pas: de même que les juifs ont porté le nom de Jacob-Israël, de même nous sommes, depuis le Christ (annoncé comme Israël par les prophètes), appelés Israël, nous qui sommes de sa race? Ne serait-ce pas parce que Justin emprunte la citation à un document qui l'invoquait dans le seul but d'y trouver la prophétie du Christ comme Israël et Jacob?' See also his conclusion on p. 309: 'Au ch. 123 Justin commence à démontrer que les chrétiens sont le véritable Israël. Mais bientôt il bute sur la citation d'Is. 42: 1–4, texte qui, dans sa source, est utilisé à deux fins: pour annoncer les noms du Christ, et pour justifier la prétention des chrétiens à être le véritable Israël. Justin se laisse entrainer à interrompre son développement pour insérer (*Dial.* 123.7–129) tout le chapitre de sa source vers lequel l'oriente Is. 42. Cette parenthèse une fois fermée, notre auteur recommence à puiser dans le chapitre universaliste dont il avait entrepris la mise en œuvre (*Dial.* 117–123.6). Voilà pourquoi on retrouve Is. 42: 1–4...puis Jer. 31: 27, Ez. 36: 12 etc....'

this demands a complete taking over of the name 'Israel'. In the context of each of these statements there is a contrast between 'you' and 'we' which often comes to the surface in an exclusive sense, as e.g. in 134.3: 'Now Leah is your people and the synagogue (ὁ λαὸς ὑμῶν καὶ ἡ συναγωγή) but Rachel is our Church' (ἡ ἐκκλησία ἡμῶν), or in a comparative sense as in 118.3: 'we [are] of more understanding and of more religion than you who think yourselves lovers of God and men of understanding'. By the middle of the second century the Church in its apologetic has effected a total transposition. This is not surprising, for (in the words of E. R. Goodenough[1]):

in a community which considered itself as having accessible for every man that Entire Law which made the partial Law obsolete, a new group feeling would inevitably arise on the Pauline suggestion that the Christian communion was the true Israel...The sense of superiority had been sharpened by a century of controversy and amplification.

Goodenough goes on, however, to say in the same place: 'It is only remarkable that Justin should still have been liberal enough to admit communion with the conservative party...', and this liberality is remarkable.[2] One is constantly struck by the reasonable tone, and by the hope that is often expressed.[3] This appears in connection with the second coming of Christ, when he hopes 'that some of you can be found to belong to [the seed] which...is left over unto eternal salvation' (32.2).[4] The most generous and expectant features are, first, the fact that

[1] *The Theology of Justin Martyr* (Jena, 1923), p. 122.

[2] So also Williams, *Justin*, p. viii: 'The treatise in fact implies a very much closer intercourse between Christians and Jews in the middle of the second century than has been commonly accepted.' Cf. L. W. Barnard, *VT*, XIV, 4 (1964), 395–406.

[3] Cf. A. L. Williams, *Adversus Judaeos: A Bird's Eye View of Christian Apologies until the Renaissance* (Cambridge, 1935), p. 42: '...the discussion was conducted in a seemly way, and the impression that we get from it is far more favourable than that which we get from the majority of our treatises... Both were earnest and sincere, and neither shows any sign of desiring merely a verbal victory...there is no Dialogue as such which is conducted on quite so high a level of courteousness and fairness until Gilbert Crispin's at Westminster at the end of the eleventh century.' Cf. A. Puech, *Les Apologistes Grecs du 11ᵉ siècle de notre ère* (Paris, 1912), p. 147.

[4] Cf. also 14.8; 35.8; 38.2; 39.2; 44.1; 102.7; 108.7.

such a conversation is accepted as possible about A.D. 160; and secondly, the irenic conclusion to the discussion in 142.3. Justin, in spite of his exclusive tendencies, still allows for Jews and Gentiles to be co-heirs in the Kingdom.[1]

The characteristics, then, of Justin's *Dialogue* are: (1) a sharp, though not absolute, discontinuity between the old people of God and Jews after the cross; (2) a similarly sharp discontinuity between Gentiles and Jews as possible recipients of the grace of God in Jesus Christ; (3) a close relationship between the righteous in the old times and the new people of God, the Christians; (4) yet, in spite of all this, the Church and Jews can still talk reasonably together.

There are two difficulties requiring explanation. The first is how to account for Justin's being the first to apply 'Israel' to the Christian Church, particularly in the light of Gal. 6: 16, which could readily have been taken to have such an application.[2] What new factor had begun to operate to make the transposition more complete? And this raises the second question: How can one account for the irenic tone of the dialogue when some of the preceding apologetics are harsher on the basis of a less thorough take-over? One would expect that the end of the apologetic development would be accompanied by an abandonment of the Jews to their fate, and a bitter polemic against them. In Justin we are confronted with neither.

We point here only to one factor: in Justin we find for the first time a fusion of the Greek philosophical spirit and Christianity.[3] Previously, Christian apologists had either been so closely tied to Judaism (by birth or by Jewish Christian influence), or else so antagonistic to it (because of the challenge it presented), that the dual characteristics found in Justin had not arisen. Here we have one who both values Judaism and is

---

[1] E.g. 140.1, although this is ambiguous.

[2] That Gal. 6: 16 is not cited in the earliest literature is made clear by J. B. Lightfoot, *Galatians* (rev. ed. London, 1896), pp. 85 ff.; cf. 227 ff. Harnack, *Judentum und Judenchristentum in Justins Dialog mit Trypho* (Leipzig, 1913, *T.U.* 39.1) raises the more general problem with respect to Paul: Why did not Justin use either Paul's letters, or even his name, in dealing with similar problems?, pp. 49 ff., 88.

[3] See L. W. Barnard, *Justin Martyr, his Life and Thought* (Cambridge, 1967), esp. pp. 169 ff. Cf. A. W. F. Blunt, *The Apologies of Justin Martyr* (Cambridge 1911 = *Cambridge Patristic Texts*), pp. xii, xvi.

set free from any attraction to it. In his attempt to present Christianity on a sound philosophical basis he uses a ready-made opening: the correlation between Israel and the People of God. His demonstration that Christ is Israel and Jacob, and that therefore the Church is Israel and Jacob, is the vital step. Here is a proposition which would appeal to his philosophical interests, an argument which had not been previously used. The Church has superseded Israel and taken over its status as a respectable philosophy.

CONTINUITY AND DISCONTINUITY

Justin has provided a fixed starting-point for the Church/Israel relationship. Moving back in time, a lack of unanimity on these matters is uncovered. It is a tempting procedure to read back into a fluid period a later fixed idea, by adducing only the evidence for that particular view.[1] But, if one begins with the presupposition that there is no unitary view of the relationship between Christianity and Judaism, much of the stereotype disappears. In the period with which we are concerned circumstances are very important in determining each writer's attitude to the question. This variety is reflected in almost every subject, and not least in the matters in which we are interested:[2] the

---

[1] This is A. von Harnack's most serious error, *The Mission and Expansion of Christianity in the First Centuries* (1908, repr. New York, 1962); see ch. 7, 'The Tidings of the New People and of the Third Race...'; and excursus, 'Christians as a Third Race in the Judgment of their Opponents'.

[2] J. B. Lightfoot, *The Apostolic Fathers* (rev. edition, London, 1890), I, I, *St Clement of Rome*, pp. 8 f., makes the attitude of the fathers to Judaism the chief aspect of their differences: 'Though the writers are all apparently within the pale of the Church, yet there is a tendency to a one-sided exaggeration, either in the direction of Judaism or of the opposite, which stands on the verge of heresy. In the *Epistle* of Barnabas and in the *Letter to Diognetus* the repulsion to Judaism is so violent that one step further would have carried the writers into Gnostic or Marcionite dualism. On the other hand, in the *Teaching of the Apostles*, in the *Shepherd* of Hermas, and possibly in the *Expositions* of Papias...the sympathy with the Old Dispensation is unduly strong, and the distinctive features of the Gospel are somewhat obscured by the shadow of the Law thus projected upon them. In Clement, Ignatius, and Polycarp, both extremes alike are avoided.' This edition is used for the texts of Clement, and Part II (1889) for Ignatius and Polycarp. For *Apology* of Aristides, see below; for *Didache* and Hermas the text in Lightfoot, *The Apostolic Fathers* (one-vol. edition, London, 1891).

relation of the Church to Israel, the *tertium genus* idea, newness and the use of the OT.

Since the take-over of 'Israel' was central to the discussion of Justin, we shall begin the examination of the earlier Patristic literature with the same word.[1] In all the literature only one reference to Israel approaches the force which Justin gives the word—*1 Clement* 29.2. This is a quotation from LXX Deut. 32: 8 f.,[2] in which the main idea, reinforced by Clement's second combined quotation (from Deut. 4: 34; 14: 2?), is the choosing of a special nation. That is made clear by his introduction to the OT text: ὁ πατὴρ ἡμῶν ὃς ἐκλογῆς μέρος ἡμᾶς ἐποίησεν ἑαυτῷ.[3] The introduction of the name Israel is incidental to his argument; the assertion that Christians are Israel, far from being explicit (as Lightfoot's translation suggests), is not made. In para. 30 a part of the quotation is explicitly applied to the Christians, but not the reference to Israel: 'seeing then that we are a special portion (μερίς)'. We may also draw attention to *1 Clement* 8 where 'all his beloved', whom God wants to come to repentance, includes both Israel from the preceding sentences, and the Christian flock in para. 9. That the harsh quotations of *1 Clement* 15 are not applied to Israel but to Christians, and that *1 Clement* 59.4 speaks of 'the wanderers of Thy people' seem to indicate the same kind of respect for the historic people of God.[4] Of the references to

[1] E. J. Goodspeed, *Index Patristicus sive clavis patrum apostolicorum operum*... (1907, repr. Napierville, Illinois, 1960), lists 19 instances, all in *1 Clement* (4.13; 8.3; 29.2; 31.4; 43.5, 6; 55.6) and Barnabas (4.14; 5.2, 8; 6.7; 8.1, 3; 9.2; 11.1; 12.2 *bis*, 5; 16.5).

[2] Verbatim, except for the omission of one καί.

[3] Lightfoot, *Fathers*, I, 2, 93, comments: '...the ἐκλογῆς μέρος is the Christian people, the spiritual Israel, who under the new covenant have taken the place of the chosen people under the old...' But the point I wish to establish is that neither Clement nor any of his fellow sub-Apostolic writers actually makes such a complete transposition; they always stop short. Thus Lietzmann's remark is not acceptable (*A History of the Early Christian Church* (repr. Cleveland and New York, 1961) I, 196): 'This meant...that this people belonged to the host of those who were denoted by the allegorical name of "Israel"...' 'Israel' is *not* used allegorically.

[4] Though in 59.4 *laos* is applied to Christians. This may indicate that the earlier reference is to Christians going astray, but I think it unlikely. Πλανάω is very often used of Jews in the literature.

Israel in Barnabas,[1] one is a citation (9.2) and the rest are all historically oriented. Only one is important for us (5.2), where, in a passage we shall look at again, Barnabas lays down one of his cardinal rules of interpretation: 'For the scriptures concerning him contain some things relating to Israel, and some things relating to us', but he does not equate the two, in fact he consciously avoids the transposition. If Clement of Alexandria's *Stromateis* 6.5.43.3 is genuinely a part of *Kerygma Petri* (φησὶν ὁ Πέτρος), that work recognizes the possibility of the conversion of Israel: ἐὰν μὲν οὖν τις θελήσῃ τοῦ 'Ἰσραὴλ μετανοήσας κτλ, although in the context it appears to be limited to a 12-year period.[2] It is unfortunate that the conclusion of this statement cannot be recovered: either, 'That period is now over, and we are finished with Israel...' or: 'Now that we have given our first and undivided attention to Israel, we proceed to hold out salvation to both together...'[3] These are the only significant instances of the word 'Israel'. Nowhere from the close of the NT canon to Justin is the Church explicitly said to be Israel.

What is the measure of continuity and discontinuity between these two groups? One aspect of continuity is seen in *1 Clement* 7 and 17, in both cases a discussion of those who have turned to God through 'the blood of Christ...from generation to generation' (7.5) including Noah, Jonah, Elijah, Elisha. The references to scriptural examples in 45.1; 46.1; and 63.1 also support this sense of historical continuity in *1 Clement*. The most impressive instance is 32.4: 'all men that have been from the beginning' (ἀπ' αἰῶνος) are justified by faith. Ignatius also maintains this continuity, expressed in *Phil.* 9 in much the same way as in *1 Clement* 32.4: Jesus Christ is 'the door of the Father, through which Abraham and Isaac and Jacob enter in, and the Prophets and the Apostles and the whole Church: all these things combine in the unity of God (εἰς ἑνότητα θεοῦ)'. It is noteworthy that this comes after the repudiation of a challenge

---

[1] The most convenient text is found in H. Windisch, *HNT* (Tübingen, 1920) and K. Lake, *The Apostolic Fathers*, 2 vols. (Loeb Classical Library, London, 1949).

[2] On the significance of this, see E. von Dobschütz, *Das Kerygma Petri* (*TU*, XI, i, Leipzig, 1893), pp. 52 ff. and Exk. pp. 136–50.

[3] Cf. also *Epistle of the Apostles* in M. R. James, *The Apocryphal NT* (Oxford, 1924, repr. 1945), p. 495, para 30.

from a gnosticizing Judaism,[1] in the course of which there is no polemic, and at the end of which there is no call to separation, only a sense of oneness with historic Israel. This restraint is paralleled by *Mag.* 8–10 (cf. *Eph.* 8.1) where there is a somewhat sharper attitude to the failings of Judaism, yet it concludes in 10.3 with an assertion of Judaism's belief in Christianity. Clearly he believes that Christianity is the superior entity, but holds a real continuity between the two.[2] The remark in *Smyr.* 1.2 about the oneness of the Church 'whether among Jews or among Gentiles', works toward the same conclusion. The *Epistle to Diognetus* often implies a sharp break; yet nowhere does he completely repudiate Judaism.[3] He is concerned primarily to correct an overemphasis on the continuity, as 3.1 makes clear: 'I fancy that thou art chiefly anxious to hear about their [Christians] not practising their religion in the same way as the Jews.' The *Apology* of Aristides is difficult to assess because of the increased harshness of the Greek version, just at the

[1] See L. W. Barnard, *VC*, xvii (1963), 193–206, particularly p. 200: 'It is then certain that these heretical teachers were not themselves circumcised, and did not require their followers to be circumcised. This is a Judeo-Gnosticism which taught by myths or fables.' Cf. Lietzmann, *The Early Christian Church*, i, 247.

[2] J. Weiss, *Earliest Christianity* (New York, repr. 1959), ii, 768, categorically opposes this: '...one may perhaps say that he loses too completely the consciousness of a historical connection with the religion of Israel'. F. J. Foakes Jackson, *The Rise of Gentile Christianity* (London, 1927), p. 176, adopts the same attitude. More recently, H. Riesenfeld in *Studia Patristica* iv (*TU* 79, Berlin, 1961), pp. 312–22, maintains that Ignatius is not a Jew, nor a Jewish proselyte, but a Hellenist who is 'still unaware of the problem of the exegesis of the OT in the Christian Church' (313). There is 'no controversy against Judaism in its orthodox form in the letters of Ignatius...'

[3] Cf. H. G. Meecham, *The Epistle to Diognetus* (Manchester, 1949), pp. 29 ff. and 35 ff. It is tempting to side with Dom P. Andriessen on the date of the letter of apology; see *VC*, i (1947), 129–36, a review of earlier articles; *idem*, on Quadratus in *Sacris Erudiri*, ii (Steenbrugge, 1949), pp. 44 ff., in which he concludes that it cannot be ascertained with any certainty whether Quadratus' *locus* was in Asia Minor. J. Quasten, *Patrology* (Brussels, 1950), i, 248 f., allows that this thesis that *Ep. to Dg. = Apol. Quad.* reopens the discussion of the authorship. *Per contra*: R. H. Connolly, *JTS*, xxxvi (1935), 347–53; J. G. O'Neill, *Irish Ecclesiastical Record*, lxxxv (1956), 92 ff.; see also discussion in Meecham, *Epistle to Diognetus*, pp. 16–19; and in H. I. Marrou, *À Diognète* (*Sources Chrétiennes*, 33, Paris, 1951), pp. 241–68, with his instructive table of proposed dates.

point where it is most important for our purpose, in para. 14.[1]
The same feature is found in para. 2 (Syr.), where it is stated
that Jesus was born of a Hebrew maiden (so also Arm.; Greek
in para. 15 = ἐκ παρθένου ἁγίας) and was born of the tribe of
the Hebrews (omitted in Greek). In para. 14, dealing with the
Jews, there are many differences; the Syriac ascribes to Jews
qualities which it later applies to Christians, all of which are
absent from the Greek. In the Syriac the key phrase is that 'they
appear to be much nearer the truth than all the peoples, in that
they worship God more exceedingly and not his works'. With
this must be contrasted the Greek: καί εἰσι παρόμοιοι τῶν ἐθνῶν,
κἂν ἐγγίζειν πως τῇ ἀληθείᾳ δοκῶσιν, ἧς ἑαυτοὺς ἐμάκρυναν.
The main criticism of them in Syriac is that they serve
angels, and observe (and not even perfectly) sabbaths and
new moons, the passover and the great fast, circumcision
and cleanness of meats. This is mild treatment,[2] emphasizing
that, in the form in which the Jews still exist, they are in a
substantial measure of continuity with those who follow in
paras. 15–17.

When we consider the other side, we must first recognize that
the adoption of OT titles of honour by the Church is very
common, and that we must look to more specific expressions of
the gap between Christians and Jews to establish the discontinuous motif. *The Martyrdom of Polycarp*, by associating Jews
and Gentiles so closely together, seems to make Jews and

---

[1] See Appendix A, where it is suggested that the Syriac is closer to the
original. One of the papyrus fragments covers part of para. 15: it is considerably closer to the Syriac in content, with the Greek dependent upon it for
its terminology. Cf. J. Geffcken, *Zwei griechischen Apologeten* (Leipzig and
Berlin, 1907), p. 83: 'Es ist ganz deutlich, daß hier, wo es sich um christ-
liche Dogmatik handelt, also nicht um Dinge die wie die heidnischen
Anschauungen einfach traditionell fortgepflanzt wurden, der späte by-
zantinische Mönch sein Lichtlein leuchten lassen will, während der zeitlich
frühere Syrer diese Tendenz weit weniger besessen haben dürfte. So ist es
denn ganz klar, daß der Grieche die Reihenfolge verwirrt und mehrere
Zusätze gemacht hat...'

[2] Geffcken, *Apologeten*, p. 82: 'Wir kommen nun zu den Juden, die der
Autor ja ziemlich milde behandelt.' Cf. n. 1: 'G. hat eine ganz törichte
tendenziöse Schilderung, die den Juden sogar den häufigen Rückfall ins
Heidentum vorwirft, gegeben.' In his text Geffcken follows the Syriac
completely in this section, except for the opening sentence. 'G. hat demnach
nur wenig vom Originale bewahrt' (*ibid*).

Christians totally separate.[1] This, however, is quite late. In the so-called *Second Letter of Clement* it is probable that 'those who seemed to have God' (2.3) refers to Jews, whom Christians have superseded.[2] Christians are of the first Church which is spiritual[3] and not of that which has become a den of robbers, although one may move from one to the other by not doing God's will.[4] The *Shepherd* of Hermas reflects a later stage in the separation of the Church from Judaism in its emphasis on the Church and the Church alone. In *Sim.* 8–9, particularly, none of the 'rods' represents a concern for the Jews.[5] In these same chapters in the metaphor of the building there is no conception that Israel, the prophets, or the patriarchs form a part of the foundation. Israel is neglected. *Kerygma Petri*, so far as we have it, emphasizes newness so much that it also separates Jew and Christian radically. Christian worship is different and new, so new that it is a third way.[6] This is primarily an apologetic concerned with worship, and not polemic, though this does not

[1] Cf. Foakes Jackson, *Gentile Christianity*, p. 199: 'It may be assumed therefore that, at Smyrna at least, the rivalry of Church and Synagogue was very bitter. But the death of Polycarp was evidently due to the desire of the authorities to placate the mob, and prevent a serious riot...this is possibly the only example of the Jews being accused of inciting the heathen to persecute, and there is no conspicuous instance in well-attested early martyrdoms of the Jews coming forward as witnesses against the Christians.'

[2] In the same paragraph, 'He spoke of us...our Church...our people... having believed we have become more...'

[3] 14.1: ἐκ τῆς ἐκκλησίας τῆς πρώτης, τῆς πνευματικῆς.

[4] J. de Zwaan, in *Aux Sources de la Tradition Chrétienne: Mélanges offerts a M. M. Goguel* (Neuchâtel, 1950); 'Some Remarks on the Church-idea in the Second Century', pp. 270–8: 'This whole chapter is singular and important as showing the way in which the eschatological stress was transformed in a mystic sense. Of course the "pre-existent church" falls into a line with the rabbinical notions, about the pre-existence of the Thorah, etc. The whole trend here is distinctly moving away from the NT and moving towards speculations about a "numinous" character of the empirical church' (p. 274).

[5] Or Gentiles or outsiders of any kind, except for occasional remarks that Gentiles are headed for judgment. Even *Sim.* 9.19 refers not to Jews (so v. Dobschütz, *Das Kerygma Petri*, p. 36 n. 1) but to Christian apostates who have worshipped the Emperor and have helped the authorities to convict other Christians, hence there is no repentance.

[6] Frags. 4 and 5: καινῶς τὸν θεὸν διὰ τοῦ Χριστοῦ σεβόμενοι...ὑμεῖς δὲ οἱ καινῶς αὐτὸν τρίτῳ γένει σεβόμενοι χριστιανοί; this is what v. Dobschütz, *Das Kerygma Petri*, p. 48, calls 'die absolute Neuheit des Christentums'.

reduce the measure of separation. The *Epistle to Diognetus* also stresses that Gentiles and Jews are mistaken in their worship.[1] That Christians do not participate in these things is therefore commendable (4.6); indeed the reason for their aloofness is stated at the very beginning.[2] This is a positive apologetic,[3] and not a negative polemic against the Jews.[4] Chapters 11 and 12 seem to represent a more explicit rejection of the Jews, and there is a greater tendency here to make the Church completely Gentile.[5] This same bias appears tentatively in ch. 9, though it might be better to take it simply as a paean of praise to God, rather than as an assertion of exclusiveness.

Barnabas is an important witness on this subject;[6] he adopts an exclusivist line in his assessment of the Church and Israel.[7] This seems to be motivated by his desire (or the necessity) to

[1] Sabbath, circumcision, fasting and new moons are mentioned (4.1) as self-evidently foolish.

[2] 1.1: καὶ τί δήποτε καινὸν τοῦτο γένος ἢ ἐπιτήδευμα εἰσῆλθεν εἰς τὸν βίον νῦν καὶ οὐ πρότερον;

[3] Harnack, *Mission*, p. 247, misconstrues *Ep. to Dg.* when he suggests that the author tries to prove that 'they have a legitimate claim to be ranked as a special "nation"'. The whole point of 5–6 is that they share all aspects of life with the rest of the world, and that they have not withdrawn from the world, even though it is opposed to Christianity. Cf. n. 1, p. 253.

[4] He speaks of the senseless persecutions of Christians as coming from both Jew and Gentile; i.e. blame is not shifted as far as possible to Jews as in *Mart. Poly.*, an easy step to have taken here. It reflects a situation in which Jews and Christians are *de facto* separated.

[5] Generally taken as a later addition but accepted as genuine by Andriessen; in fact these chapters are crucial to his theory. Note that in 11.1 the author is a διδάσκαλος ἐθνῶν; in 11.3 the Word ὑπὸ λαοῦ ἀτιμασθείς... ὑπὸ ἐθνῶν ἐπιστεύθη.

[6] There is no overwhelming agreement on the questions of date and background of the author: see the recent synopsis by L. W. Barnard in *Studia Patristica*, IV, p. 263; contrast J. A. Robinson, *JTS*, xxxv (1934), 123 and 145; Windisch, *HNT*, pp. 412 f.; Lightfoot, *Fathers*, I, 2, 503 ff.

[7] Though some overstate it; e.g. J. Donaldson, *The Apostolical Fathers* (London, 1874), p. 253; J. Parkes, *The Conflict of the Church and Synagogue: A Study in the Origins of Antisemitism* (Cleveland, repr. 1961), p. 84: Foakes Jackson, *Gentile Christianity*, p. 172. J. A. Robinson, *JTS*, xxxv (1934), 127, is more balanced: 'The gentiles, through the teaching and labours of St Paul, had claimed and secured equal privilege with the Jews in a Christian society. It was becoming evident that the future of Christianity was mainly with the gentiles, and that the Jews, as a people, had finally refused to admit that in this joint inheritance lay the fulfilment of the promise to the Fathers ...Christianity could not forget its Jewish origins.'

retain the OT but to transfer its meaning, and leads to an extreme in biblical hermeneutics which has been only rarely exceeded.[1] But the very fact that he deals with Judaism thus harshly is indicative of a residual continuity with Judaism which he wanted to overthrow.[2] We can do little more here than to call attention to some specific instances of this attempt. In Jesus Christ, God has annulled (κατήργησεν) sacrifices (2.6), law (3), the Mosaic covenant (4.6–8, 14.1, 4), circumcision (9.4), the Sabbath (15.8), the Temple (16); in fact there is no provision for their once having had value. Israel[3] was led astray (πλανώμενοι, 2.9), rejected because they refused the Lord, and then filled up the measure of their sins by slaying him.[4] The climax is reached when Barnabas claims that, though 'certain persons' say 'our covenant remains to them also', in fact the Jewish people lost it right after it was given to Moses and it is now 'ours' (ἡμῶν μέν; 4.4–8). These two words sum up the author's theology. Christians alone are the 'heirs of the covenant of the Lord' (6.19); 'a second creation, made at the last' (6.13); 'we have been created anew' (6.14); and therefore are 'the people (λαός) he had prepared in his well-beloved' (3.6).

[1] Barnabas is a necessary first step to Marcion's elimination of the OT altogether.

[2] The often quoted remark of J. A. Robinson (*JTS*, xxxv, 1934, p. 145) 'After reading the Epistle again and again I find no trace of animosity against the Jews' is true, but it needs to be supplemented by what follows: 'Severe things are said about them as a people, but with the definite purpose of showing that they have forfeited their privileges in the divine covenant, which has thus passed justly from them to the New People, whom God foresaw...to Barnabas Judaism is a blank failure from the beginning... *This is the extreme to which no NT writer proceeds. Nor was Barnabas followed in this respect.*' Robinson also insists that the author uses Eph., in which case it is interesting that he did not use Eph. 2: 11 ff., especially *v.* 15.

[3] Barnabas means all Israel: we reject the thesis of S. Lowy, *Journal of Jewish Studies* (London), xi (1960), 1–33, that Barnabas is confronting a Jewish Messianic movement which offered a dangerous alternative to Christianity. It is based on the theory that Barn. intentionally fails to stress the important points (p. 32), a tenuous postulate.

[4] 5.11; 8.1 ff.; cf. 1 Thess. 2: 16 (see below) and note the discussion of the relationship between Barn. and Thess. by J. Oesterreicher and K. Thieme in *ZKT*, lxxiv (1952), 63–70: 'Um Kirche und Synagoge im Barnabasbrief: ein offener Briefwechsel zwischen J.O. and K.T.'

'TERTIUM GENUS'

The starting-point for a consideration of *tertium genus* must be Harnack's treatment.[1] He tries to sustain the thesis that

the triad of 'Greeks (Gentiles), Jews, and Christians' was the church's basal conception of history...But so far as I am aware the blunt expression 'We Christians are the Third Race' only occurs once in early Christian literature subsequent to the *Preaching of Peter* (where moreover it is simply Christian worship which is described as the third class), and that is in the pseudo-Cyprianic tract *de Pascha Computus* (ch. 17) written in 242–243 A.D.[2]

He later adduces evidence from Tertullian (*ad Nat.* 1.8) to show that by A.D. 200 in Carthage the heathen were calling Christians the third race[3] but the general conclusions he draws from this do not necessarily follow. In another place he says:

Israel was thus at all times the pseudo-church...This is the unanimous opinion of all writers of the post-Apostolic age. Christians were the true Israel; and therefore all Israel's predicates of honour belong to them. They are the 12 tribes, and therefore Abraham, Isaac and Jacob are the Fathers of the Christians. This idea, about which there was no wavering, cannot everywhere be traced back to the Apostle Paul...[4]

How far is the idea of Christianity as a *tertium genus* normative for the Church in this period? The first and clearest witness is *Kerygma Petri*.[5] The crucial statement is found in Clement of

---

[1] *Mission and Expansion*, chapter 7 and excursus 3. Cf. M. Simon, *Verus Israel* (Paris, 1948), pp. 135–9, who points out that this is a transitory apologetic motif which later gives way to a bipartite division.

[2] *Mission and Expansion*, p. 250; it is a mark of his greatness as a historian that all the qualifications necessary are present, even though he does not heed them sufficiently.

[3] In a short contribution to the *G. A. Kohut Festschrift* (New York, 1935), Leo Baeck considers 'Das dritte Geschlecht' from the point of view of its Jewish background, and concludes: 'Jedenfalls steht es fest, daß unser Wort den palästinensischen Judentum zugehört. Von hier ist es dann in einen Sprachgebrauch der Kirche gelangt und hat im Munde ihrer Gegner zu Spöttereien den Anlaß gegeben' (p. 46).

[4] *History of Dogma* (1900, repr. New York, 1961), I, 179; and also note 3; cf. p. 148 and note 1; pp. 177 ff.

[5] Texts, commentary and discussion in E. von Dobschütz, *Das Kerygma Petri* (*TU*, XI, 1, Leipzig, 1893). It is not clear when *Ker. Petr.* was written, but the first quarter of the second century is a fair guess.

Alexandria's *Stromateis*, 6.5.41: νέαν ὑμῖν διέθετο, τὰ γὰρ Ἑλλήνων καὶ Ἰουδαίων παλαιά, ὑμεῖς δὲ οἱ καινῶς αὐτὸν τρίτῳ γένει σεβόμενοι χριστιανοί.[1] Harnack has already been quoted above on the point that *genos* is used of 'manner' of worshipping, not as a third 'race'; so that, while *Kerygma Petri* does not yet use a thorough *tertium genus* idea, it represents an important step on the way.[2] The second piece of evidence is the *Epistle to Diognetus*, but it can only be accepted as testimony to a *tertium genus* concept with reservations. In para. 1 he mentions 'the religion of Christians', some lines later 'the gods of the Greeks', and then 'the superstition (δεισιδαιμονία) of the Jews',[3] suggesting in the next line or two that Christianity is a καινὸν γένος ἢ ἐπιτήδευμα. The structure and language together might just be sufficient grounds for holding that *tertium genus* constitutes the background of this passage. Christians stand as a new thing over against Jews and Greeks. As we have noted, the author's insistence in 11.3 that Christians are a Gentile product, not continuous with Jews, may reinforce this.[4] Of the other writers in this period, it is impossible to deduce anything about a *tertium genus*; there is nothing in *1 Clement, Didache*, Polycarp or Hermas.[5] The only other writing which has any light to shed is the *Apology* of Aristides. Para. 2 (Gr.) holds to a three-part division. However, as Appendix A shows, there is good reason for believing that the four-part division is original, and this carries with it important implications for the plan and structure. Consequently only one work prior to A.D. 150 thought of Christianity as a *tertium genus*, and that in the context of worship.

If Christianity did not generally think of itself as a third

[1] Frag. 5. It is possible that this whole statement is a comment by Clem. Alex., but we shall here assume that it is genuine.

[2] *Ep. to Diog.* and *Apol.* Arist. may have known and used this work; see discussion in Robinson, *Texts and Studies*, 1, 1 (Cambridge, 1891), 86–99; and v. Dobschütz, *Das Kerygma Petri*, pp. 80 ff.

[3] 'Superstition' is too weighted a translation; it is a more neutral word, as E. H. Blakeney suggests, *The Epistle to Diognetus* (London, 1943), p. 43.

[4] Which we include tentatively beside 1–10.

[5] V. Dobschütz, *Das Kerygma Petri*, p. 36 n. 1, thinks he detects this idea in Herm. *Vis.* 1.4.2: δίκαιοι, ἔθνη, ἀποστάται; and Herm. *Sim.* 4.3 f.: δίκαιοι, ἔθνη, ἁμαρτωλοί; and in Herm. *Sim.* 8.6.4; 9.19.1 he takes ἀποστάται of the Jews. This is extremely doubtful as evidence for *tertium genus*.

thing, did it consider itself a *secundum genus*, over against some other group immediately present in the author's situation?[1] This could mean that Christianity is contrasted to Jews, Gentiles, or the world. While there need be no temporal progression,[2] the *tertium genus* is a more sophisticated presentation of Christianity and may imply greater separation. It is true that a *secundum genus* presentation can be equally harsh. Barnabas is a good example, where only Jewish/Christian relationships are discussed, of the opinion that Christianity is separated from Judaism. The contrast between 'we' and 'they' and the use of *prōtos* in 13.1 is important: 'Let us see whether this people or the first people has the inheritance, and whether the covenant had reference to us or to them.' The rest of the discussion in 13–16 and the preceding section, 2–6, leave little doubt as to his intention: Christianity is the greater, Judaism the lesser: μείζων ὁ λαὸς οὗτος ἢ ἐκεῖνος (13.3; cf. 13.5).

Ignatius also thinks of Christianity as a *secundum genus* with the rest of the world as the only other category (cf. *Rom.* 3.3; *Eph.* 10.1) which included even those Christians who denied the reality of Christ's suffering (*Trall.* 10; cf. 6–7).[3] The passage which at first seems to support the opposite argument (*Smyr.* 1.2) is the most persuasive demonstration that the division between Jews and Gentiles has no real validity; both can coalesce in the one body of his Church, and the corresponding entity comprises those who do not believe, with no special emphasis on their origin. Clement of Rome has no interest in this question, but two things combine to make it likely that he belongs in this category. First, he quotes the OT extensively, but in his use of it he nowhere suggests that Christianity is set over against Israel, or that Christianity is a *tertium genus*.[4] The

---

[1] The term is not used in the literature; but cf. Barn. 13.1; *2 Clement* 14.1.

[2] *Contra* Simon, *Verus Israel*, pp. 135–9.

[3] C. C. Richardson deals with this general problem of heresy in *The Christianity of Ignatius of Antioch* (New York, 1935), pp. 51–4 and 81–5. He takes it that there are two heresies: docetism and Judaism.

[4] Cf. W. K. L. Clarke, *The First Epistle of Clement to the Corinthians* (= *Translations of Early Documents*, London, 1937), p. 23: 'The Church also felt itself to be one with the people of God in the OT, and unsuspiciously took over the sacred books as its title deeds. The battle with Judaism which St Paul had been compelled to wage belonged to a past era.'

second is his emphasis, as in 59.2, 3, that Christians are taken out of all the nations of the world with no distinction between Jewish or Gentile origin. Similarly 'all those who do not believe' are taken from all nations, with no distinction as to origin. The tendency of *1 Clement* is in the direction of Christianity as a *secundum genus*.

It is difficult to assess the *Second Letter* ascribed to Clement, but there are some indications that the unknown author thought in similar terms. In 17.4, 5, unbelievers (ἄπιστοι) are the complementary group to Christians, and these, presumably, are found in all peoples, tribes and tongues. In 13.2, 3 the same group is referred to under the heading Gentiles. When, in 14.1, he refers to 'the first Church' (ἡ ἐκκλησία ἡ πρώτη) which implies an 'unspiritual' complementary entity (as others have referred to Judaism), the implication is not made precise, nor does the author draw these two diverse thoughts together and set out a scheme of three things. In the *Martyrdom of Polycarp* the author's basic distinction is seen readily in 16.1: καὶ θαυμάσαι πάντα τὸν ὄχλον, εἰ τοσαύτη τις διαφορὰ μεταξὺ τῶν τε ἀπίστων καὶ τῶν ἐκλεκτῶν. This categorization, 'unbelievers' and 'elect' is found throughout. In para. 3 the multitude is set over against the γένος τῶν χριστιανῶν (cf. also 12.2; 9.2). While a distinction can be drawn between Jews and Gentiles (e.g. 13.1), it has no real significance for the author; together they are simply the multitudes of unbelievers who are quite separate from the Christians.

Different circumstances create three solutions to this problem of the division between people and their relationships. The one, often overemphasized, is to consider Christians/Jews/Gentiles as the basic divisions; the second is to deal only with Christians and Jews; and the third singles out Christians from the unbelieving world. This variety, a constituent factor in the sub-Apostolic writings, leads to as many views on the relationship of the Church and Israel. No one view in the sub-Apostolic period is normative. In each case the particular approach adopted is a function of the situation in which the author is set, together with his theological tendencies. None of them buttresses his position with any reference to the NT.

NEWNESS, AND THE OLD TESTAMENT

'Newness' is often stressed in a passage which emphasizes discontinuity, so it is useful to note the scope of this idea in our literature.[1] Newness is not always considered a positive advantage to these writers; Clement points out that one aspect of Christianity (its ministry) is not new at all but is identical to that referred to in the OT: 'And this they did (*sc.* appointing bishops and deacons) in no new fashion (οὐ καινῶς); for indeed it had been written concerning bishops and deacons from very ancient times.'[2] His denial of newness and his emphasis on continuity between Judaism and Christianity are consistent with what we have seen earlier of Clement. Another aspect of the stressing of continuity under the heading of newness is found in Ignatius, *Mag.* 9.1: 'If then those who had walked in ancient practices attained unto newness of hope... (εἰς καινότητα ἐλπίδος).' It is 'hope' which is new for those coming from the old ways of Judaism; the essential continuity is expressed in the reference to οἱ ἐν παλαιοῖς κτλ, and in the following assertion that the prophets were Christ's disciples.[3] Ignatius follows the NT in his use of 'new' in *Eph.* 20, where Jesus is the 'new man'. Similarly, but rather cryptically, Hermas *Sim.* 9.12.2–3 refers to Jesus as older than creation, yet a 'new door' through which believers enter into the presence of God. *Epistle to Diognetus*, 11.4, maintains the same conundrum: οὗτος ὁ ἀπ' ἀρχῆς, ὁ καινὸς φανεὶς καὶ παλαιὸς εὑρεθεὶς καὶ πάντοτε νέος ἐν ἁγίων καρδίαις γεννώμενος. Οὗτος refers back to Christ as ὁ λόγος, recalling 2.1

[1] From Goodspeed, *Index*, we find the following figures for καινός and derivatives: Justin 28; Barn. 5; Ign. 5; Diog. 4; Herm. 4; *1 Cl.* once.

[2] In 42.5; the citation misreads the LXX and gratuitously introduces διάκονοι.

[3] This is in the context of the Lord's day: very different from this is Barn. 15.7, whose point is that Sabbath observance was never very valid because men have never been fully justified. It is only possible when all things have been made new in the eschatological consummation. For the present we keep the eighth day, when Jesus rose from the dead. Cf. P. Prigent, *Les Testimonia dans le Christianisme Primitif, l'Épître de Barnabé, i–xvi et ses Sources* (EtBib, Paris, 1961), pp. 65–70. 'Il précise donc, avec une fine pointe polémique, que cette observance véritable du sabbat est impossible actuellement, tant que la justification parfaite n'a pas été opérée, ce qui n'est pas encore le cas, c'est là un des aspects typiques de la théologie personnelle de Barnabé (cf. 4.10 et 6.9)' (p. 68).

where ὁ καινὸς ἄνθρωπος seems to refer to the new ethical creation (but may have a double reference to Christ also, note ἐξ ἀρχῆς). He then speaks of having confessed λόγος καινός, which is probably not 'story' (so all commentators) but Christ the Word.[1] There are two references in Barnabas to the new creation: 6.11, 'He renewed us (ἀνακαινίσας) in the remission of sins, he made us to be a new type (ἄλλον τύπον)...as if he were re-creating us' (cf. 6.13; 6.14); and 16.8 'receiving the remission of sins...we became new (ἐγενόμεθα καινοί) created afresh from the beginning'. Such statements go beyond the NT concepts, but they are still in line with them. However, his reference to the new law of Jesus which replaces the old law now done away with (2.6) is out of line with the NT. Ignatius *Mag.* 10 says that Christians are the new leaven (νέος) which replaces the old leaven of Judaism.

All these are apologetically conceived validations of the Christian contention that the new way is better than that of Judaism from which it grew. The outward and most characteristic manifestation of newness is seen in their worship, and it is this facet of newness that *Kerygma Petri* emphasizes in Frags. 4 and 5.[2] A more general 'way of life' is mentioned in *Epistle to Diognetus*, 1.1, where *genos* is used in the same way as in *Kerygma Petri*. Christianity is pragmatically different from the others. It is also a theoretically different entity; but it is striking that the new practice of Christians is nowhere connected with the theoretical statement that they are the 'new people'. This latter is the most sweeping claim based on the word καινός. The idea is found in Barnabas 5.7: αὐτὸς ἑαυτῷ τὸν λαὸν τὸν καινὸν ἑτοιμάζων κτλ (cf. 7.5): and in *Apology* of Aristides (Syr. only) at 16.4: 'Truly this people is a new people, and there is something divine mingled with it.'[3] These two are the first to use the combination καινὸς λαός.

The two early authors who stand most clearly in the tradition of the NT, Clement and Ignatius, use *kainos* with careful reserve. Two motives are distinguishable in the others; an

---

[1] If so, this reinforces Andriessen's contention that 11–12 form an integral part of *Ep. to Diog.*

[2] Note also the one occurrence of 'new covenant' in this literature (Frag. 5).

[3] Accounting for the Greek not having this is difficult.

attempt to establish the grounds of the Christian difference from Judaism (new covenant, law, leaven); and an attempt to explain the results of the new Christian revelation (new creation, worship, way of life). Only Barnabas and Aristides use *kainos* to apply to Christians as a social grouping, although it is an easy step from the one association to the other.

The use made of the OT varies greatly. Some (Ignatius, Polycarp, *Martyrdom of Polycarp*, *Epistle to Diognetus* and Hermas) scarcely mention it.[1] Of those who use it, Clement is most important; he does not repudiate the OT but quotes from it and applies it without abusing it.[2] This 'legitimate' use of the OT is found also in the *Didache*, where there is little or no allegorization. These are the only two early writings where we feel a sympathetic handling of scripture, and an acceptance of the old people of God portrayed there. The likeliest reason for this is that both arose in churches having a close affinity with Jewish antecedents where regard for Israel was still felt.[3] One aspect of the relationship to the OT is the common idea that the prophets have a special link with Christianity. *Epistle to*

[1] It is surprising to find Ignatius in this list. The pastoral concern (of a different kind from Clement's which uses the OT widely) may account for the lack. *Ep. to Diog.* on the other hand is concerned with Judaism, and his failure to use the OT to his advantage is due to either his lack of regard for it, or his moderate tendencies on the re-application of it.

[2] Lietzmann, *History*, I, 195 ff., has a useful discussion of Clement's use of the OT but he mis-states the case when he says: 'The OT had therefore already been wrested from the Jews and had become the special property of the Christians to such an extent that its commandments could be regarded as "types"...' (See also pp. 199 ff. on the proselyte origin of the Roman church.) Cf. Harnack, *Dogma*, I, 156: 'The exposition of the OT...turned it into a Christian book. A historical view of it, which no born Jew could in some measure fail to take, did not come into fashion...' Contrast Lightfoot, *Fathers*, I, 2, p. 205: '...the genuine Clement...looks upon himself as a descendant of the Patriarchs, as an heir of the glories of the Israelite race; and (what is more important) he is thoroughly imbued with the feelings of an Israelite, has an intense knowledge of the OT scriptures...In short his language and tone of thought proclaim him a Jew...'

[3] Cf. Foakes Jackson, *Gentile Christianity*, pp. 201–2: 'When...[the Jewish leaders]...passed away the majority of Christians were gentiles, not only by race but in thought and feeling. They had never been Jews and never therefore broke with Judaism. All they retained of the ancient religion was the OT as necessary to prove the Messianic claims of their Lord...' *1 Cl.* and *Did.* are prior to the stage described here.

Diognetus, 11.6, speaks of knowing the grace of the prophets; Barnabas refers to the 'prophets, receiving grace from him, prophesied concerning him' (5.6); and *Kerygma Petri*, frags. 9 and 10, repeats the same type of statement, noting more fully what can be found in the books of the prophets. Ignatius also shares this view, suggesting that the prophets lived 'in expectation of a coming deliverer and a redemption' (*Mag.* 8.2; cf. *Phil.* 5.2; *Mag.* 9.3). He says that they both looked forward to Christ and are disciples of Christ. Unfortunately we have no adequate indication of how *Epistle to Diognetus*, Ignatius or *Kerygma Petri* might use the OT.

Barnabas and *2 Clement* represent the radical school of exegesis. *2 Clement*'s practice of allegorization and re-application to refer solely to the Church is obvious in the first instance in which he quotes the OT (2.1). The author's claim that 'he spoke of us' is far removed from Clement's use. His handling of the OT places him at a point where it had already become the special property of Christians. 14.2 reaches a climax of misused typology: 'God made man, male and female. The male is Christ and the female is the Church' (contrast Eph. 5: 31 f.). With Barnabas we are in the same atmosphere, although it may be at an earlier stage in the development of this type of exegesis.[1] His primary hermeneutical principle is found in 5.2: γέγραπται γὰρ περὶ αὐτοῦ ἃ μὲν πρὸς τὸν Ἰσραήλ, ἃ δὲ πρὸς ἡμᾶς.[2] On occasion the two applications of scripture are held in close juxtaposition, but not often;[3] it is more usual for him to draw a single lesson, either in reference to Israel or to the Church. Whether or not his use of the OT includes *testimonia* is incidental to us:[4] the important point is that the final result involves a consistent hermeneutic that has not yet been taken quite to its

---

[1] Note his emphasis on the principle of γνῶσις (e.g. 6.9). Cf. H. Windisch, *HNT* (1920), pp. 307 ff., on a dual use of γνῶσις in Barn.

[2] Windisch, *HNT* (1920), p. 315, adds a second principle: 'alles ist in Jesus befaßt und zieht auf ihn ab 12.7. Für letztere Regel ist bedeutsam, daß Christus selbst als Sprecher in der Bibel anzusehen ist.'

[3] As e.g. in 2.7 and 2.10; or 3.1 and 3.3; in the latter case his exegesis drives the two halves of a single passage apart.

[4] Windisch, *HNT* (1920), pp. 313–16. Prigent, *Testimonia*, finds three basic types of material in Barn.: polemical anti-Jewish *testimonia* (against sacrifices, fasting, circumcision, covenant, sabbath and temple), Messianic testimonia, and Midrashic traditions.

logical conclusion.[1] Barnabas grounds his argument fully on Judaism, and then rejects it.[2] His attitude, then, to the Church/ Israel problem, while involving what we have called a *secundum genus* approach, is actually more radical than the *tertium genus* conception to which, in other respects, he often corresponds. This 'yes-and-no' in which he is involved is his downfall. Others may have followed him, but eventually he leads into a dead end. The tragedy is that later writers are infected by a similar allegorical method and the same repudiation of all historical and spiritual value in Judaism, coupled with a new moral legalism.[3] He was not the originator of this methodology, for the same elimination of historical truth in favour of an allegorized modern application had been common in Alexandria before, but he may well have been the popularizer of it within Christian circles.

The problem of the OT reaches its peak in the controversies with the Jews in later literature.[4] Even in the literature surveyed here, one of the purposes is to establish that Christianity is the inheritor of the spiritual legacy of the old covenant: i.e. it is the 'new Israel'. There is a correspondence in the position the writer adopts to Israel and to its scriptures. There is insufficient evidence for certainty, but it is likely that the formative factor is the author's attitude to Judaism, and then (consciously or subconsciously) his hermeneutical principle would follow.[5] If

[1] This is well said by Harnack, *Dogma*, I, 178 n. 6: 'It is a thorough misunderstanding of Barnabas' position towards the OT to suppose it is possible to pass over his expositions in ch. 6–10 as oddities and caprices, and put them aside as indifferent or unmethodical. There is nothing here unmethodical and therefore nothing arbitrary. Barnabas' strictly spiritual ideas of God, and the conviction that all (Jewish) ceremonies are of the devil, compel his explanations. These are so little ingenious conceits to Barn. that, but for them, he would have been forced to give up the OT altogether' (cf. pp. 291 ff.). In *Mission and Expansion*, pp. 65 ff., esp. p. 69 n. 1, Harnack points out that Barn. avoided the repudiation of the OT by a 'resolute re-interpretation of the literal sense' (cf. also ch. 8).

[2] As e.g. in 13–14: this people and the first people are the only two entities, but the one had no covenant so we only are the 'first' people.

[3] Cf. T. F. Torrance, *The Doctrine of Grace in the Apostolic Fathers* (London, 1948), p. 107.

[4] See M. F. Wiles, *SJT*, VIII (1955), 113–26.

[5] His attitude to Judaism will depend on many things, including whether or not he is a Jewish Christian, in what kind of Christian environment he is

so, this isolates an important presupposition of each author, and elevates to a place of greater importance his assessment of the Church/Israel relationship.

CONCLUSIONS

The various factors alluded to in chapter I (particularly 'theological') can be seen to be at work throughout this literature. The one constant factor is a growing, though not uniform, tendency to emphasize discontinuity and to forgo continuity. The writers grope for a formulation which will answer to the historical and social problems of the day, especially those concerning the Church and Israel. Hesitantly they move towards the statement that Christianity is the 'true Israel', a conclusion reached, as we have seen, in Justin's *Dialogue with Trypho*. The late date is evidence of considerable restraint, even though as early as Barnabas it seemed an inevitable conclusion.

Barnabas, however, is not just a 'whipping boy'; he represents the farthest advance in the literature to A.D. 150, at which point Justin takes the mantle from him. These two are not alone; Justin, Barnabas, the *Epistle to Diognetus* and *Kerygma Petri* have in common a primary concern to make an apologetic presentation of Christianity as over against Judaism,[1] as well as the Gentiles. Each, therefore, has a tendency towards harshness to Judaism, and views it as a temporary phenomenon which is passing away because its revelation has been superseded by a new revelation teaching a better, uncluttered worship. At the same time this group of writers is freest in the use of *kainos*, and in the take-over of Jewish prerogatives. Of these, the two most thorough in emphasizing discontinuity have extensive OT quotations while the other two have none.[2] The heirs of this approach to Judaism are on the one side Marcion and on the other the Apologists.

nourished, what stage separation beteeen the two groups has reached, how important an apologetic statement of Christianity *vis-à-vis* Judaism has become.

[1] This is true even in *Apol. Arist.* and *Ker. Petr.*, where each author is interested in settling the confusion between Jew and Christian.

[2] Perhaps because of a Gentile audience?

The *Apology* of Aristides should have belonged to the previous group by virtue of its form and content; and yet it must stand apart from them because of its emphasis on continuity and its irenic quality. It has this in common with the pastoral letters of Clement of Rome and Ignatius. These all seem to be addressed to, or arise out of, churches which have a living Jewish background. All are aware of the deficiencies of the old beside the new in the light of the coming of Christ, but they do not deny spiritual value to the old, and seem to be hopeful of further fruitful contact with Judaism.[1] The *Epistle* of Polycarp, which could be included with this group, has nothing to say to our problem. The *Martyrdom of Polycarp* and *2 Clement* are pastoral in intent, but falling at the end of the period exhibit a more exclusive view of the Church and, in the case of the *Martyrdom of Polycarp*, an antagonistic attitude to the Jews. In all this group 'newness' is not emphasized; in fact, only Ignatius and Clement use the word. Generally, the farther one moves into the second century the more separated are Judaism and the Church. The same principle applies to the use of the OT in *2 Clement*: being more recent it assumes a greater hermeneutical discontinuity. Hermas and *Didache* have had little relevance to our inquiry.

In this period there is much variety—a function of the time, kind of writing, and background of the author and persons addressed. Specifically, there is variety on the question of the division of the world into parts, and on the place of Christianity in that division: the writers of the period hold no brief for a *tertium genus* concept, nor do they feel any necessity to assert that Christianity is the true Israel until after the break becomes a well-established fact. Two important steps are taken: the first is to neglect Judaism or treat it as useless; the second is to develop a hermeneutic of discontinuity.[2] But, however we view this period, we do not find here the decisive transition for which we are looking in this investigation.

[1] This is true of Justin too, of course, although the others in the previous group are more doubtful.

[2] The farthest point the NT reaches is found in Hebrews, but this letter does not seem to lie consciously in the background of any of the sub-Apostolic authors.

CHAPTER III

POLITICAL FACTORS
IN THE
SEPARATION

INTRODUCTION

There are a number of external factors which must be assessed in a documentation of the Church's growing separation from Israel: the relationship of nationalistic movements to local Palestinian authority; the relation of the Church to this nationalism; and the relation of the Church and the Diaspora to local and Roman government. The authorities' attitude to Christians and Jews influences the need for identification and separation in the consciousness of each as, for example, in the conflicts between Rome and a Judaism temporarily swayed by a nationalistic fervour. For this question Roman law is an important factor. The events requiring discussion are, therefore, the wars of A.D. 66–73 and A.D. 132–5; the alleged persecutions by the Emperors from Claudius to Hadrian; local Jewish persecutions including the Synagogue Ban. It will be argued that none of these traumatic incidents provides either the sharp break or the grounds for the break which is under examination. Their importance lies in the encouragement they provide for each of Judaism and Christianity to go its own way, and in the opportunity for self-assessment. The incidents also provide grounds for later polemic and apologetic justification for the break as it develops, but they are symptoms and not first causes of the rupture.

JEWISH REVOLTS

The revolt led by Bar Cochba in A.D. 132 was initiated by extremely provocative action of Hadrian towards the Jews: the proscription of circumcision[1] and the establishment of Jeru-

---

[1] It is difficult to be certain whether this came before or after the war; see Simon, *Verus Israel*, p. 126.

salem as a thoroughly hellenized city, Aelia Capitolina.[1] The effects of this uprising have been generally underrated. M. Simon, in his very penetrating study, is one of the few to give due weight to the importance of this event. A.D. 135 is for Jewish/Christian relationships, if not more significant, at least as significant as A.D. 70. This is particularly true if K. W. Clark is correct in suggesting that temple worship continued in truncated form after A.D. 70.[2] If so, A.D. 135 becomes the point of absolute cessation of sacrifice, as well as the last hope of Israel's identity as a nation. The State is now smashed. There is from this time forward (as is particularly evident from Justin) a new possibility of spiritualizing the name 'Israel' without its being grossly misunderstood as related to Zealot ideals. Jews, especially in the Diaspora, after A.D. 135 live not so much in relation to a recognizable political entity as to a past history,[3] and to a tradition propagated by the Schoolmen at Jamnia.

Two other factors make A.D. 135 an important break in Jewish/Christian relationships. On the one hand, Bar Cochba's claim, and semi-official acceptance of that claim by R. Aqiba and many (most?) Palestinian Jews, must have 'appeared as the final and irrevocable Jewish rejection of the Christ Jesus';[4] and on the other, the Christians' refusal to aid in any way in the struggle led to their persecution by the messianic pretender, the first instance for which we have evidence that the rupture resulted in mass persecution over a question of nationalism from the Jewish side. This date, then, represents the point at which positions had been taken, even though the problem of

---

[1] For a good brief analysis of the events, see F.-M. Abel, *Histoire de la Palestine depuis la conquête d'Alexandre jusqu'à l'Invasion Arabe*, II (Paris, 1952), 83 ff.; I. Abrahams, *Campaigns in Palestine from Alexander the Great* (London, 1927, the Schweich Lectures for 1922), pp. 37 ff.; Hans Bietenhard, 'Die Freiheitskriege der Juden unter den Kaisern Trajan und Hadrian, und der messianische Tempelbau', *Jud*, IV (1948), 57–77, 81–108, 161–85.

[2] In 'Worship in the Jerusalem Temple after A.D. 70', *NTS*, VI (1959–60), 269–80; see also J. R. Brown's study, *The Temple and Sacrifice in Rabbinic Judaism* (Evanston, 1963, Winslow Lectures for 1963). E. Schürer allows for this view although he finally rejects it; *A History of the Jewish People in the Time of Jesus Christ* (Edinburgh, 1905), Div. I, II, 268 ff.

[3] J. Jocz, *The Jewish People and Jesus Christ* (London, 1954), pp. 173 f., emphasizes the new political situation after A.D. 135.

[4] S. W. Baron, *A Social and Religious History of the Jews* (New York, 1952), II, 132.

relationships still remained.[1] It is the closest approximation to a point at which the break is complete.

In the study already referred to, M. Simon points out that there is a parallelism between A.D. 135 and A.D. 70.[2] In each case the Roman authorities conclude successfully a bloody struggle against nationalist Jews. In each case Christians might hope to benefit from the state of affairs by showing their loyalty.[3] Their non-participation in the revolution of 66–70—wherever their sympathies may have lain—and their flight to Pella from Jerusalem were more negative in their effect upon Jewish/ Christian relationships than the later events of 132–5.[4] In this earlier revolt the year A.D. 68 marked the point at which the lunatic fringe took over control in Jerusalem, forcing many of the reasonable people to leave.[5] A sharp rupture, while a possibility after A.D. 70, is not required by the nature of the case, since the subsequent leaders of Jamnian Judaism failed in the same way as Christians to support the revolutionaries. There is little to distinguish R. Yohanan from the Jerusalem church so far as attitude to the revolt is concerned. Subsequent opposition must not be construed as a function of the polemic of a faithful nationalistic Jewish party against a non-faithful party of Christians.[6]

---

[1] So Simon, *Verus Israel*, p. 91.   [2] *Ibid.* pp. 146 f.

[3] The apologetic literature of the second century would support this for A.D. 135. The *in bonam partem* references to the state might support this for the NT, if their dates were established satisfactorily; some, though, are before A.D. 70 (Rom. 13: 1) and some adverse comments are certainly after (Rev. 13).

[4] There are insufficient grounds for maintaining that this is either unhistorical or happened earlier. J. Neusner, *A Life of Rabban Yohanan ben Zakkai; ca. 1–80 C.E.* (Leiden, 1962 = *SPB*, VI) makes a good case for Christians and R. Yohanan leaving Jerusalem for the same reasons and about the same time, i.e. winter 67–68 C.E. (p. 112 n. 4).

[5] See Cecil Roth's illuminating article on the groups involved in the revolutionary forces: 'The Zealots in the War of 66–73', *JSS*, IV (1959), 332–55, especially pp. 340 ff.; *idem*, 'The Constitution of the Jewish Republic of 66–70 A.D.', *JSS*, IX (1964), 295–319.

[6] The failure of the Diaspora to support the revolution is also an important point on this matter. Within the Greek communities the attitude of Christians and Jews towards the revolt seems to have been the same. On the Roman policy in this, Neusner is important; *Yohanan*, pp. 107, 124–6; cf. also Baron, *History*, I, on the non-participation of the Diaspora, pp. 231, 247.

The year A.D. 70 is widely held to be a major turning-point both for Judaism and for Christianity. That it was for the former cannot be disputed; for the latter it is more questionable, but the question need not seriously detain us.[1] We are concerned with the effects of A.D. 70 on the relationship of Christians and Jews. The most obvious effect was that it taught Christians to stay completely aloof in the future from Jewish nationalist movements, a lesson they had learned well by A.D. 132. There seems to have been a tendency for Christians to be associated with nationalist movements from the beginning, even though Jesus himself indicated a firm repudiation of such tendencies.[2] Christians, faced with the difficulties imposed by the War of 66–73, would be of two minds, and it was not until the flight to Pella that this tension was resolved. This is not to say that there was a sharp break with the Jewish people on nationalistic grounds.[3] They saw in the Fall of Jerusalem the judgment of God (and in retrospect a punishment for not believing in Christ)[4] in common with many other Jewish commentators on the tragedy.[5] But the Christian writings which we have make

[1] S. G. F. Brandon, *The Fall of Jerusalem and the Christian Church: A study of the Effects of the Jewish overthrow of A.D. 70 on Christianity* (London, 1951), is the most complete attempt to document this. This work has already been criticized by many. The majority of his work is irrelevant to this study; pp. 183 f. is the most significant part. See also E. Fascher, 'Jerusalems Untergang in der urchristlichen und altkirchlichen Überlieferung', *TLZ*, LXXXIX (1964), 81–98.

[2] W. R. Farmer, *Maccabees, Zealots and Josephus: an Inquiry into Jewish Nationalism in the Greco-Roman Period* (New York, 1956), ch. 8; cf. O. Cullmann, *The State in the NT* (London, 1957), esp. chs. 1 and 2; H. W. Montefiore, 'Revolt in the Desert', *NTS*, VIII (1961–2), 335–41. R. Eisler's thesis goes much too far; *Messiah Jesus* (London, 1931). On the other side, K. Nickle, *The Collection* (*SBT*, XLVIII, London, 1966) has suggested that the Zealot problem operates on a different level in the early Church. He finds them a factor in the Galatian and other situations, encouraging Gentile Christians to be circumcised so that they will conform to a minimal nationalist Judaism. This is unlikely on any meaningful interpretation of 'nationalism'.

[3] M. Hengel, *Die Zeloten* (Leiden, 1961, *AGSU*, 1) concludes his definitive study with a list of further studies necessary, one of which deals with this problem and NT attitudes to the State based upon the Zealot struggle with Rome. This has not yet been done.

[4] See Eusebius, *The History of the Church*, 3.5.

[5] Neusner, *Yohanan*, pp. 129 ff.

very little of this until after A.D. 135.[1] Christians did not, as a result of the revolt, abandon all concern for Israel as a people, even though Jews had been discredited by the events of the revolution and any associations with them would be suspect. Had this been so, they would have hesitated to assert their continuity with Israel, and especially would have been reluctant to admit any transference of names and privileges. The assertion of continuity is a constant factor in Christianity. Moreover it is virtually impossible to date disputed NT books (e.g. Hebrews) on the basis of pre- or post-70 allusions. We must reject the attempt to insert A.D. 70 into the history of Jewish/Christian relationships as the decisive date.[2] W. D. Davies, rightly, says: 'Any undue emphasis on the fall of Jerusalem is, therefore, to be avoided.'[3]

The conflicts between the Roman State and nationalistic Judaism served to make the Church, as well as many of the Jewish nation, conscious of the gap that separated them from Jewish Zealots.[4] The Church was encouraged to emphasize the 'spiritual' nature of many of their claims; e.g. the new and spiritual Jerusalem, Israel, circumcision, worship, law. But, though these factors were at work, the Jewish conflict with Rome did not itself create the need or the occasion for Christians to separate from Jews. Both Christians and Jews in Palestine

[1] Cf. C. F. D. Moule, *The Birth of the NT* (London, 1962), pp. 121 ff., see esp. p. 123 n. 2; cf. L. E. Elliott-Binns, *Galilean Christianity* (London, 1956, *SBT*, xvi), p. 64. B. H. Streeter, *The Primitive Church* (London, 1929), p. 42, has underlined the great gap between the Church in Jerusalem pre-70 and post-135.

[2] M. Goguel, *Les Premiers Temps de l'Église* (Neuchâtel, 1949), pp. 140, 153, points out that 60–70 is important because internal and external crises very nearly correspond chronologically. He fluctuates between putting the decisive date in 64 (pp. 195 f.) and 70 (p. 153).

[3] In his excellent article, 'The Apostolic Age and the Life of Paul', *Peake's Commentary on the Bible* (Edinburgh and London, 1962), pp. 870–81; the quote is from para. 768b. W. M. Ramsay, in *The Church in the Roman Empire before A.D. 170* (London, 1894, 3rd ed.), p. 364, regards the critical step as passed by A.D. 70 (in this case in the context of the development of the ministry).

[4] It is an arguable hypothesis that the original version of Josephus, *Wars of the Jews* (see 3.108), was intended to propagandize both Judeans and Diaspora Jews in order to dissuade them from revolting; see H. St J. Thackeray, *Josephus the Man and the Historian* (New York, 1929), pp. 23 ff.; H. St J. Hart, 'Judaea and Rome', *JTS*, n.s. III (1952), p. 183 n. 4.

failed to participate in the revolt, just as Christians and Jews in the Diaspora adopted much the same attitude to the revolts as a result of the exigencies of having to live under the Roman authority.[1] An analysis of the two revolts would lead us to place rather more emphasis upon the later than upon the earlier, at least so far as sealing the breach. The earlier revolt is important for what it reveals about the relationships, but has provided no evidence that it was a formative factor in creating a breach and a consequent take-over of prerogatives. To say, as some do, that this marks the beginning of a totally new 'dispensation' is a gross confusion of the realities of the situation.

ROMAN LAW AND PERSECUTION[2]

There is an immense literature on the subject, on which we can barely touch, but it is reduced to manageable proportions if we insist, so far as possible, on dealing only with the way the official attitude of the State reacted upon the growing distinction between the Church and Synagogue. The main issue is persecution by the State, though to one side must be left the extent of

---

[1] On the matter of the *Fiscus Judaicus*, there is some question about the extent of the requirement to pay the poll-tax to the Temple of Jupiter Capitolinus; see references in Josephus, *B.J.* 7.6.6; Suetonius, *Domitian*, 12; Dio Cassius, 66.7; and also comments by Schürer, *History*, II, 1, 251; II, 2, 266 f.; G. F. Moore, *Judaism in the First Centuries of the Christian Era: The Age of the Tannaim* (Cambridge, U.S.A., 1927), I, 234, 350 f., '...exacted from those who...lived like Jews as well as born Jews who concealed their race...'; and Baron, *History*, II, 105 ff. We should like to know if, in the collection, it was decreed that Christians were still 'Jewish' enough that they had to pay the tax, or if only Jewish Christians (or circumcised Christians) paid, or if their Christianity rendered them exempt from it. The sources do not allow us to say how the Roman authorities exercised their prerogative at this point. For a full bibliography of the subject and a new explanation, see I. A. F. Bruce, 'Nerva and the Fiscus Judaicus', *PEQ*, XCVI (1964), 34–45.

[2] The best short introduction is A. N. Sherwin-White in *JTS*, III (1952), 199–213. A useful treatment, though old, is H. B. Workman, *Persecution in the Early Church* (London, 1923, 4th edition); Ramsay, *The Church in the Roman Empire*, is still important; W. H. C. Frend, *Martyrdom and Persecution in the Early Church: a Study of a Conflict from the Maccabees to Donatus* (Oxford, 1965), is a definitive study, though unsatisfactory in many respects; cf. *idem*, 'The Persecutions: some links between Judaism and the Early Church' in *JEH*, IX (1958), 141–58.

persecution,[1] the charges associated with persecution, and the means whereby the charge was given legal effect.[2] The following is based on the view that Christians were prosecuted under the *coercitio* procedure rather than on the basis of a *lex*, and that this was in connection with the transgression of the edicts of the Roman Emperor on the subject of *collegia*.[3] By the time Christians were recognized as distinct from Jews, enough was known about the Church and its practices to make possible a judgment based upon a confession of being a Christian, although the basic charge was still predicated upon *collegia* laws. It is possible to say that they were being persecuted for the name, though this itself was not formulated as a crime,[4] since the admission of the *nomen* was sufficient indication of adherence to the *flagitia* of the cult.

There were instances of persecution under Hadrian, Trajan, Vespasian, Nero, Claudius and Tiberius. The best starting-point is still Trajan's rescript to Pliny the Younger.[5] He does

[1] Older historians have tended to exaggerate the extent; recent historians, convincingly, have reduced it considerably; see *inter alia* R. L. P. Milburn, *CQR*, cxxxix (1944–5), 154–64; J. Moreau, *La Persécution du Christianisme dans l'Empire romain* (Paris, 1956).

[2] The best introductory article and résumé is by H. Last in *RAC*, ii (1954), cols. 1208–28; cf. J. Vogt, *ibid.* cols. 1159–1208, and more briefly K. Wessel, *RGG*, i (1957), cols. 1730–2. Three recent works in English are particularly relevant; S. L. Guterman, *Religious Toleration and Persecution in Ancient Rome* (London, 1951, no bibliography is later than 1932); A. N. Sherwin-White, *Roman Society and Roman Law in the NT* (Oxford, 1963, Sarum Lectures for 1960–1); A. H. M. Jones, *Studies in Roman Government and Law* (Oxford, 1960).

[3] A good treatment of these, from a sociological and non-legal standpoint, is found in S. Dill, *Roman Society from Nero to Marcus Aurelius* (London, 1905, 2nd edition), pp. 251–86. *The Cambridge Ancient History*, volumes x and xi (Cambridge, 1934 and 1936), also have useful descriptive and background materials.

[4] The dispute on this matter breaks into two basic positions: that of Th. Mommsen, that the judicial procedures are occasional and a function of the prefects' or proconsuls' *imperium*; and that of Callewaert, that there is an *institutum Neronianum* specifying the crime. On the Neronic question, see J. W. Ph. Borleffs in *VC*, vi (1952), 129–45, who argues that this *institutum Neronianum* is nothing more than 'le sens de coutume, d'usage de condamner et de punir les chrétiens'. The question of *religio licita* and *illicita*, as F. C. Grant shows (*Studia Patristica* iv, Berlin, 1961, *TU*, 79) is irrelevant here.

[5] Book x, 96–7: a convenient text and notes are found in Lightfoot,

not answer the question, posed by Pliny, whether the *nomen ipsum* is sufficient charge. But the implications are that participation as a Christian in the cult or *collegia* is justification for punishment, and on the other hand that adherence to the 'name' itself is to be subordinated to the necessity that they be hard-core Christians—*si deferantur et arguantur, puniendi sunt.* There is not an automatic relationship between profession of the name and punishment, but confession of the name is compromising in the eyes of the State, unless it is repudiated.[1] By this time (A.D. 112), in spite of many misunderstandings, Christianity is known by the officials in the provinces as a religion distinct from Judaism.

There is less clarity, however, in the evidence for persecution under Domitian.[2] In the notorious execution of Flavius Clemens and the exile of his wife Flavia Domitilla (the charge against whom was ἀθεότης = *sacrilegium*, which may be associated here with a vague charge about Jewish practices)[3] a difficulty is posed by the archaeological evidence which has been held to indicate that Domitilla (and therefore also her husband?) was a Christian sympathizer if not a Christian herself. If the suggestion of Dio Cassius that the charge was related to Jewish practice be substantiated, then this supposes a confusion about the separate identities of Jews and Christians in the time of Domitian.[4] This is difficult to believe; it is more likely that Dio's account has become garbled, or that the catacomb evidence has had a rather more definite construction placed upon it by scholars than is actually possible. The evidence for

Fathers (London, 1889), II, I, 50 ff., together with a full list of notices relating to Trajanic persecution; documents relating to Hadrian, Pius, and Marcus (pp. 476 ff.); and in I, I, 104 ff. to Domitian.

[1] Sherwin-White, *JTS*, III (1952), 209, calls this Pliny's 'try-out' of the custom of persecution in view of the jurisdictional freedom granted to him by virtue of his *imperium*. He goes on (p. 210) to point out that, though disproval of the *flagitia* should result in toleration, in fact one *crimen* was replaced by another as the *cohaerens scelus*. The reasonable demand to participate in the worship of the Emperor did not make Christians guilty of *maiestas* upon refusal, but rather of *contumacia*.

[2] See especially R. L. P. Milburn, *CQR*, cxxxix (1944–5), 154–64.

[3] τὰ τῶν Ἰουδαίων ἔθη: Dio Cassius, 67.14. This is found only in a late and abridged (and therefore worked over) manuscript. Suetonius says (*Dom.* 15) that it was 'upon some very slight suspicion'.

[4] See the discussion in J. Moreau, *Persécution*, pp. 36 ff.

a widespread Christian persecution under Domitian is late, probably exaggerated, and largely irrelevant here.[1]

It is possible, but not proven, that there was persecution under Vespasian; it is indeed certain that he expelled the *philosophi* from Rome.[2] Material for our quest is lacking. More important is the Neronic persecution of the Christians as a result, says Tacitus, of the need to find a scapegoat for Nero for the great fire (*ergo abolendo rumori Nero subdidit reos...*).[3] Tacitus' account suggests total identification of Christians as a separate entity: 'Auctor nominis eius Christus Tiberio imperitante per procuratorem Pontium Pilatum supplicio adfectus erat... erumpebat, non modo per Iudaeam, originem eius mali, sed per urbem etiam...' By mentioning the place of their origin and the generating cause Tacitus implies that civil recognition is total by A.D. 64.[4] This is the first evidence of such recognition. To what extent it is due to Poppaea's influence is pure speculation,[5] but it is quite within the realm of possibility

[1] It is difficult to conceive any possible reason for the 'Jewish' reference in Dio, if Clemens were executed as a Christian. It will not do to say that the phrase (see p. 40 n. 3) points to his being a Christian when it is long after the break is perfectly observable. If we take the language at its face value, and accept Dio's account, we must suppose a blurring of distinctives in A.D. 95. In his careful analysis of this, J. Vogt (*RAC*, II, 1167–70) concludes that it is 'possible' that the charge against him was sympathy with Christianity, even though the real reason may have been otherwise.

[2] See Ramsay's theory that 1 Pet. reflects a situation in the late 70s and that Peter may have been martyred therefore under Vespasian, *Church in the Roman Empire*, pp. 279–95.

[3] *Annals*, 15.44, cf. 15.38. Text in G. O. Holbrooke, *Annals of Tacitus* (London, 1882); translation by M. Grant (London, 1959, 2nd edition, repr. 1964); see H. Fuchs, 'Tacitus über die Christen', *VC*, IV (1950), 65–93.

[4] How far this may be taken to represent the real attitude of Nero's day is a moot question. The substance of the account must be true, and this carries with it the distinction between Jew and Christian. Suetonius (*Nero*, 16) also knows of Christians as a recognizable entity, punished by Nero, but not with reference to the fire.

[5] Cf. Josephus, *Antiquities*, 20.8.11; *Vita*, 3; she was Nero's wife during the period of the fire (cf. Suetonius, *Nero*, 35; Tacitus, *Annals*, 13.45 f.; 16.6; and see Schürer, *History*, Div. 2, II, 238 f. n. 74). It is of some interest that Poppaea's father had been ruined by his friendship with the notorious Sejanus (Tacitus, *Annals*, 13.45). M. Goguel suggests that it was largely due to Josephus, who was in Rome about this time (*Vita*, 3), that the distinction was made known (*Les Premiers Temps de l'Église*, Neuchâtel, 1949, p. 194).

that by this time Jews themselves were actively propagating the distinction from their side, and used Poppaea's position to that end.[1]

When we turn to Suetonius' account of Claudius' expulsion of the Jews from Rome (*Claud.* 25),[2] and also that under Tiberius (*Tib.* 36), it is clear that Suetonius does not distinguish between Jews and Christians. This may be either because he knows it would be an anachronism, or else because it simply does not occur to him to do so, even in the case where he mentions one *Chrestus*.[3] Even though this is a common name, it is difficult to escape the notion that Suetonius is referring to a riot between Christian and non-Christian Jews.

There are two very important factors arising out of this brief analysis: in the imperial city Christians are distinguished from Jews by A.D. 64, but not as early as A.D. 49. The State's recognition of their separate status occurred somewhere between these two dates according to the Roman sources. Secondly, there was in Rome the necessary situation for this distinction being pressed from the Jewish side but not from the Christian side: there was, first, the Jews' indignation at having been expelled from Rome because of the Christians in A.D. 49 and, secondly, the presence in the imperial court of one or more influential persons who could press the Jewish point of view. Persecution *per se* played no role in the actual separation from the Christian side, although it provided the reason, within the context of the governing authorities, for both the original move towards

---

[1] J. Moreau, *Persécution*, p. 35: Frend, *Martyrdom*, p. 164, agrees but makes the attempt too premeditated and grandiose.

[2] On the expulsion see H. J. Léon, *The Jews of Ancient Rome* (Philadelphia, 1960), pp. 23 ff. He inclines to an earlier date (closer to 41) rather than a later date (49–50). For an interesting conjecture about the effects of the expulsion, see E. Bammel in *ZTK*, LVI (1959), 294 ff.; cf. F. F. Bruce, 'Christianity under Claudius', *BJRL*, XLIV (1962), 309–26.

[3] Unless in *Tib.* 36 *similia sectantes* alludes to sects which are offshoots of Judaism, but this is generally rejected. If this were sustained, it would be a case of unusual historical accuracy to call Christians a sect in A.D. 49 but later to refer to them under their own name in the year A.D. 64. Note also his suggestion in *Dom.* 12 (re *Fiscus Judaicus*) that there is a confusion in this later period between (*a*) Jews, (*b*) those who lived as Jews, (*c*) those who did not publicly profess to be Jews but lived like them, and (*d*) those who concealed their Jewishness. Whether Christians are involved in one or other of these is a matter of conjecture.

separation and the continuing reason (after A.D. 64) for Jews maintaining that separation. After A.D. 70 it may have become to the Christians' advantage, in part at least, to maintain the distinctiveness of Christianity, but this would be primarily a case of perpetuating a recognized state of affairs. In the provinces, at least by A.D. 112 and very likely earlier, this distinction had been noted officially and pressed home. It is germane to this discussion that in Palestine, Asia Minor, Macedonia, and Achaia from the Jewish side again, the distinction between Jew and Christian was evident as early as Paul's ministry. It is therefore possible that disturbances resulting in official action in the provinces were reported to Rome in the 50s, and these, together with the other factors mentioned, gave rise to the new situation which begins some time around 55–64: a confession that one participates in a *collegium* that, according to the authorities, has such antisocial tendencies that it is in effect proscribed, can lead to court proceedings (if not summary justice). It is sufficient to confess the *nomen ipsum*.

JEWISH AUTHORITIES AND PERSECUTION

Jewish persecution of adherents of the Messianic sect played an important part in the break between the Church and Judaism. Probably this was a factor as far away as Rome, as early as the fifties. We turn now to the Palestinian persecution reflected in nearly all books of the NT,[1] in the Apostolic Fathers, and even in the Apologists. Sometimes this took the form of outright persecution, sometimes proscription of Christians from Jewish activities.[2] The most important event in this state of affairs is the Synagogue Ban against the *minim*,[3] which we may tentatively date somewhere between A.D. 80 and 90. R. Gamaliel II, who went to Rome to see the Emperor Domitian on behalf of the Jews, inserted this into the *Shemoneh Esreh* as the twelfth Benediction; in one form it explicitly excludes not just *minim*

---

[1] C. F. D. Moule, *The Birth of the NT* (London, 1962), ch. 7: 'What can be identified is mainly Jewish rather than imperial...' (p. 124); '...Judaism bulks by far the largest among the antagonists of Christianity which have left their stamp on the NT' (p. 105).

[2] See J. Jocz, *Jewish People*, pp. 45 ff. on Jewish liturgical alterations.

[3] For bibliography, see Schrage, ἀποσυνάγωγος in *TWNT*, VII, 845 ff. Note especially the discussion in Jocz, *Jewish People*, pp. 51–7 and 174–90.

but also *nozrim*.[1] This interpolation by the Jamnian authorities was propagated officially among the synagogues of the Diaspora so that its effect was spread fairly quickly over the Mediterranean world.[2] Hence, not long after the fall of Jerusalem we find the leaders who, with Christians, evacuated Jerusalem in A.D. 68 creating a test designed to accelerate (if not conclude) the breach between Christians and Jews.[3]

Perhaps the fact that this negative and exclusive action is taken by the authority newly reconstituted in Jamnia, in place of a more hostile form of action, is indicative of the new care required on their part in the face of Roman distrust after the revolution.[4] A turning-point of sorts has been reached; from now on opposition is more subtle.[5] The general reaction to exclude is preceded by a series of actions against Christians by the Jewish authorities. It is important to note that these are directed against specific individuals[6] and more specifically, understandably, against Jewish Christians, never against Gentile Christians. The line stretches from James the Just,[7] back through Paul,[8] the imprisonment of Peter and the execution of James the brother of John by Herod Agrippa, to the condemnation of Stephen by the council (εἰς τὸ συνέδριον, Acts 6: 12). If we add to this the random allusions to the Jerusalem authorities actively engaging in what amounts to police action

---

[1] See S. Schechter, *JQR*, x (1898), 654–9.

[2] However, in view of later references to Christian worship in Synagogues (see Baron, *History*, II, 188 and notes) the measure was not entirely effective.

[3] Whatever *minim* actually meant, its intention was in large part directed towards Christians; *nozrim* properly interprets this. 'Die Einführung dieser Benediktion in das Schemone 'Esre u damit in die Liturgie der Synagoge durch R. Gamaliel II, um 90 n. Chr. entschied definitiv über den radikalen Bruch zwischen der chr. Kirche u dem Judt.' (Schrage, *TWNT*, VII, 848.)

[4] See J. Neusner, *Yohanan*, pp. 125 ff., 147 ff.

[5] It is consistent with this that it is not until the renewed Zealot government of A.D. 132–5 that one hears directly of Jewish persecution of Christians again. The references in Rev. 2: 9 and 3: 9, e.g., presuppose opposition, but not necessarily overt persecution.

[6] Though cf. Acts 8: 1: διωγμὸς μέγας (καὶ θλῖψις D (h sa)); almost the same authorities add ἐπὶ τοὺς πιστούς at 12: 3 (D sy^hmg sy^p); note also 1 Thess. 2: 14.

[7] Condemned either by Jewish courts alone, or by crowd action.

[8] Whose *delatores* must have gone to Rome to press the charges against him; it was a formal accusation to the Roman governor after the unsuccessful attempt to lynch him by mob action.

in the near countries (if not farther afield also),[1] and if we take into account the local opposition in centres in Asia Minor and Macedonia and Achaia about which we read in Acts, we find a consistent picture of sporadic outbreaks of the fullest use of the authorities' powers together with a more persistent illegal attempt to hold back the Christian sect.[2]

However, against this activity must be balanced the facts which were noted in connection with the Apostolic Fathers. The persecution is real and at times very violent, but it is not so thorough that it precludes continuing contacts.[3] The evidence portrays, for the most part, a strictly occasional persecution, prompted generally by a specific affront, though there was, perhaps, considerable variety.[4] On the one hand, Jewish opposition in the early period was more provoked than a stated policy; on the other hand, it was historically inevitable as an instinctive reaction. The challenge which Christianity presented to the Judaism of its day was clear:[5] it believed not just

---

[1] We have already noted Justin's preoccupation with this activity in his day.

[2] On the competence of the *synedrion* and for a full bibliography see Lohse, *TWNT*, vii, 858–69, especially pp. 862 ff. The description by Harnack, *Mission*, pp. 57 f., is too strong: 'The Jews now sought to extirpate the Palestinian Churches and to silence the Christian missionaries. They hampered every step of Paul's work among the gentiles; they cursed Christians and Christ in their synagogues; they stirred up the masses and the authorities in every country against him; systematically and officially they scattered broadcast horrible charges against the Christians, which played an important part...in the persecutions as early as the reign of Trajan; they started calumnies against Jesus; they provided heathen opponents of Christianity with literary ammunition; unless the evidence is misleading they started the Neronic outburst against the Christians; and, as a rule, whenever bloody persecutions are afoot in later days, the Jews are either in the background or the foreground...'

[3] The literary disputes alone are evidence of this, apart from the information within the literature. Cf. J. Parkes, *Conflict*, ch. 4; contrast Harnack, *Mission*, p. 59.

[4] Perhaps the persecutors varied too, and the background against which the persecution was to be understood; see Bo Reicke in *Studia Paulina: in hon. J. de Zwaan* (Haarlem, 1953, ed. J. N. Sevenster and W. C. van Unnik), pp. 172–87. J. Weiss, *Earliest Christianity: A History of the Period A.D. 30–150*, i (New York, repr. 1959), 138 ff., 169 ff., 186 ff., and ii, 709 ff. (on James), is overly sceptical about the accounts and the charges noted. He takes the death of Stephen as one of the great turning-points in the early Church, p. 140.

[5] Cf. F. V. Filson, *A NT History* (London, 1965), pp. 173 f.

in the teaching of a teacher who had been rejected, but in the Messiahship of one who was branded as an impostor and the divinity of one condemned for blasphemy. When challenged to retract their judgment and accept as true his claims, the Jewish leaders could do no other than exercise to the fullest extent their authority. Whatever the specific occasion for proceeding against a Christian, the underlying reason was necessarily christological.[1] There is a direct line between the part played by the Jews in the death of Jesus and their part in the subsequent persecutions of those who followed him.[2]

The persecution of Christians by Jews in the thirties, forties and fifties is both a cause of the rupture, and a result of the recognition of the distinctive aspects of Christianity. In this situation it would beg the question to apportion 'blame': Christian teaching (rightly) gave offence to orthodox Jews, and the inevitable result was opposition aimed at stamping out Christianity. If Jesus was put to death as a blasphemer (on the Jewish interpretation) and a Zealot (from the Roman side), it was impossible for his followers not to be regarded in much the same light as long as they were vocal about their beliefs.[3] During the first years Christians would have been regarded as a heterodox party still within Judaism, and any punishment might be viewed as necessary internal correction. This is the atmosphere in Stephen's death and Saul's commission. The persecution is better called 'discipline' at this stage, even though it be of the most severe kind. This discipline, as so often is the case, resulted in the hardening of each party's attitude and created a sympathetic hearing for Christians among the populace. But continual discipline slides into persecution, and

[1] So J. Jocz, *Jewish People*, pp. 157–63, especially pp. 162 f.: 'The process of separation began immediately after the death of Jesus, and was necessitated by an inner logic which made compromise impossible; between the two diametrically opposed groups stood the crucified Messiah. The inevitable persecution which thus arose hastened the process...' Similarly L. Goppelt, *Christentum und Judentum im ersten und zweiten Jahrhundert: ein Aufriß der Urgeschichte der Kirche* (Gütersloh, 1954), pp. 72–5.

[2] It is strange that Frend, *Martyrdom*, makes no assessment of the importance of Jesus' death upon his disciples' attitude. One cannot speak of persecution in this context apart from christology.

[3] Does Gamaliel's speech in Acts 5: 35–9 reflect a situation in which Jews thought of Jesus' disciples as Zealots? This misunderstanding could be possible in the early years, but hardly for very long.

46

persecution of one group by another demands separation. We have not sufficient evidence to know when the internal correction shifts over to external opposition. In Palestine, where the Christian group was entirely Jewish in background, this would happen later than in the Diaspora, where the additional offence created by the admission of Gentile converts without circumcision, and the inability to discipline these from inside, create a more volatile situation.

Jewish persecution, then, because it was originally an *intra muros* controversy, played a more creative role than did Roman opposition. The latter was concerned with Christianity only after it became separate, the former helped to make it a separate entity and to see that it was recognized as such by the Roman authorities. To this point we have had to concentrate upon the factors prompting a self-conscious recognition of separation from both Jewish and Christian sides. The place of persecution is important, particularly in so far as it helps in making more precise the timing of the stages of the break. But the events and writings surveyed so far have not determined the date at which separation became either desirable or necessary, nor the internal and theological reasons which led up to the breach. It has described the external effects of the 'inner logic' of the break. We must turn now to an analysis of that logic itself beginning from the life and teaching of Jesus.

CHAPTER IV

JESUS AND HIS DISCIPLES

INTRODUCTION

To this point we have looked at evidence, external to the New Testament, which describes or might help to describe the Church/Israel relationship. Two facts have emerged: (1) in the post-apostolic period the relationship is not assumed to be a simply defined chasm which precludes interest in the other party; on the contrary, there is considerable uncertainty about the Church's approach to Judaism, and only a late take-over of the title 'Israel' by the Church. (2) No one event or group of events is responsible for the break. From these facts we may infer that the eventual separation only gradually developed. It does not abruptly become an impassable gap, even though points can be isolated at which the gap noticeably widens. We may infer also that the decisive factor is not an event in Church history but, on the contrary, a number of internal (and often unobserved) shifts in opinion and practice consequent upon the event of Jesus' death and resurrection, and the inner logic following from this. The description of the externally observable phenomena in the situation of increasing separation has been a necessary preliminary to the description of the internal factors.

In this chapter we shall lay the groundwork for this assessment by stating Jesus' appraisal of his role within Judaism; his attitude to the Judaism of his day; his view of a newly formed people of God; and his expectation of a mission beyond Israel.[1] We can concentrate only upon certain basic questions

---

[1] Parallel to our treatment is that of N. A. Dahl, *Das Volk Gottes: eine Untersuchung zum Kirchenbewußtsein des Urchristentums* (Oslo, 1941; 2nd edition, Darmstadt, 1963, unrevised); especially pt 3, ch. 1. Cf. G. Johnston, *The Doctrine of the Church in the New Testament* (Cambridge, 1943), especially chs. 3–4; R. Newton Flew, *Jesus and His Church: A Study of the Idea of the Ecclesia in the New Testament* (London, 1945, rev. edition), pt 1. O. Linton gives an excellent discussion of the history of this problem up to 1932, *Das Problem der Urkirche in der neueren Forschung, eine kritische Darstellung* (Uppsala Universitets Årsskrift, Uppsala, 1932).

as they impinge upon our thesis. We must leave many matters to one side. In particular, the question whether or not Jesus intended to found a church is displaced in favour of the question concerning the relationship of Jesus' followers to Israel. We shall examine only the views of Jesus himself; the rather sketchy treatment of the material will be partially rectified when we examine the individual evangelists later (ch. 6). This is the first stage in tracing from the beginning the growth of the idea that Christians are 'True Israel', a development which, as we have seen, comes to fulfilment by *c.* A.D. 160.

JESUS AND HIS MISSION

The most fundamental question about Jesus of Nazareth is concerned with his self-consciousness.[1] The evidence is of two kinds: Jesus' teaching (using the best critical procedures to come close to his *ipsissima verba*), and an analysis of the implications of his actions. Neither of these facets—which themselves are not finally separable—can lead to an assured answer. Taken together, the teaching and the actions reinforcing each other, there is a good case for the assertion that, at the end of his career, Jesus consciously knew himself as the Anointed One of Israel.[2] The evidence points to this being a growing awareness, stronger and more complete at the end of his ministry than at the beginning.[3] Whether there is a precise event which crystallizes the loosely associated indications of it is still open to

[1] Many today would dismiss this question immediately, holding that it is an illegitimate one. But, if a certain amount of naïvety may be permitted, it seems to be an essential part of the task. It is interesting to note that the question 'Who is Jesus of Nazareth?' is a very frequent one among inquiring University students. O. Cullmann, *The Christology of the New Testament* (2nd edition, London, 1963) is a basic work, in spite of a number of shortcomings; beside this should be placed the more critical *The Foundations of New Testament Christology* by R. H. Fuller (London, 1965).

[2] R. H. Fuller, *The Mission and Achievement of Jesus* (London, 1954, *SBT*, XII), p. 116, would prefer to say the 'pre-Messianic' consciousness of Jesus; cf. the same writer's later treatment, *Christology*, ch. 5.

[3] G. Bornkamm, *Jesus of Nazareth* (New York, 1960), p. 172, rejects this, and mentions a 'movement of broken Messianic hopes'. He goes on to say that the 'Messianic character of his being is contained *in* his words and deeds and *in* the unmediatedness of his historic appearance' (his italics, p. 178).

question.[1] Here we cannot pause to discuss this matter, but shall assume that Jesus is aware of having a special mission to his people given to him by God, and that this *Selbstbewußtsein* colours his teaching and is the origin of many of his actions.

His self-consciousness has no meaning apart from the Jewish background of certain ideas and the Jewishness of Jesus himself.[2] As a member of his race, he has a strong attraction to and appreciation of the scriptures, but he stands apart from fellow Jews in his conviction that God is, in him, fulfilling the scriptures. Only on this premise can sense be made of Jesus' claims in relation to the Law, tradition, and Jewish institutions. When he uses the famous ἐγὼ δὲ λέγω ὑμῖν (or the less emphatic λέγω ὑμῖν)[3] he is asserting his function as reinterpreter of the Law and as judge of people's attitude to it in the present.[4] This, however, is not simply a negative judgment, as the Q saying in Luke 6: 46 //Matthew 7: 21 makes clear: the reinterpretation demands a positive obedience, not because of the statement's intrinsic worth and self-authentication, but because it is said by this man who speaks with authority:[5] τί δέ με καλεῖτε· κύριε κύριε, καὶ οὐ ποιεῖτε ἃ λέγω;

The heart of 'what I say' is a double demand, to receive the

---

[1] T. W. Manson (*The Teaching of Jesus*, Cambridge, 1963, *passim*) has made the strongest case for the confession by Peter being such an event; H. W. Montefiore in *NTS*, VIII (1961–2), 135–41, has suggested the feeding of the five thousand which comes shortly before this. Others would suggest the Baptism of John, the Temptation, the Entry into Jerusalem, and so on.

[2] However, J. Klausner, *From Jesus to Paul* (E.T. 1953, repr. Boston, 1961), p. 5 (cf. *Jesus of Nazareth*, London, 1925, pp. 369–407), speaks of the 'quantitative exaggeration of a thing which turns it into a new quality' so that Jesus' Jewishness becomes non-Jewish.

[3] In the antitheses, some of which are beyond dispute (Matt. 5: 21 ff.); cf. also Matt. 5: 18 and 20 about the law and righteousness. For the former see W. D. Davies, *The Setting of the Sermon on the Mount* (Cambridge, 1963); for the latter see G. Barth, in Bornkamm, Barth and Held, *Tradition and Interpretation in Matthew* (London, 1963), pp. 64 ff.

[4] See J. A. Baird, *The Justice of God in the Teaching of Jesus* (London, 1963), pp. 245 ff., 248 f. For the eschatological significance see Fuller, *Christology*, pp. 104 f.

[5] Baird, *Justice*, p. 247; cf. R. Bultmann, *Theology of the New Testament*, I (London, 1952), 9 f.; he distinguishes between the call to decision which Jesus makes and his pointing ahead to a coming Messianic Son of Man.

good news and to repent of sin.[1] This proclaiming and teaching activity of Jesus[2] is not confined either by the prophetic or rabbinic examples, but goes beyond anything seen before. Both the opposition and amazement which it engenders in the hearers validate the evangelists' reports of the teaching: ὡς ἐξουσίαν ἔχων (Mark 1: 22//Matt. 7: 29; cf. Luke 4: 32). The evangelists are all aware of the relationship between the ministries of teaching and healing.[3] Healing pericopes often indicate a relationship between all the basic factors: healing, repentance, forgiveness, and the reception of the good news (e.g. Mark 2: 1 ff. pars.). In the one person, Jesus, this variety of functions is associated indivisibly.[4] The significance of the concentration of attention upon his own person by Jesus' acts and teaching is appreciated by the observers, though misunderstood.[5] It constantly creates consternation where there is no commitment (and often even where there is commitment) to that person.

Jesus seeks committed followers because he is confident that he can point them to God, with whom he is conscious of standing in a specially close relationship. This relationship with God is discussed at some length in the gospel of John. Apart, however, from that treatment, it is clear that his claims depend for their legitimacy on the question whether or not Jesus is the eschatological prophet and teacher. If he is the one who is to break into history at the end of days and point conclusively to the conclusion of history, then his sometimes obscure references to his relationship with God take on additional point. For the one who ushers in the last days and inaugurates the Kingdom of

---

[1] Luke at this point omits the reference to forgiveness (4: 14 f.) which Matthew and Mark share. Only Mark (1: 14 f.) emphasizes εὐαγγέλιον; Luke stresses the teaching function—though he later quotes from Isa. 61: 1 f. and 58: 6, in which both Mark's and Matthew's words are prominent.

[2] Stressed again in Mark 1: 21 ff.//Luke 4: 31 ff.

[3] Matthew particularly; a section of healing stories follows a section of teaching (5–7; 8–9); he organizes the characteristics of the ministry in 4: 23 and 9: 35 (teaching, preaching, healing); he replaces with ἐθεράπευσεν (19: 2) Mark's ἐδίδασκεν (10: 1). Note also Mark 6: 12//Luke 9: 6.

[4] Cf. the Q account of John's disciples' question in Matt. 11: 2 ff. par. with the same demand for acceptance of 'me'.

[5] Most notably the disciples' amazement as a result of the stilling of the storm: τίς ἄρα οὗτός ἐστιν;; the general disturbance about who Jesus is in Mark 6: 14 ff. pars., cf. Mark 8: 27 ff. pars; the tentative answer of his opponents in Mark 3: 20–30 pars.

God has, by definition, a special position with respect to God. Is it perhaps for this very reason that John the Baptist decisively repudiates his own Messianic status? Is it not for this reason that Jesus affirms it?[1] John points men to the one who points them to God; Jesus is the way to God. He accepts this role of leader to which he knows himself divinely appointed, and with this confidence he calls for followers (Mark 8: 24 ff. pars.).

As leader he sends out others in his name[2] who announce with equal authority the dawn of the Kingdom of God.[3] Because this is God's mission to which they have been appointed, the task can be carried out without fear (Matt. 10: 26 ff.) and with the certainty that God will confirm it by the presence of the Holy Spirit (Luke 12: 2 ff.). Now, the centre of this message is the kingly rule of God, which is made available through a commitment to Jesus. He sweeps away conventions and traditions which impede God's control over men and claims superiority over the leaders of Judaism as an interpreter of what God wants. As a result Sabbath, Temple, Law, sacrifices are christologically re-

[1] Basic to his position is his conviction that he is 'Son of Man', a matter into which we must avoid digressing. Out of the immense literature, see M. Black, *BJRL*, XLV (1963), 305–18; H. E. Tödt, *The Son of Man in the Synoptic Tradition* (London, 1965; E.T. of 2nd German edition); A. J. B. Higgins, *Jesus and the Son of Man* (London, 1964); E. Sjöberg, *Der Verborgene Menschensohn in den Evangelien* (Lund, 1955 = *Skrifter Utgivna av Kungl. Humanistiska Vetenskapssamfundet i Lund*, 53); F. Kattenbusch, 'Der Quellort der Kirchenidee' in *Festgabe von Fachgenossen und Freunden A. von Harnack zum 70ᵉⁿ Geburtstag* (Tübingen, 1921), pp. 143–72; J. Coppens and L. Dequeker, *Le Fils de l'homme et les Saints du Très-Haut en Daniel vii, dans les Apocryphes et dans le NT* (Louvain, 1961) (= *Analecta Bib. et Orient.* Ser. III, Fasc. 23); Cullmann, *Christology*, ch. 6; Dalman, *The Words of Jesus* (Edinburgh, 1902), pp. 234–67; R. Otto, *The Kingdom of God and the Son of Man* (London, 1943, 2nd edition).

[2] The authoritative 'I send you' (Luke 10: 3//Matt. 10: 16) implies what is made explicit in the disciples' exclamation on their return that the demons are subject to them *in Jesus' name* (Luke 10: 17).

[3] The Kingdom of God in the teaching of Jesus is a large matter, and one that directly affects his self-consciousness and the eschatological character of his ministry. See R. Otto, as above; J. Héring, *Le Royaume de Dieu et sa Venue* (Paris, 1937); N. Perrin, *The Kingdom of God in the Teaching of Jesus* (London, 1963); G. Lundström, *The Kingdom of God in the Teaching of Jesus* (Edinburgh, 1963); R. Schnackenburg, *God's Rule and Kingdom* (Freiburg, 1963); note also the very important attempt to go against the current by S. Aalen, '"Reign" and "House" in the Kingdom of God', *NTS*, VIII (1961–2), 215–40.

interpreted by the One who is greater than them all.[1] The previous commitment to these institutions demanded by the leaders is replaced by a commitment to the God of Israel alone, made known by this one new leader.[2]

Jesus' mission of teaching, preaching, healing, of calling disciples, of ushering in the Kingdom does not imply that Israel is supplanted. Consistently his activity is set within the context of the Temple or synagogue,[3] and apparently he accepts both the form and fact of these institutions.[4] His personal superiority to these does not involve a total repudiation of the institutions. Similarly, whenever he steps outside the bounds of Israel itself, it is regarded as extraordinary.[5] His intention is to work within regularly constituted Judaism, to verify and express his self-consciousness within the context of the expectation of his own day. That the working-out of this consciousness does not conform to the general expectation is obvious from the accounts, and this fact is necessary to account for the incidents leading up to Jesus' death. Nevertheless, this discrepancy between the two does not result in a determination to move outside Israel and carry on the work in new surroundings. Instead, it leads to an increasingly violent confrontation between Jesus and the representatives of institutional Judaism.

JESUS AND THE OLD ENTITY

Jesus works almost entirely with Israel—its institutions and peoples.[6] His synagogue ministry seems to have been extensive,

[1] None of these claims could have been created by the Church. The contrast between his own personal superiority to this tradition and the tradition itself is too bold; e.g. Mark 3: 1 ff. pars. (cf. Mark 2: 23 ff. pars.).

[2] This does not mean, as Goguel suggests (*The Life of Jesus*, London, 1933, p. 319, cf. p. 585), that Jesus unknowingly brought a new religion.

[3] E.g. Mark 11: 11, 15, 27 pars.; and Mark 1: 21, 39; 3: 1; 6: 2 pars.

[4] He encourages obedience to the requirement of the Law by the leper whom he heals; Mark 1: 44 pars.

[5] This is stated most energetically by J. Jeremias, *Jesus' Promise to the Nations* (London, 1958, *SBT*, xxiv), ch. 1, B and C.

[6] For this section see L. Goppelt, *Jesus, Paul and Judaism* (New York, 1964), pt 1, pp. 44–96; cf. Goguel, *Life*, p. 321, who holds that Jesus later despaired of the nation and thought that the structure and privileges of Judaism would be abolished, 'but the time was too short for him to act on this conviction'.

and when he moves to Jerusalem it is appropriate for this prophet of Israel to carry out his ministry in the Temple precincts. But while he accepted these institutions he did not hesitate, while in them, to make what could only appear to be blasphemous statements,[1] and to act in ways which appeared questionable.[2] There is an element of judgment in his actions within the synagogue and Temple. In Mark 1: 44 pars. the man who is cured of leprosy is to go into the Temple with the required offering, εἰς μαρτύριον αὐτοῖς. It is not clear what is intended here, but it may involve both an acceptance of the Law and the custom,[3] and also a judgment upon the leaders for failure to believe what Jesus is doing among men.[4] The phrase is used later in the little apocalypse *in malam partem* of testimony before synagogues.[5] In each case the synagogue is both accepted and rejected. The same ambivalence is found in his attitude to the Temple—he both cleanses it and speaks of its destruction;[6] the Law—he affirms it and reinterprets it;[7] the Sabbath—he acknowledges it and yet he frees it; sacrifice—he accepts it and portrays himself as a replacement.[8] Even the leaders of Judaism

[1] Luke 4: 16–30; cf. Mark 6: 1 ff.//Matt. 13: 53 ff., both of whom omit the nature of the offence.

[2] The inherent authority of the teaching and healing, and the newness of the implications right in the place committed to maintaining and expounding the tradition, can hardly be overestimated (Mark 1: 27 par.; 3: 6 pars.). This leads to opposition, though perhaps not so quickly as Mark implies.

[3] And a reply to the accusation that Jesus teaches non-observance?

[4] Μαρτύριον need not imply accusing testimony, but simply 'evidence'. Here it may be a more passive evidence of what God is doing in Jesus. See L. Hartman, *Testimonium Linguae* (*Con. Neot.* 19, Lund, 1963) on Luke 21: 13 (pp. 57–75).

[5] Mark 13: 9//Luke 21: 13; Matt. places it elsewhere (10: 18; 24: 14) coupled with ἔθνεσιν. In Mark 6: 11 it has the same judging function (Luke reads ἐπ᾽ αὐτούς, 9: 5). The only other place it is found with a dependent dative is Jas. 5: 3 where again it speaks of judgment: εἰς μαρτύριον ὑμῖν.

[6] N. Flew, *Jesus and His Church*, p. 40, expands this to mean that the old Israel will be destroyed, but he fails to discern the tension which is so prominent in Jesus' attitude to these institutions. See B. Gärtner, *The Temple and the Community in Qumran and the New Testament* (Cambridge, 1965, *SNTS Monograph Series*, no. 1), pp. 105 ff.

[7] So also J. Jocz, *The Jewish People and Jesus Christ* (London, repr. 1954), pp. 21 ff., in a good brief study.

[8] This is at least a part of the significance behind the words at the last meal, which are indubitably authentic: τὸ αἷμά μου...τὸ ἐκχυννόμενον

are accepted (what they say he enjoins his disciples to follow; Matt. 23: 3) and yet superseded by the one who is the Way.

The leaders within Israel are continuously presented as opposing Jesus.[1] In Mark the scribes secretly accuse him of blasphemy, hinting at discussion with Jesus about the significance of his activity, possibly at an early point in his ministry (2: 6 ff.). Later, scribes and Pharisees question Jesus' associations with undesirables (2: 16 ff. pars.). In Mark 2: 18 ff. the issue is fasting, though with less condemnation (and this time probably including John's disciples). Mark continues this series in which the leaders take the initiative against Jesus in 2: 23 ff. pars., accusing him of profaning the Sabbath; and in 3: 4 ff. pars., again of the Sabbath, where for the first time Jesus answers back indignantly. Mark steps up the pace by claiming (editorially, in 3: 22) that scribes were sent from Jerusalem who accuse him of being an agent of Beelzebul (cf. also Mark 7: 1). In this preliminary skirmishing there is remarkably little indication of Jesus' view of the leaders; the issue is usually pressed from the other side. Relief is given (Mark 5: 21 ff. pars.) when one leader (ἀρχισυνάγωγος) comes and begs help.[2] From Mark 7: 1 ff., where the opposition is Jerusalem-centred, Jesus begins to counter-attack the leaders; he refuses to give them a sign to help them (Mark 8: 11 ff. pars.) and warns his disciples against them (Mark 8: 15 pars.). This is followed closely by the prediction of his death at the hands of the leaders.[3] From here on Jesus continues to show outspoken opposition to the leadership

ὑπὲρ πολλῶν (Mark 14: 24 pars., with variations but the same sense). In assessing this Flew, *Jesus and His Church*, pp. 71 ff., makes this the moment when 'the new Israel was constituted' (p. 76). This is later theologizing. See, for a better treatment, H. Wenschkewitz, *Die Spiritualisierung der Kultusbegriffe: Tempel, Priester und Opfer in NT* (Leipzig, 1932, ΑΓΓΕΛΟΣ Beih., 4), pp. 87–106. Cf. E. Trocmé, in *RHPR*, XLIV (1964), 245–51.

[1] There is little editorial agreement on the addressees of many pericopes; see A. F. J. Klijn in *NT*, III (1959), 259–67; A. W. Moseley, *NTS*, x (1963), 139 ff. G. Baum, *Jews, passim*, uses the 'leaders' too readily as a way out of all difficulties. Caution is required before making the identity of the opposition definite.

[2] Note also the friendliness of Joseph of Arimathea (Mark 15: 42 pars.) and the special Lukan statement that Pharisees warned Jesus of Herod's plot (13: 31). Each of these incidents acts as a foil to the others.

[3] Mark 8: 31 pars.; this is missing from the second prediction (9: 30 ff. pars.), but present in the third (10: 32 ff. pars.).

of Judaism (e.g. Mark 10–13, plus additional Q material in Matt. and Luke).[1] It is impossible to allocate 'blame' for the antagonism between the authorities and Jesus.[2] In general the picture is: initially the leaders individually question and reproach Jesus; soon the central authorities at Jerusalem become involved;[3] as the pressure upon him increases, Jesus takes the offensive, charging them with misuse of their position and false leadership. In a number of his sayings,[4] and also parables,[5] he encourages the common folk to reject their inferior position with respect to the leaders, not by revolution but by acceptance of God's good news. While the intention of this is partly to undermine the authority of the leaders, it is aimed primarily at releasing the people from bondage to an incorrect conception of what God is like and what he wants from men.[6]

The dangerous opposition to Jesus stems from the authorities, and this is underlined by the paucity of evidence for a broader-based opposition by the people themselves. Two special cases are Gerasa, where the people are frightened by the power unleashed among them (Mark 5: 17 pars.), and Nazareth, where they reject his wisdom and his power, as well as his prophetic office, because they know his family too well.[7] A more general lack of receptivity and possibly opposition lies behind the diffi-

[1] The Markan construction of events which we have followed is theologically oriented; but we have no order if we abandon the Markan one, unless we follow the Johannine order (E. Stauffer, *Jesus and His Story*, London, 1960, pp. 17 f.). Without going into this problem, it is evident that the same picture is painted; the mass of leaders are opposed, although individual leaders are disposed towards him; e.g. John 2: 13–25, 3: 1 ff.

[2] J. Jocz, *Jewish People*, p. 34, rightly regards Jesus' teaching as insufficient to account for the cleavage; it is ultimately 'the claim to unique authority' (cf. 147 ff.).

[3] John involves Jesus with the Jerusalem authorities quite early (cf. Mark 3: 22) by making him go to the Temple (John 2: 12 ff.).

[4] Especially the sheep-without-shepherd sayings (e.g. Mark 6: 34 pars.; Matt. 10: 6; 9: 36 par.; and cf. 15: 24) and sheep–wolf sayings (e.g. Luke 10: 3 par.) merged in John 10: 1 ff. (see J. A. T. Robinson in *SBT*, xxxiv, London, 1962, pp. 67–75).

[5] E.g. Matt. 22: 1 ff. par.; 21: 33 ff. pars.; 21: 28 ff. and perhaps 24: 45 ff. par.

[6] Cf. Fuller, *Mission*, p. 47.

[7] Mark 6: 1 ff. par.; Luke 4: 15 ff. puts the incident much earlier and couples it with an example of his preaching, at which offence is taken.

cult pericope on parables (Mark 4: 10 ff.), the instructions to the disciples as they are sent out (Mark 6: 11 pars.), and the crowd scene in the trial (Mark 15: 6 ff. pars.).

Is there then something special about 'this generation'[1]— leaders and people—which renders them hardened[2] to God's activity amongst them?[3] The classic passage is Mark 4: 10 ff. pars., about which it is maintained often that Jesus intends to say that Israel has been rendered obtuse purposely, so that it will not understand the message (= Mark's ἵνα).[4] We shall have to restrict the discussion to several brief points:

(a) It is very likely that the saying has been introduced here by Mark out of context.[5]

(b) Mark's motive for its introduction here is twofold: it is the first full parable in the Markan account, providing the earliest opportunity for the attraction of ἐν παραβολαῖς to a parable proper; and that parable is suitable for the editorial attraction, since both have to do with response.

(c) It is certain that Matthew's more thoroughgoing dualistic contrast is secondary, as is his full citation of Isaiah 6: 9 f., although in the original tradition there was a recollection of the passage.[6]

---

[1] Used *in malam partem* at Mark 8: 12 pars.; 8: 38; 9: 19 pars.; 13: 30 pars.; Matt. 12: 41 par.; 12: 42 par.; 12: 45; 23: 36 par.; Luke 11: 50; 17: 25; 7: 31.

[2] Πώρωσις is used only once of leaders or crowds (Mark 3: 5, no pars.), and πωρόω twice of the disciples (Mark 6: 52; 8: 17, no pars.). Further, ἀσύνετος, ἀπιστία, σκληροκαρδία or cognates are used equally of disciples and Jewish opposition in Mark, but the others shift away from this.

[3] E.g. Mark 3: 22 pars.; when confronted by the clearest evidence of the working of God, the explanation offered by the opponents is: 'he is possessed by Beelzebul'.

[4] See J. Gnilka, *Die Verstockung Israels: Isaias 6: 9–10 in der Theologie der Synoptiker* (München, 1961). The literature is cited there.

[5] So J. Jeremias, *The Parables of Jesus* (London, 1963, 2nd edition), pp. 13 ff.; cf. T. W. Manson, *Teaching*, pp. 75 ff. C. F. D. Moule, *Birth*, pp. 149 ff., treats it as a 'bridge passage' (a frequentative generalization) which leads into the explanation of the parable in *vv.* 13 ff. The inconsistent use of the plural 'parables' in Mark 4: 11 and 13 is recognized by Matt. and Luke and altered by a singular in the second instance and changing the verb in the first.

[6] Cf. W. Wilkens, 'Die Redaktion des Gleichniskapitels Mk 4 durch Matth', *TZ*, xx (1964), 304–27; L. Cerfaux, *NTS*, ii (1955–6), 238–49, has tried, unconvincingly, to demonstrate Matt.'s priority.

(d) 'Εν παραβολαῖς is probably to be understood as an adverbial phrase 'parabolically'. Only Matthew has it depend upon an explicit λαλῶ; Mark makes it dependent upon an impersonal πάντα γίνεται, and Luke upon δέδοται (understood).[1]

(e) While the Greek of Isaiah 6: 9 f. is teleological, behind both the Hebrew of Isaiah and the underlying Aramaic of Mark 4: 12 is a Semitic blurring of purpose and result.[2]

(f) The 'hardening' which the ἵνα and the Matthean quotation express is not a part of Jesus' purpose in his ministry; the earliest onlookers interpreted the facts as a theologically 'necessary' fulfilment of Isaiah's words, and consciously read back purpose into the saying.[3]

(g) The four independent sayings in Mark 4: 21–5 par. each substantiate that there is a gracious purpose in Jesus' teaching: it is like a light, it is meant to unveil, it is meant to be received. The fact that when it is refused one is left worse than before constitutes a part of the 'hardening'.

(h) Further, Mark underlines (4: 33 no pars.) that the parabolic method is used καθὼς ἠδύναντο ἀκούειν.[4]

(i) 'Privacy' (Mark 4: 34; 4: 10; and implied by τοῖς ἔξω in 4: 11), which is not so obvious in Matthew and Luke, is a special (overemphasized) Markan motif related to his theologically constructed secrecy and opposition themes.

To sum up, there need be little doubt that a saying of Jesus lies behind this, referring however not to Jesus' method of teaching but to the results of an incorrect hearing.[5] Even the disciples do not hear well, and the parables need to be explained to them. We conclude that there is no theory of the hardening of the people of Israel, and that Jesus is not himself an agent to this end.

---

[1] It is not impossible that this saying might have referred originally to acts rather than words, or the totality of words and actions.

[2] See Moule, *Idiom*, pp. 142 f.

[3] Note Matt.'s ἀναπληροῦται.

[4] Matt.'s omission of this phrase, together with his omission of Mark 4: 21 ff., makes his attempted softening of Mark 4: 11 less credible. Luke stands midway between.

[5] Cf. Bornkamm, *Jesus*, p. 71; he accepts that a genuine word lies behind it, and that its fundamental point is that the parables contain a mystery, which he expounds on existential grounds.

But if this generation has not been hardened, is it possible that Jesus thinks that God has let go his people? There is some additional evidence for this which has not yet been mentioned. The Q saying which Matthew has made follow upon Jesus' exclamation about the Centurion (Matt. 8: 10: 'Not even in Israel have I found such faith'[1] = Luke 7: 9) is very strong; and to this is added: 'but the children of the kingdom ('you' in Luke 13: 28) will be thrown into the outer darkness' (Matt. 8: 12).[2] The similarity of the saying to that of John Baptist in Matt. 3: 9 par. is striking.[3] Both Jesus and John expect a *coming* judgment upon those who exalt themselves in Israel, and a *coming* extension to all the poor and outcast. But in neither case has Israel been abandoned; instead, there is a definite possibility that many will bring abandonment upon themselves.[4] The crisis parables which Luke has gathered together in chs. 14–15 are originally warnings to repent, addressed to the leaders of Judaism concerning their critical situation. Sometimes these are given a secondary conclusion by the evangelist (e.g. Luke 14: 24) which speaks of abandonment; and although there is indisputably a floating saying of Jesus about the first and last changing places this may be only a shift in relative position and not an absolute rejection (e.g. Matt. 19: 30 pars.). There is little support in the earliest tradition for the idea that the people of Israel have been let go.[5]

[1] Πίστις is prominent in Matt. 15: 28 (but not Mark 7: 28 f.) when again Jesus goes beyond Israel; and also in Luke 17: 19 with respect to the Samaritan leper.

[2] Jesus originally used this polemically, against the privileged members of Judaism, in a way which implied some form of universalism. Prof. Moule has suggested to me that Matt. 8: 12 is an allusion to Ps. 111: 10 with a transference from Gentiles to rejected Israelites.

[3] Compare also the story of Zacchaeus (Luke 19: 1 ff.) ending with a difficult reference to a 'child of Abraham'. Even taking a weakened sense for καθότι (Moulton/Turner; p. 318, Bl–D/Funk, 456.4) there is a strange logic in the way salvation comes to his house.

[4] This is no doubt the intention of the other Q saying in Luke 10: 21// Matt. 11: 25: 'You have hidden these things from the wise and intelligent, and revealed them to the childlike.'

[5] See also Goppelt, *Jesus, Paul*, pp. 52 ff., 91 ff. Relevant to this whole question is G. B. Caird's proposal to interpret Jesus' intention as a *national* call to repentance which involves *national* survival. Certainly it is correct to emphasize the fact that Jesus is concerned for the whole nation, but when Caird goes on to relate failure in this enterprise to the destruction of

On the basis of this brief review it seems correct to stress that:
(1) Jesus did not despair of his own people, nor did he teach his
followers to abandon them; (2) on the contrary, he maintained
a consistent ministry to them, only rarely going outside the
bounds of Judaism; (3) he expected a response from them, and,
though this was often negative, it does not submerge the
expectation of a positive response from many; (4) the harshest
statements are made about the leaders, and the most hopeful
references are to the ordinary people.

JESUS AND THE NEW ENTITY

What is the relationship between those who make a positive
response to Jesus and the People of God? Do these disciples
constitute a 'new' People of God, a true community of the
faithful, the Remnant? Is this society, in Jesus' day, the
'Church'? At the outset we must say that the gospels (correctly)
reflect little in the way of community self-consciousness amongst
Jesus and his disciples.[1]

Matthew has a tendency to portray Jesus as a new *Torah-
lehrer*, whose teaching is addressed to a community representing
the true Israel.[2] The Beatitudes with their emphasis on future
rewards, the Antitheses which include some community
interests, the Salt and Light sayings (note the emphatic ὑμεῖς
ἐστε), as he records them all presuppose a community; the
emphasis of these authentic sayings has been shifted by Matthew
to the community from the original emphasis on Jesus' authority.
He claims to be sent from God and demands that those who

Jerusalem and the coming of the Son of Man (with implications about the
Gentile's inheritance of a new place in God's scheme) he is in danger of
falling into a new dispensationalism; see *Jesus and the Jewish Nation* (London,
1965).

[1] See Olaf Linton, *Problem der Urkirche*, particularly ch. 5 and pp. 157–83.
The most difficult problem we have to face is the tendency on the part of the
later community to alter subtly Jesus' words in favour of their Church-
awareness at the time of writing. Sometimes this is clear (especially Matt.),
but many times we cannot be sure how much the words have been given
new content.

[2] But cf. N. A. Dahl, *Volk*, pp. 160 f.; while Jesus was a teacher he did not
teach a *Sonder-Halachā* which would be necessary to constitute a *Sonder-
Kenishtā*. Matthew's tendencies are discussed later. On Matt. see especially
W. Trilling, *Das wahre Israel* (3rd edition, *SANT*, x, München, 1964).

hear his teaching and accept its validity should follow him. This call to discipleship is basic both to his position and to his intention.[1] By calling men to repentance and a new way of life he creates followers.[2] This was a fluid group, including both those who actually travelled with Jesus from time to time and those who had been captured by his teaching and personality without continual attendance on him. None the less, the fluidity must not be mistaken for laxity;[3] the challenge to follow, as in Mark 10: 21 pars., is made difficult to accept because of the extensive demands (Mark 10: 29 ff.). Refusal to follow is much easier, but that raises in its harshest form the question: who can be saved? When one follows, this question is proleptically answered.

A special group of followers are the twelve. Certainty is impossible on such a matter, but it appears that there is no thought in Jesus' mind that they are to represent 'Israel'. They are called to associate with the Son of Man in his ministry, to serve in the same way he serves. They are true Israelites but not 'true Israel',[4] and their significance in relation to Israel is primarily evocative and not constitutive.[5] Their importance does not lie in any attempt to constitute a 'remnant' by Jesus[6] but rather in their very close relationship to, almost identity with, Jesus. Is it for the reason that the twelve are so closely tied to him that a collective term is rarely applied to them? In spite of the fact that they do not fully understand Jesus, their signific-

[1] See E. Schweizer, *Lordship and Discipleship* (London, 1960, *SBT*, xxviii), ch. 1; and G. Lundström, *Kingdom*, p. 235.

[2] The two peaks are the original call (Mark 1: 16 ff. pars.) and the reaffirmation of the demands of discipleship (Mark 8: 34 ff. pars.). Both could have some later Church-theology overtones, but the idea of following is so consistent as to be Jesus' own intention.

[3] Re Jesus' practice of eating and drinking with undesirables, J. Jeremias ('Der Gedanke des "Heiligen Restes" im Spätjudentum und in der Verkündigung Jesu', *ZNW*, xlii (1949), 184–94) has pointed out that this is an essential part of his Messianic character. We must distinguish between his rejection of an incorrect exclusiveness and the demand to follow closely once one is caught by the truth of the claims he makes.

[4] So Dahl, *Volk Gottes*, p. 162; *per contra*, J. W. Bowman, *The Intention of Jesus* (London, 1945), pp. 184 f.

[5] Cf. Bornkamm, *Jesus*, p. 150; Dahl, *Volk Gottes*, p. 159; 'Zeichen, Typen für die eschatologische Gottesgemeinde'.

[6] So Jeremias, *ZNW*, xlii (1949), 184–94.

ance derives wholly from him. In connection with this, it is instructive to note that there is no suggestion in the gospels that either Jesus or the evangelists allowed for fluctuation in the term 'Son of Man' between Jesus himself and the twelve. A corporate sense of the term is a legitimate deduction from Daniel 7 and 1 Enoch 71, but it has not been demonstrated that Jesus thought of himself as Israel and that the disciples were included within this designation as a corporate extension of the primary personal sense.[1] Beyond question, the narrow circle of the twelve has a special function in the foundation of the Church, but this is primarily a post-Resurrection matter: even if foreseen by Jesus, it was not communicated in such a way that it is observable in the gospel tradition.[2]

The larger group of followers is simply the group of those who repented and believed and are saved. They have submitted to God's rule over them, so that for them the kingdom (βασιλεία τοῦ θεοῦ) has drawn near through the person of the Son of Man, and they are assured that they shall enter that kingdom.[3] However, it is remarkable in the gospels how seldom collective language which implies a community self-consciousness is applied to this group.[4] We have referred to the Sermon on the Mount and the tendency of Matthew's gospel.[5] When Matthew

---

[1] See Manson, *Teaching*, pp. 211 ff., 235, 269 (n. 2); M. Black, *BJRL*, XLV (1962–3), 305–18; only John 15: 1 can support such a claim (in the 'vine' metaphor). Our position is shared in essence by W. G. Kümmel, 'Kirchenbegriff und Geschichtsbewußtsein in der Urgemeinde und bei Jesus' (*SBU*, I, Lund, 1943), esp. pp. 30 f., 34 ff.; *per contra*, P. Nepper-Christensen, 'Wer hat die Kirche gestiftet?' (*SBU*, XII, Lund, 1950, pp. 23–35). Also similar is E. Schweizer, 'The Disciples of Jesus and the Post-Resurrection Church', *USQR*, XV (1960), 281–94.

[2] So Tödt, *Son of Man*, excursus III, especially pp. 310 f.; and P. G. S. Hopwood, *The Religious Experience of the Primitive Church* (Edinburgh, 1936), pp. 234–6.

[3] The denial of a relationship between 'Son of Man' and 'Kingdom of God' is, as Black shows (*BJRL*, XLV, 1962–3, 310 f.), ill-considered and forces the evidence.

[4] S. Aalen, *NTS*, VIII (1961–2), 232, takes 'kingdom' itself to be such a word. But βασιλεία and οἰκία in Mark 3: 24 f. pars. cannot bear this weight. The contrast in Mark 4: 10 ff. is considerably weakened when we push back to the original, for οἱ ἔξω becomes a general expression, and ὑμῖν implies only the present hearers.

[5] Cf. also Matt. 13: 16 f. with its emphatic Ὑμῶν δὲ μακάριοι οἱ ὀφθαλμοί, Matt. 13: 24–30 and 36–43 where a community is presupposed but not given

applies the term ἐκκλησία (whatever we think of the originality of the word) to those who *will* follow, he follows it with non-collective terms: εἴ τις θέλει...ὃς γὰρ ἐὰν θέλῃ...ὃς δ᾽ ἂν ἀπολέσῃ.[1] In 18: 17, there is more emphasis on the group as a whole, yet the conclusion brings out the occasional nature of the gathering: 'two or three in my name'. Matthew also adds to his version of the parable of the vinedressers to give it a more community-centred application.[2] The same impression is created by Matt. 22: 1–14. Apart from Matthew there is very little that points to a distinctive community which is the creation of Jesus.[3] In Jesus' lifetime the continual emphasis was on 'discipleship', on confirming one's 'Judaism' and becoming a 'true Israelite'. His disciples had no collective identity except the way they related to Jesus himself.[4]

Indubitably there are sayings and parables of Jesus that have a community application, but this does not mean that they presuppose a distinct organizational entity, or that they are intended to aid in setting up such a unit.[5] Nor is it the case that the disciples' commission to preach the gospel requires a

a collective title except υἱοὶ τῆς βασιλείας. The same is true of 13: 47–50. Cf. Dalman, *The Words of Jesus* (Edinburgh, 1902), pp. 115 f.

[1] Matt. 16: 24 f. Note the future in Matt. 16: 18 (οἰκοδομήσω). See P. Vielhauer, *Oikodome, das Bild vom Bau in der christlichen Literatur vom NT bis Clemens Alexandrinus* (Karlsruhe–Durlach, 1940), pp. 70 ff.

[2] Δοθήσεται ἔθνει (Matt. 21: 43); in *v.* 41 he has ἄλλοις with Mark and Luke.

[3] So also E. Schweizer, *Church Order in the NT* (London, 1961, *SBT*, xxxii), 2 b (p. 22); cf. Dahl, *Volk*, pt 3, ch. 1; Johnston, *Church*, chs. 3–4. It is Flew's purpose (*Jesus*, pt 1) to prove the opposite, although he recognizes the inferential nature of his task (p. 36).

[4] In the last week the sense of community appears to grow, perhaps partly under the pressures of being so closely identified with Jesus in a situation of conflict. On the way to Jerusalem and at the entry the twelve would have been prominent, though at the trial they faded into the background. A relationship with Jesus was dangerous (e.g. Luke 22: 54 ff.); but it must be stressed that there is never a suggestion that the disciples are implicated in Jesus' guilt. The saying about judging Israel (Luke 22: 30), while it has implications, perhaps, that we cannot recover, does not bring to the foreground the idea that in the disciples Israel is reconstituted. To the end of Jesus' life the emphasis is so strongly on commitment to Jesus that community consciousness is always subordinated.

[5] Luke 22: 24–30 pars.; Matt. 25: 14–30 pars.; Matt. 24: 45 ff. par.; Mark 13: 33 ff. pars. etc.

communal identity as an extension of the witness of Jesus.[1] As they go out in twos they represent not their community but Jesus himself.[2] In the same way the man who is healed is told to go to his own people (πρὸς τοὺς σούς, Mark 5: 19) and tell what the Lord (Luke, 'God') has done, and so he goes and tells what *Jesus* has done. 'Telling' is not restricted to the intimate band, and it is not carried out during the life of Jesus as a community operation. Rather, it is carried out by those who are excited by the evidence they observe that in Jesus God is doing something new in Israel. Moreover, other functional distinctions are lacking which might suggest that this gathering of 'disciples' was set over against Israel. It had no rite, creed, locality, name of its own which separated it from Israel.[3] The only possible pieces of evidence are the Lord's Prayer and the Last Supper. If, in the latter, the Lukan phrase is original (22: 19) there may be a reference to continued remembrance (ποιεῖτε), and an implicit establishing of a group within Israel. It is, however, more likely that it should be interpreted in terms of the one event—the last supper of Jesus with his disciples. If so, the gospel tradition knows of no community act, dominically constitutive of a group, that goes beyond the Jewish *chaburah*.[4] The difference lies in the fact that it is an eschatological act pointing to (and partaking of the nature of) the Messianic feast. As for the Lord's Prayer, there is nothing in the account which requires corporate as over against individual application.

Jesus did not establish a *Sondersynagoge*;[5] the evidence for such

[1] A. T. Hanson, *The Pioneer Ministry* (London, 1961), has tried to show that the mission of the Church is the mission of the OT remnant, and that therefore the Church is identified with the Remnant (pp. 15 ff.); however, he cannot show that Jesus considered his disciples to have this identity. Manson, *Teaching*, pp. 175 ff., distinguishes between a 'saved' and a 'saving' remnant; the latter is the 'key to the NT' (p. ix); but again he cannot demonstrate that this is Jesus' own conception. He must jump to the later NT writers to substantiate it, pp. 199 ff.   [2] So Dahl, *Volk*, p. 160.

[3] As Schweizer, *Church Order*, 2a, points out. This is negative evidence, but still very important as an indication of Jesus' intention. Even in the last week when, as we have suggested, there might be an increase in the sense of corporateness, everything seems to be pointing ahead to the totally new situation that will arise after the death of Jesus.

[4] This is, of course, a question which has been widely debated; we cannot digress to consider it more fully.

[5] Or even a *Sondergruppe* (K. L. Schmidt's term, *TWNT*, III, 530).

a step is lacking. The new entity is a band of disciples who follow Jesus the Son of Man because of the evidence they see of God's rule appearing through him. They live dependently upon him, though he cannot depend upon them. When faced with his death, they are prepared to disband and go their own way, so little is their community self-consciousness and so great their concentration upon him. Even the last week does not prepare them for the shock. It requires a divine manifestation to overcome this despair and to weld them into a cohesive group.[1] Any claim that Jesus intended to establish in his lifetime a new Israel to supersede the old Israel founders on this lack of self-conscious community, for this Jewish group could hardly conceive, in those few years, that it was representing Israel.[2] Jesus' relationship to this small segment of Judaism is that of leader to followers, God's messenger to the redeemed and forgiven.[3] Only after the Resurrection can anything be said about the Church or the claim be considered that the Church/community is the True Israel.[4]

Jeremias, *ZNW*, XLII (1949), 184–94, suggests that 'die alle umfassende Heilsgemeinde des neuen Gottesvolkes sammelt Jesus'. It is not clear that at this stage one should speak of a *new* people of God being gathered. C. K. Barrett (*The Holy Spirit and the Gospel Tradition*, London, 1947, p. 137) says more correctly: 'Until his life had been given, the many, though some of them were gathered together in the entourage of Jesus and lived in fellowship with one another, were only an aggregation of individuals, and not Israel.'

[1] Barrett, *Holy Spirit*, pp. 138 f. The Holy Spirit is given as a substitute for the presence of Jesus and it is he who creates a new sense of community. Luke, in the early chapters of Acts, is trying to portray this happening. That he does not do this in the gospel is a tribute to his historical sense. See C. K. Barrett, *Luke the Historian in Recent Study* (London, 1961), esp. p. 24.

[2] See the important article by G. Lindeskog, 'Christianity as Realized Judaism' in *Horae Soederblomianae 6: Pistis kai Erga* (Lund, 1964), pp. 15–36.

[3] Cf. Herntrich, art. λεῖμμα, *TWNT*, IV, 198 ff.; esp. p. 215: 'Dann ist der Messias der Grund, auf dem sich die neue Gemeinde aufbaut...Hier (*sc.* Deuterojesaja) ist der Ebed, der die Sünden "der Vielen" getragen hat, der Repräsentant des Gottesvolkes, und allein in ihm hat die neue Gemeinde ihren Bestand.'

[4] Cf. Dahl, *Volk*, pp. 163 ff.: the Church is the creation of the Resurrection (p. 167); and Fuller, *Mission*, pp. 118 f.: Jesus allowed for an interval between his death and the End, to which period the *ecclesia* belongs. 'But the interim period is qualitatively different from the time which preceded it, including the time of Jesus' ministry' (119); and we may say, the community also is qualitatively different in this interim from the community in the time of Jesus' ministry.

GENTILES IN THE DISCIPLES' MISSION[1]

Jesus' mission was Israel-centric. His activities were contained almost entirely within Israel, and directed solely towards Israel, with the end in view that Israel should turn to God by acknowledging the truth of Jesus' diagnosis and of his cure. He remains a true Jew in this task. On at least one occasion he sends out followers whom he has called to him as extensions of his own ministry with functions and powers parallel to his own. As well, he looks forward to a time when these would go out again and have to suffer for their testimony to him, but during his lifetime he forbids these witnesses to go to Gentiles (Matt. 10: 5 f.).

In the instruction given on this and other occasions there are vague indications that the mission was not to be completely confined to his own nation. Apart from the post-Resurrection saying recorded by Matthew (28: 16–20) we note the following points: (1) there is little specific evidence; some of it is brought in by the judicious addition (editorially) of a word or two;[2] (2) had he taught specifically on this subject we might expect a recollection of a challenge to it, especially in view of his challenge on the inadequacy of a Jewish mission to the rest of the world; (3) however, there are some statements with a claim to interpretation as sanctioning a Gentile mission; (4) on occasion he did go beyond Judaism himself, though this was exceptional;[3] (5) he stands in the prophetic tradition which looks for a gathering of all nations at Jerusalem.[4]

The main evidence is all related in private discourse to the

---

[1] See most recently F. Hahn, *Mission in the NT* (*SBT*, XLVII, London, 1965), pp. 26–46; and D. Bosch, *Die Heidenmission in der Zukunftschau Jesu* (*ATANT*, XXXVI, Zürich, 1959).

[2] Matthew's addition of ἔθνει at 21: 43 is typical.

[3] Three times: the Centurion's servant, the Syrophoenician's daughter, and the Gerasene (probably). All three show a refusal (which is overcome), and a maintenance of the distinction between Jew and Gentile (so Jeremias, 'The Gentile World in the Thought of Jesus', *SNTS Bull.* III, 1952, pp. 18–28).

[4] B. Sundkler, 'Jésus et les Païens' (*RHPR*, XVI (1936), 462 ff.); and J. Jeremias, *Jesus' Promise*, have discussed this conveniently. Jeremias maintains that Matt. 8: 11 par. is a summary of the OT conception of the Gentile pilgrimage to Zion, which embraced five main points: (1) Epiphany of God; (2) the call of God; (3) the journey of the Gentiles; (4) worship at the world sanctuary; (5) the Messianic Banquet.

disciples, chiefly in the so-called Little Apocalypse of which Mark 13: 9 ff. is the primary account.[1] Both Matthew (10: 17 ff.; 24: 9 ff.) and Luke (21: 12 ff. and 12: 11 ff.) have dual accounts. Luke retains the primary version in his little apocalypse, and puts the secondary version elsewhere; Matthew has only a truncated version in the apocalyptic discourse and the fuller version elsewhere. There is no literary dependence between either of the Matthean and either of the Lukan versions. Moreover, in both Lukan accounts every reference to Gentiles is omitted, while in both Matthean accounts Gentiles are included, in each case with a dative following εἰς μαρτύριον.[2] As compared with Mark 13: 10, it appears that three accounts (representing possibly three sources: special Luke, Q, and special Matthew) understand the statement concerning preaching to the Gentiles as independent of the context. One source (Matt. 10) seems to find it in its present place, but omits the 'preaching' saying, and links ἔθνη to αὐτοῖς by altering εἰς plus accusative to a dative. In Matthew's second case (24: 14) the same thing is said, retaining the Markan language, but changing the sense;[3] the gospel is to be preached throughout the world, not specifically *to* the nations, but for a witness to them. Again three witnesses (Matthew twice, Luke 21: 13 and probably Mark 13: 9 also[4]) agree that the objects of μαρτύριον include Gentiles either by inference or

[1] See G. D. Kilpatrick, 'The Gentile Mission in Mark and Mark 13: 9–11' in *Studies in the Gospels, Essays in Honour of R. H. Lightfoot* (ed. D. E. Nineham, Oxford, 1955), pp. 145–58; F. C. Burkitt, *Christian Beginnings* (London, 1924), appended note, pp. 145–7; C. H. Turner, *JTS*, xxvi (1924–5), 19 f. and 152 f.; J. Jeremias' two works noted above. On the priority of Mark see G. R. Beasley-Murray, *Jesus and the Future* (London, 1954), pp. 226 ff. Jeremias dismisses these accounts with a few footnotes on the assumption that the Matthean form is original. One cannot avoid the other parallels, whose evidence underlines the priority of Mark. Oral tradition shaped the later splitting of the material by Matt. and Luke, but they do not agree in the extent or placing of the other material.

[2] A Q account may be behind Luke 12, with its different terminology, and if so this was probably a parallel to the Markan version. Possibly the omission of ἔθνη from the Q account has influenced Luke to omit Mark 13: 10 when he constructs his apocalyptic discourse.

[3] This, together with Luke's total omission of the verse, leads to rejection of attempts to repunctuate Mark 13: 10; *contra* Burkitt and Kilpatrick.

[4] If ἡγεμών is a *terminus technicus* for Roman authorities.

explicitly, and this 'witness' (even in Matthew 24: 14) is judging as well as evidential.[1] The conclusion must be that the original saying was an undivided unit and that, as with much of the discourse in Mark, it is to be interpreted independently of its context.[2]

This being the case, the saying, found variously in Mark and Matthew, refers in the first instance to the extent of the proclamation: the whole world must hear the good news.[3] Because of the association of 'councils and synagogues' and 'rulers and kings' it seems that the Jewish reference is primary. The mission to Jews is to the forefront, including not just Palestinian Jews but also those who are in daily contact with Gentiles. This preaching will in the course of things be heard by Gentiles who attend the synagogues without having been initiated into membership in Israel. All of this will create conflict with Jewish authorities; and this will lead to trouble with Gentile authorities. Thus the gospel will be proclaimed in the world, among the nations. We must then affirm two things in tension; the gospel is not intended by Jesus to be proclaimed directly to the Gentiles but all the steps are foreseen which are necessary for the ultimate evangelizing of the Gentiles.[4] When taken together with the expectation of the eschatological ingathering of the nations, the very occasional precedent for Gentile salvation in Jesus' own ministry, and—we may now mention it—the post-Resurrection saying of Matt. 28: 16–20, it seems clear that, in spite of the Palestinian church's reluctance to take this

[1] Cf. Strathmann, art. μάρτυς κτλ, *TWNT*, IV, especially pp. 508 ff. See also Matt. 12: 41 f. par., though it cannot be used as evidence for or against Gentile mission.

[2] Cf. Beasley-Murray, *Jesus*, and also his *A Commentary on Mark 13* (London, 1957). He summarizes his view in the latter, p. 11 n. 1; and *Jesus*, p. 197, where he notes the absurdity in arguing that *v.* 10 is a later insertion when it is likely that all of *vv.* 9, 10, 11, 12, 13 have been conjoined to form a section. Cf. also W. G. Kümmel, *Promise and Fulfilment: the Eschatological Message of Jesus* (London, 1957, *SBT*, XXIII), p. 98.

[3] Mark (14: 9) and Matt. (26: 13) also agree in the saying about the woman's anointing Jesus: ὅπου ἐὰν κηρυχθῇ τὸ εὐαγγέλιον (+ τοῦτο: Mark) ἐν ὅλῳ τῷ κόσμῳ (εἰς + τοῦτο: Mark). This variation exactly parallels the variation in Mark 13: 10 and Matt. 24: 14 in an exactly similar context, and probably with the same effect.

[4] Cf. Jeremias, *Jesus' Promise*, pp. 55 ff. For the shift in the tradition, and for the temporal problem, see ch. 6 below; cf. Kümmel, *Promise*, pp. 95 ff.

step, Gentile mission (when it happened) was founded on a legitimate deduction from, and as an expression of, Jesus' own intention.[1]

Jesus' particularistic concern is not absolute. There is no question but that he is primarily concerned for all Israel, to such an extent that he refuses to establish a new Israel, or to designate a group within Judaism as the remnant. None the less, two factors moderate the national concern. One is the clear assumption by Jesus that not all within Israel will accept his call to repentance and renewal. While he does not call out a remnant, he does recognize that a sifting is taking place. Secondly, there is a universalism in his thought; Gentiles and Jews will all assume the same position before God in the resurrection and be judged on the same basis. They will be brought in (centripetally) to worship God. Yet there is also evidence that they are to be reached secondarily as a result of the mission to Israel in its broadest scope as it embraces the Diaspora. It is Jesus' Israel-centric ministry that lends weight to the view of those early Jewish Christians who were reluctant to step outside the bounds of Judaism at all. But it was the men who followed through the implications of Jesus' incipient universalism who were truest to his intentions. Only in this way could Daniel's vision of the Son of Man be fulfilled, 'that all nations, races and folk of every tongue should serve him' (Dan. 7: 14; Moffatt).

[1] R. H. Lightfoot's suggestion (*The Gospel Message of St Mark*, Oxford, repr. 1962, pp. 60 ff.), that the cleansing of the Temple expresses this intention by declaring the universalizing of Jewish worship, is a possible construction of Mark's theology, but not likely the original meaning of the event. T. W. Manson, *The Servant Messiah* (Cambridge, repr. 1961), pp. 81 ff., supports Lightfoot (independently I believe) in his assertion that it was a 'vindication of Gentiles' rights in the Temple itself' (p. 83); and cf. T. W. Manson, *Jesus and the Non-Jews* (London, 1955).

CHAPTER V

PAUL

INTRODUCTION

We turn from our brief consideration of Jesus to a longer treatment of Paul, without considering what is often called 'primitive Christianity'.[1] Our justification for this hiatus in tracing the development is fivefold: (a) the sources are meagre and secondary (primarily Acts);[2] (b) while this primitive Christianity is unquestionably important, the sources are highly selective, making it impossible to assess its uniformity and variety; (c) Church consciousness must have progressed rapidly in this early period, under the impetus of Jesus' post-Resurrection appearances and teaching, because of the intensity of the Spirit's filling, and because of the needs of this new group for material sharing and participation;[3] but to detail the growth in community is largely outside our scope, and we need only assume the existence and organization of the Church; (d) it is not possible, because of the absence of theologically oriented sources, to observe the transformation taking place during the period called primitive Christianity; (e) Paul's theological position can be assessed independently of other early developments as a function of the teaching of Jesus and the mind and background of Paul himself, and moreover provides sufficient sources to watch developments and the circumstances that give rise to them.

Consequently, we shall presuppose that there are distinctive

[1] See especially the attempt to define and describe this by R. Bultmann, *Theology of the NT*, I (London, 1952, repr. 1959), 33–183. He mishandles the sources by not making careful reservations in the way one document may be used to interpret another. The little-known but exciting book by P. G. S. Hopwood, *The Religious Experience of the Primitive Church* (Edinburgh, 1936) is another attempt in the same direction.

[2] It is this lack of primary sources which Bultmann neglects.

[3] Hopwood, *Religious Experience*, makes a strong case against a decision to neglect primitive Christianity; but in his chapter on Church consciousness he can only assess the Acts' evidence and make assertions *ex hypothesi*.

rites, practices, and teaching which identify the Church as a special group. Paul works within this Church, and adds to it through his activity as a herald and an interpreter of Jesus. But into this relationship between Paul and the gospel of Jesus must be inserted not only cultural variations and the needs of non-Palestinian (often non-Jewish) groups, but also the excogitations of one who is faced with the problem of commenting on problems arising from but not answered by Jesus' teaching. The interpretative element becomes in Paul a fundamental issue.

We can clear the ground by stating our presuppositions about the Pauline corpus. We accept the authenticity of the four 'great' letters, of the two Thessalonian letters, of the four 'prison' epistles (though with some doubt in the case of Ephesians). Since the Pastorals touch but lightly on our problem we can avoid the question of authenticity. Chronologically we hold Galatians to be the earliest letter, and are disposed to an Ephesian imprisonment for Philippians, though not for Colossians, Philemon or Ephesians.[1]

The two basic contentions which follow are: first, that Paul uses 'Israel', not of the Church, but in a way that retains a large measure of continuity with the old entity; and secondly, that Paul adopts the viewpoint of Jesus on mission, though under the influence of the situation in which he is involved he pushes this as far as possible while still remaining true to it.[2] The best example of this is the tension between his practice of going in each city first to Jews, and his teaching concerning the necessity of the Gentiles' being saved before the fullness of the Jews. He retains Jesus' concern for Jews, but alters his theory somewhat under the influence of the new conditions created by the proclamation of the gospel in the Diaspora. The concepts necessary for a complete breach are latent within Paul's

---

[1] See article by F. F. Bruce, *Peake's Commentary on the Bible*, ed. Black and Rowley (London/Edinburgh, 1962), pp. 929–39, for a close approximation to this view.

[2] Cf. A. Schweitzer, *The Mysticism of Paul the Apostle* (London, 1953, 2nd ed.), pp. 113 f., who makes this point about eschatological conceptions: '...Paul is forced by the position (*sc.* altered world-circumstances) to take, in his teaching, an original attitude alongside Jesus. But in this he is merely recasting in accordance with the conditions of the time the fundamental conceptions, derived from eschatology, which are common to them both. He does not abandon Jesus but continues his teaching.' (P. 114; cf. 172 f. and 186.)

writing, but are not developed by him. He stands as a middle factor between Jesus and the early Church. Others, even close friends of Paul, tend increasingly to dissolve the tension either through misunderstanding, or through the needs of a changed situation.[1] We shall describe to what extent Paul is responsible for the separation, and in a later chapter discuss post-Pauline developments.[2] One important aspect of the problem is the later absence of concern for the salvation of Israel.[3]

Paul's first interest is the practical missionary situation, and the theoretical questions (when discussed) derive from this. He focuses attention upon the respective responses to the gospel by Jew and Gentile, and this causes him to consider the logic behind the generally negative response of the Jew and the positive response of so many Gentiles. The solution to the Church/Israel relationship is viewed in the context of these varied responses. We shall investigate those sections in the Pauline letters which express Paul's attitude to contemporary Judaism, his understanding of the Gentiles' relationship to Israel, and to some extent his view of the Church. Important to this inquiry is the extent of the transposition of particular Israelite designations and attributes to the Church, and what this implies for the nature of the relationship of Israel and the Church. The Jew/Gentile relationship within the early Church is a specific case of the broader question.

[1] Schweitzer, *op. cit.* pp. 203 f.: '...the theory was already prepared in the Pauline Epistles and the Pauline tradition. The original meaning of the Pauline freedom from the Law was as little understood by this new generation as was that of the eschatological mysticism from which it sprang. But it made its entry through the breach which the artillery of the Apostle of the Gentiles had opened for it.' This overstates the case but is essentially true.

[2] What A. Schweitzer, *Paul and his Interpreters, a critical history* (London, 1912, repr. 1948) described as the task of historical science: 'to point out the geological fault and dislocation of the strata, and enable us to recognize the essential continuity of these formations by which they have taken their present shape' (p. viii).

[3] This may be illustrated by an observation by F. C. Grant, *Ancient Judaism and the NT* (Edinburgh, 1960), p. 164, on the way the early Church outgrew, reinterpreted and then rejected the *Menschensohndogmatik*: 'The shift took place between the days of Paul and those of Justin Martyr, Irenaeus and Origen...In fact Paul, who never mentions the term "Son of Man", was probably the one who did the most to bring about this change in usage. For him, "the Son of Man" was either an unknown or at least an unused title...'

We shall maintain that an important aspect of the logic of the problem is Paul's and Jesus' expectation of the salvation of 'Israel'. As long as a part of 'Israel' is expected to come to repentance, it is unlikely that the name would be appropriated exclusively as a self-designation of the nascent group. 'True Israel' might adequately represent what they are and feel themselves to be, but as long as they remain in contact with the larger whole they cannot be expected to assume the privileged title. Consequently it is unlikely that the designation 'Israel' will be used to describe Christians until the break is irrevocable.

In what follows we deal with each letter in what is probably the chronological order. We shall emphasize the part played by polemic in encouraging the take-over of some titles and the spiritualizing of others.[1] In these aggressive apologetic sections the two factors, relationship of Church to Israel and transposition of attributes, coalesce. The doctrine of the Church as such is not the main thrust of our examination, but it will be seen that the growing concentration upon the theory of the Church corresponds to its growing separation from Judaism. The development which we describe is not a straight line, though it is true that the answer given in one letter for particular circumstances may be in mind when Paul answers another set of difficulties.

There are numerous general studies which cover some part of the ground we are covering. Since the following observations are largely exegetical and analytic we have not referred to these as often as we might, for to do so would involve also a consideration of each person's thesis.[2] They have all contri-

---

[1] See Appendix C on polemic in the sects and parties of Judaism.

[2] E.g. N. A. Dahl, *Das Volk Gottes* (Oslo, 1941); A. Oepke, *Das neue Gottesvolk* (Gütersloh, 1950); A. Schlatter, *The Church in the NT Period* (London, 1955); L. Cerfaux, *The Church in the Theology of St Paul* (New York, 1959); W. L. Knox, *St Paul and the Church of the Gentiles* (Cambridge, 1939, repr. 1961); J. Munck, *Paul and the Salvation of Mankind* (London, 1959); H.-J. Schoeps, *Paul, The Theology of the Apostle in the light of Jewish Religious History* (London, 1961); W. D. Davies, *Paul and Rabbinic Judaism: Some Rabbinic Elements in Pauline Theology* (London, 1955, 2nd edition, repr. 1962); L. Goppelt, *Jesus, Paul and Judaism* (New York, 1964); L. Goppelt, *Christentum und Judentum* (Gütersloh, 1954); G. Baum, *The Jews and the Gospel* (London, 1961); G. Dix, *Jew and Greek, A Study in the Primitive Church* (London, 1953, repr. 1955); from the mass of periodical literature, we note especially O. Michel, 'Polemik und Scheidung. Eine biblische und religions-

buted something either by persuasion or by reaction, but unless acknowledged it is not a specific dependence. With reference to Dahl's book, whose section on Paul runs parallel to our attempt, it is important to note that, whereas he accepts as a presupposition that Paul applies 'the Israel of God' to the Church (cf. his preface), the following is intended to establish the illegitimacy of such a presupposition, and to explain how this finally does come about. On many other important points we agree extensively.

GALATIANS 6: 16

In earlier chapters we have claimed without full proof that Justin Martyr was the first to identify the Church with Israel. It will now be our first task, in the discussion of Paul's attitude on these matters, to substantiate this assertion by refuting the usual claim that Galatians 6: 16 equates the Church and Israel. Some modify the common position by claiming that the phrase refers to Jewish Christians only. We shall suggest that this should be taken as a reference to the contemporary continuation of Israel, and not the whole Church or a select part of it.

In the paragraph Galatians 6: 11–18 we have Paul's *ipsissima verba*. This paragraph is not only his autograph to the letter to show its genuineness to the recipients,[1] it is also his own handwritten summation of the key points of the letter.[2] It is valuable to recover a passage in an almost uncontested textual condition[3] which expresses, without the intermediary effects of an amanu-

---

geschichtliche Studie', *Jud*, xv (1959), 193–212; G. Lindeskog, 'Israel in the NT—Some few remarks on a great problem', *SvExArs*, xxvi (1961), 57–92; and his 'Christianity as Realized Judaism' in *Pistis kai Erga* (Lund, 1964), pp. 15–36.

[1] On autographs see O. Roller, *Das Formular der paulinischen Briefe, ein Beitrag zur Lehre vom antiken Briefe* (*BWANT*, 4. Folge, Heft 6, Stuttgart, 1933), pp. 187 ff. and notes 499, 501, 502. He believes Paul wrote the whole of Gal. and Philem.

[2] See J. Moffatt, *An Introduction to the Literature of the NT* (Edinburgh, 1918, 3rd edition), p. 88; G. Milligan, *NT Documents* (London, 1913), pp. 21–8; M. Dibelius, *A Fresh Approach to the NT* (1936, n.p.), pp. 144 f.; E. J. Goodspeed, *An Introduction to the NT* (Chicago, 1937), p. 33; R. M. Grant, *A Historical Introduction to the NT* (London, 1963), p. 186.

[3] See below for *v.* 13; we accept the short form in *v.* 15; οὔτε γὰρ περιτομή and στοιχήσουσιν in *v.* 16.

ensis, the thought of Paul himself.[1] In other cases also Paul
pens a conclusion to a letter: e.g. 1 Corinthians 16: 21; 2 Thessalonians 3: 17; Philemon 19 (if he has not written the whole);
Colossians 4: 18. The evidence of 2 Thessalonians 3: 17 f. is
important for establishing the general practice of writing such
a conclusion,[2] but it does not help in the further point, which we
should like to establish, that often these conclusions are actually
a genuine Pauline summary.[3] We suggest that in 1 Corinthians
16 the greeting in Paul's own hand is from *v.* 19 to the end.[4]
There are four unusual aspects to this conclusion: love (*vv.* 22,
24, and cf. ch. 13); the end (*v.* 22 *b*, cf. ch. 15); apostolic
authority (*v.* 21, cf. chs. 1–4); and warnings (*v.* 22, everywhere
in the letter).[5] If we turn to 1 Thessalonians it may be that
5: 27 f. is the postscript, since it marks the introduction of the
1st person singular into the letter, but if it were to go back to
v. 23, there would also be an appropriate summary to the
content of the letter.[6] Romans is complicated by the textual
difficulty with ch. 16, but if we accept the theory of T. W.
Manson,[7] then ch. 16 is an integral part of one copy of the letter.[8]

[1] This is on the assumption that ἔγραψα is an epistolary aorist, and that
it does not refer to the whole letter. Some think that Paul began writing at
5: 2, but, while possible, this is not as likely a starting-point as the emphatic
statement of 6: 11. For Roller, see above.

[2] Cf. A. Deissmann, *Light from the Ancient East* (London, 1922), pp. 171 f.

[3] See now G. J. Bahr, 'Paul and Letter Writing in the First Century'
(*CBQ*, xxviii, 1966, 465–77), who agrees that the autographic conclusions
are summaries. On summaries generally see P. Bonnard, *Matthieu* (*CNT*,
Neuchâtel, 1963), p. 51 n. 1, who cites P. Benoit in *Mélanges Goguel*
(Neuchâtel, 1950), pp. 1–10, and E. Trocmé, *Le Livre des Actes et l'Histoire*
(Paris, 1957), pp. 195 ff.; both on Acts.

[4] The difficulty in establishing the extent of the autograph is a result of
the fact that no distinguishing mark except the handwriting was necessary
in the original. Note here that ἀσπασμός, which is in Paul's hand, begins
at *v.* 19.

[5] Chs. 1–4, 13, 15 represent the basic parts of the letter, the rest is
occasional in nature—the result of requests for advice from Corinth.

[6] Note 1st person plural in 5: 12, 14, a train of thought which concludes
at *v.* 22.

[7] *BJRL*, xxxi (1948), 224 ff.

[8] The argument for taking *vv.* 25–7 as Pauline is reinforced by 𝔓[46]'s
reading these after 15: 33, on Manson's hypothesis the conclusion of the
Roman copy of the letter. Thus both copies have the same conclusion. See
also Roller, *Das Formular*, pp. 193 ff.

If, as well, we accept as an inference from 'I Tertius'[1] that he stops writing at the end of that section and Paul pens *vv.* 25–7, then the conclusion may also be a Pauline summary of the content of the letter.[2] There are, then, some grounds for the view that, where Paul did close the letter in his own hand, his note was not always just a salutation but often crystallized the basic issues. The conclusion *may* clarify the real purpose of the letter, and this legitimates an approach to the letter as a whole through the conclusion.[3]

Ἰσραὴλ τοῦ θεοῦ in Galatians 6: 16 is a unique phrase. In a context where polemic is very common, this name comes immediately after a prayer for peace upon those who shall walk according to a 'rule'.[4] Those who conduct themselves as new creatures, who have obtained life in Christ and are obedient to the direction of the Spirit, will know 'peace'.[5] This is both an assured promise and a present state for genuine Christians, who stand in contrast to the pseudo-Christians (whoever they may be) who are urging a reliance upon something less than Jesus himself. Physical things, especially those deriving from a desire for exclusiveness, are of no assistance to the Christian who wants to be incorporated into Christ. All that matters for him is whether or not he is a καινὴ κτίσις. If so, peace is his.

The link between this and the next phrase is not so clear as most would like it. Occasionally in commentaries it is remarked that εἰρήνη and ἔλεος appear in an illogical order, but this rarely gives rise to any discussion of the assumption that both are

---

[1] Cf. Deissmann, *Light*, p. 236; W. M. Ramsay, *A Historical Commentary on Galatians* (London, 1900, 2nd edition), p. 465 (and note 2 misprints); F. J. A. Hort in J. B. Lightfoot, *Biblical Essays* (London, 1893), p. 323 n. 2.

[2] It underlines the value of the *kerygma* to those outside God's mercies, emphasizes the revelation of mystery, refers to the Prophets (quoted at greater length in Romans than elsewhere), and claims that the gospel is valid for all nations. These points are all made at the beginning of the letter as well (1: 1–6) in different terms, and are echoed in an intermediate summary (not an autograph) in 11: 28 ff., for which see later. Cf. Hort, *Biblical Essays*, pp. 326 ff.

[3] Cf. A. Deissmann, *Bible Studies* (Edinburgh, 1901), pp. 347 f.: 'More attention ought to be paid to the concluding words of the letter generally; they are of the highest importance if we are ever to understand the Apostle. The conclusion to the Galatians is certainly a very remarkable one.'

[4] Cf. Beyer, *TDNT*, III, 596 ff., art. κανών.

[5] See Foerster, art. εἰρήνη κτλ, *TDNT*, II, 411 ff.

intended to apply to the same group. However, the logic of the Christian life is clear: mercy precedes peace, peace flows out of God's merciful activity.[1] When χάρις also is considered, it invariably comes before ἔλεος, again in the 'correct' order logically and theologically. The basic formula χάρις καὶ εἰρήνη is a standard salutation which is never varied.[2] It appears in all the Pauline letters, including Ephesians and Titus, and also 1 Peter, varied only at 1 Timothy 1:2 and 2 Timothy 1:2 to include ἔλεος as the middle term.[3] The concluding formula: χάρις κτλ[4] is found in the whole corpus, and in almost every case as the final statement (e.g. Galatians 6: 18). Other word groupings in which progression of ideas is clear are found in Ephesians 3: 14–19 (χάρις, δόξα, πίστις, ἀγάπη → πλήρωμα); Ephesians 6: 23 f. (εἰρήνη, ἀγάπη μετὰ πίστεως → χάρις); the unique 2 Corinthians 13: 13 (χάρις, ἀγάπη, κοινωνία); and 1 Corinthians 13: 13 (πίστις, ἐλπίς, ἀγάπη).

This brief résumé adequately demonstrates that, in Pauline prayers, blessings, and liturgical formulae generally, where co-ordinate or consecutive words are used they are arranged logically. With possibly one exception the order is based on the logic of God's activity among men: source then benefits.[5] There are, however, few specific examples of the coupling of ἔλεος and εἰρήνη. Only once in LXX are the two words found closely together, and there in the correct order.[6] Generally the LXX illustrates the same pattern as the Pauline letters; in the matter

---

[1] M. J. Lagrange, *EtBib* (3rd edition, 1926), p. 166, is not convincing: 'Mais dans l'ordre des faits on peut regarder la paix comme l'état qui permet à Dieu de répandre ses bénédictions, qui viennent de sa miséricorde.' Cf. also C. J. Ellicott (1854), p. 138.

[2] See Roller, *Das Formular*, pp. 110 ff. and Tabelle 3; C. F. D. Moule, *Colossians and Philemon* (*CGTC*, Cambridge, 1962), pp. 153 f. Full bibliography in B. Rigaux, *Saint Paul et ses Lettres: État de la Question* (Paris, 1962), pp. 165 f.

[3] So also at 2 John 3; in Jude 2 only ἔλεος and εἰρήνη.

[4] Roller, *Das Formular*, pp. 114 ff., Tabelle 4.

[5] The exception, Eph. 6: 23 f., is explainable on stylistic grounds—that it is intended to build up to χάρις.

[6] Tobit 7: 12s (cf. also 6: 18s, where σωτηρία unusually precedes ἔλεος). There is also one example in the Syriac Apocalypse of Baruch (2 Bar. 78: 2). There is little to be gained by an analysis of pairs in LXX using one or other word; they are often combined, mostly in what we have called the logical order, but this is not without exceptions.

of the two words in which we are interested there is unanimity in all the instances wherever they are found.

The LXX offers other more general parallels to the separate parts of Galatians 6: 16 but no parallel can be found for the structure of the sentence with its double noun and double preposition. The closest canonical reference is undoubtedly Psalm 124: 5 (= 127: 6) εἰρήνη ἐπὶ τὸν ᾽Ισραήλ,[1] which deals with two groups: those who are good and upright, and those who turn aside whom the Lord will lead away.[2]

Another standard OT theme is 'mercy upon Israel', in most cases as a recollection of Israel's privileged place because of God's choice. Close to Galatians 6: 16 is the song of praise in Ezra 3: 11: ὅτι ἀγαθόν, ὅτι εἰς τὸν αἰῶνα τὸ ἔλεος αὐτοῦ ἐπὶ ᾽Ισραήλ.[3] Sometimes God's mercy was shown in specific acts, as here; sometimes it is a prayer that God would continue to show his mercy upon a disobedient people. The latter is present in the passage in Hosea 1 and 2. Whereas 1: 6 ff. appears to be a stark negation of the 'chosenness' of a part of God's people, 2: 23 nullifies the negation. His mercy will overcome. All too often, the mercy of God takes on a sectarian character as in the *Psalms of Solomon*. Running as a refrain through this collection is the idea that God's mercy is only for the select group.[4] This is obvious in 5: 25; 7: 10; 9: 11; 11: 9 (τοῦ κυρίου τὸ ἔλεος ἐπὶ τὸν ᾽Ισραὴλ εἰς τὸν αἰῶνα καὶ ἔτι); 13: 12; 15: 13. Often in such instances the assertion of God's mercy is linked with a demand for God's judgment on others.

The conclusion that must be drawn from the above is negative: there is little help in explaining the structure of the sentence in Galatians 6: 16. There is no example of the two terms appearing in the reverse order. This makes the one example

---

[1] Kittel, *BH*, proposes an emendation of the Hebrew to delete the former instance on the basis of an overlong line; the second instance, however, remains.

[2] It is interesting that there is the metaphor of walking (of the ethical life) here. Is it possible that Paul takes this and reverses the categories so that 'peace' is wished upon those who do good and are upright in heart, while Israel is identified with those who turn aside? It is too much to claim that this is Paul's primary intention, but it might be a part of it.

[3] חַסְדּוֹ עַל־יִשְׂרָאֵל; other examples are Ezek. 39: 25; Amos 5: 15; Zech. 1: 12–17; Isa. 44: 23; 49: 13; Joel 2: 13.

[4] See Appendix C for a broader consideration.

which is close—the *Shemoneh Esreh*[1]—more impressive. Part of Benediction XIX reads: 'Bestow peace, happiness, and blessing, grace, loving-kindness, and mercy upon us and upon all Israel thy People...'[2] 'Peace...and mercy' are found in the reverse order, as in Galatians, and this is followed by a reference to two groups—'us and all Israel'.[3] 'Us' refers to the worshippers present, and 'all Israel' to the Jewish worshipping community wherever it may be located. We may compare the presumed Hebrew and Greek of the forms as follows:

Sh.E. (Pal.) [שים] שלומך על ישראל עמך...ועל נחלתך וברכנו כולנו
δώσῃ εἰρήνην ἐπὶ τὸν ᾿Ισραὴλ τὸν λαόν σου...καὶ ἐπὶ τὸν κληρονομίαν σου.

Sh.E. (Bab.) [שים] שלום...וחסד...עלינו ועל כל ישראל עמך
δώσῃ εἰρήνην καὶ ἔλεος ἐφ᾿ ἡμᾶς καὶ ἐπὶ πάντα ᾿Ισραὴλ τὸν λαόν σου.

Gal. 6: 16:[4] εἰρήνη ἐπ᾿ αὐτοὺς καὶ ἔλεος καὶ ἐπὶ τὸν ᾿Ισραὴλ τοῦ θεοῦ.
שלום עליהם וחסד [ו]על ישראל אשר לאלהים

The similarity is close enough to make dependence or unconscious allusion plausible.[5] However Galatians 6: 16 and *Shemoneh Esreh* are not identical; importance must be attached to the variations. The *Shemoneh Esreh* has an expanding relationship between two groups ('us' and 'all Israel') whereas, on the usual showing, Paul has either the same group (Christians) or a decreasing group ('all Christians' and 'Jewish Christians').

[1] See E. L. Dietrich, *RGG*, v, cols. 1462 f. (probably goes back before Maccabean times); StrBill IV, I, Exk. 10, pp. 208–49; E. G. Hirsch, *Jewish Encyclopedia*, XI, 270–82; W. Staerk, *Altjüdische Gebete* (*Kleine Texte*, 1910); C. W. Dugmore, *The Influence of the Synagogue upon the Divine Office* (Oxford, 1944), for a convenient Hebrew text of both versions. For a contrary view of the date, see A. Marmorstein, *JQR*, n.s. XXXIV (1943), 137–59, and his references to H. I. Bell, *Fragments of an Unknown Gospel* (London, 1935), and Wahrhaftig, *JTS*, XL (1939), 376–81.

[2] Babylonian recension; the Palestinian is shorter: 'Bestow peace upon thy People Israel and upon thy city and upon thine inheritance...'

[3] The additional examples given by StrBill at Gal. 6: 16 probably stem from the liturgical precedent of Benediction XIX and are not therefore independent witnesses to this order.

[4] The BFBS edition of the Hebrew NT (Delitzsch) transposes the word order to give the usual interpretation.

[5] Cf. H. N. Ridderbos in *NLC* (1953), p. 227; he is one of the few commentators who expresses surprise at this phrase.

Moreover, the point of the benediction is the reference to all Israel; in Galatians the word is limited by τοῦ θεοῦ, an almost impossible expression in Hebrew. It is difficult to account for 'the Israel of God', but the difficulty is compounded if it refers to a more restricted group singled out for special mention. There is also a significant variation in the structure of the two which cannot be accounted for on stylistic grounds. It is precisely the style of Galatians 6: 16 that sets the major problem for the interpreter. The two passages seem to be analogous, but do not have the same structure or purpose. The Galatians sentence conveys the impression of being an interpreted reflection of the benediction.

The verse cannot be interpreted as is usually done. Three articles in *Judaica*[1] only illustrate the difficulties of the usual views. Schrenk rightly claims that Israel must be identified in some way with *das konkrete Israel*, and Dahl rightly claims that it is difficult to understand Paul referring to Jewish Christians here, for it would be admitting that, when all is said and done, Judaizers are right and he is wrong.[2] The stylistic hinge of the argument is the second *kai*. Dahl appeals to Acts 5: 11 to support his contention that it is epexegetic; Schrenk correctly replies that it is not a parallel case, and that if ἐπὶ τὸν ᾽Ισραὴλ τοῦ θεοῦ were epexegetic, *kai* were better omitted. He continues by observing that there is a very significant difference between naming two attributes and then two recipients (= εἰρήνη καὶ ἔλεος ἐπ᾽ αὐτοὺς καὶ ἐπὶ τὸν ᾽Ισραὴλ τοῦ θεοῦ) and the word order as it stands.[3] Schrenk also deals with the double *kai*, but

---

[1] G. Schrenk, 'Was bedeutet "Israel Gottes"?', *Jud*, v (1949), 81–94; N. A. Dahl, 'Zur Auslegung von Gal. 6. 16', *Jud*, vi (1950), 151–70; and G. Schrenk, 'Der Segenswunsch nach der Kampfepistel', *ibid.* pp. 170–90. In the first article there is a survey of the positions held by many exegetes. Neither allows for the possibility of the view expressed here.

[2] Since this was written D. W. B. Robinson has tried, very attractively, to create a 'Distinction between Jewish and Gentile Believers in Galatians' (*Aus. Bib. Rev.* xiii (1965), 29–48). He shares the attempt in the present work to challenge the view that Gal. 6: 16 equates the Church with Israel, but he falls into the same problems as Schrenk. Robinson's argument, based upon an interesting analysis of the use of 'we' and 'you' in Gal. 3: 13 ff. and 4: 5 ff., involves the assumption that in the early Church there are two types of churches: Gentiles and the saints at Jerusalem. This must remain a very tenuous hypothesis.

[3] *Jud*, vi (1950), 177 f.; this is the *Hauptsache*.

not successfully.[1] His main point, reserved for the end of his article, is that the Jewish prayers (noted above) predispose Paul to think of *das konkrete Israel*; and he goes on: 'Ist auch 'Ισραήλ τοῦ θεοῦ nicht hebraisierend, sondern gräzisierend, so entspricht doch τὸν 'Ισραήλ der griechischen Bibel. Unsere Auffassung, daß Israel Gottes in Gal. 6: 16 den christgläubigen Juden gelte...' The difficulty is that his two statements do not follow: he is correct in the first, but the conclusion he draws is incorrect, as Dahl quickly points out.

The dilemma stems from a failure to consider the multiple problem: double *epi*, double *kai*, and double attributes in the wrong order. There are no parallels for such a structure, though the *Shemoneh Esreh* is precedent for the illogical order. We contend that Paul has given this an ironical twist: where it has 'us' and 'them' (who are an extension of 'us'), Paul turns this into 'us' and 'them', where 'they' are people who should be connected with 'us' but are not yet. This irony depends for its bite upon the positive connection, that in both 'they' are the larger whole of which 'we' are the particular group in mind— in Galatians 'we' being Christians and 'they' all called Israel. Paul follows but modifies the illogical order of the benediction, associating only one of the attributes with each group.[2] This accounts for the word order in Galatians; he is saying something important by this variation from the *Shemoneh Esreh*. Perhaps the difficulty arises from the fact that he is making an unpopular wish in the situation addressed.

The sentence must be re-punctuated, so that it reads: εἰρήνη ἐπ' αὐτούς, καὶ ἔλεος καὶ ἐπὶ τὸν 'Ισραήλ τοῦ θεοῦ.

---

[1] 'Sieht man sämtliche Beispiele des doppelten ἐπί im NT durch, so überwiegt bei weitem jene Figur in der das zweite ἐπί die Hinzufügung eines neuen Momentes bringt' (*Jud*, v, 86 n. 10). He lists Matt. 27: 25; Luke 23: 38 (?); Acts 5: 11, cf. 11: 15; Heb. 8: 8; Rev. 20: 4; and also notes Rev. 8: 10; 19: 16; and Heb. 10: 16. These only indicate that there is no parallel to this form of double *epi* in which the second is separated from its logical position by a second noun. To examine these to deduce whether the second introduces expanding, contrasting or correlative terms is beside the point.

[2] Possibly because for him *eleos* carried a more positive content related primarily to the Christ-event. 'Mercy' is shown when one is brought to a condition of trust in Jesus; it is not simply a wish for God's blessing. Bultmann's treatment is deficient at this point; *TDNT*, II, 477 ff. (especially pp. 484 f.).

'Peace' is then applied to all who will walk according to the new possibilities of freedom and purity made available through the cross of Jesus; 'mercy' is wished upon some group which is called *Israēl tou theou*.

Who is this group? We suggest that it is those within Israel to whom God will show mercy—all those Israelites who are going to come to their senses and receive the good news of Christ. It is relevant to this, first, that *eleos* in the Pauline epistles is usually associated with God's special mercy in bringing to salvation; it has expectant overtones that cannot be confined in a formula of blessing. Secondly, the future στοιχήσουσιν may carry, by analogy, a future element into the parallel prayer dependent upon 'mercy': Israel is not yet the Christ-believing Jews, it is those who are still to believe. Thirdly, *tou theou* is not intended to be set over against *kata sarka*. The proper antithesis of *kata sarka* is only *kata pneuma*: one cannot in Pauline language contrast ἐκκλησία τοῦ θεοῦ with ἐκκλησία κατὰ σάρκα; nor can one contrast περιτομή κατὰ σάρκα with περιτομή τοῦ θεοῦ. In each case the second phrase is nonsense. Paul, in Galatians 6: 16, is not contrasting *Israēl tou theou* with *Israēl kata sarka*. The change from *kol yisrael* to *Israēl tou theou* can only be interpreted on the grounds that for Paul 'all Israel' is too ambiguous (though he uses it in Romans after a long discussion of his meaning); he expects that only a part, *Israēl tou theou*, will be blessed in the way he prays. There is an Israel (of God) within (all) Israel.

An argument remaining for consideration is the question of the second *kai*. May it not actually be necessary to Paul's purpose? If it were omitted, the sentence could be interpreted too readily in line with the position of Dahl: namely, 'peace and mercy be upon all who walk by this rule, upon the Israel of God' (= RSV), where the last phrase defines the first. But the addition of *kai* should prevent such an interpretation by calling attention to the last four words of the sentence, and by demanding for them special consideration. *Kai* may be construed as ascensive,[1] but only slightly so; the justification for needing any ascensive force at all is that, from the way Paul has argued previously in the letter, one might infer that he was condemning

---

[1] See Bl–D/Funk, 442.12; Moulton/Turner, p. 335; and cf. Moule, *Idiom*, p. 167, on displacement of *kai*.

everything about Israel. To forestall this inference he includes this prayer to God for mercy to be shown to Israel.[1]

This means that Galatians 6: 16 does not presuppose that the Church has taken over the name Israel for itself.[2] On the contrary, Paul avoids this association of ideas, and prefers to describe the Church by means of a functional, rather than a substantive, designation. Both the Church and those who are not yet the Church are the subjects of a prayer to God for blessing. The 'Israel of God' is, when Galatians is written, a part of the Israelite nation.[3] We have evidence, in Acts and

---

[1] See E. de W. Burton, *ICC* (1921), one of the best commentaries ever written, who has anticipated this position. He also points to the illogicality of the order of nouns, and to the absence of *Israël* referring to anything except the Jewish nation or a part of it. He says: 'καὶ ἔλεος becomes, then, an afterthought, to which καὶ ἐπὶ τὸν 'Ισραὴλ τοῦ θεοῦ appends a second afterthought.' More likely than afterthought is dependence upon *Sh.E.*, and the ironical reversal of categories. But he goes on: 'These facts favour the interpretation of the expression as applying not to the Christian community, but to Jews; yet in view of τοῦ θεοῦ, not to the whole Jewish nation, but to the pious Israel...including even those who had not seen the truth as Paul saw it, and so could not be included in ὅσοι...στοιχ. In this case the benediction falls into two distinct parts. In the first the apostle invokes peace upon those who recognize and act in accordance with the principle of *v.* 15, and, in distinction from them, the mercy of God...upon those within Israel who even though as yet unenlightened are the true Israel of God.' (Pp. 357 f.) Both Schrenk (*Jud*, v, 1949, 94 n. 29) and Bonnard (*CNT*, 1953, p. 131) attribute the Jewish Christian position to Burton. This is not clear, however, from Burton's language; we are left wondering about the extent of Israel's 'unenlightenment'.

[2] Strong confirmation of this position comes from the total absence of an identification of the Church with Israel until A.D. 160; and also from the total absence, even then, of the term 'Israel of God', to characterize the Church. When the change is made first, the Church is called 'the true Israel'. This great hiatus between Gal. 6: 16 and Justin's *Dialogue* creates a firm presumption in favour of the above interpretation. The earliest commentary extant on Gal. 6: 15 f., by Eusebius of Emesa, supports the usual view; see K. Staab, *Paulus Kommentare aus der griechischen Kirche aus Katenenhandschriften* (Münster i.W., 1933), p. 52.

[3] Cf. Schrenk, *Jud*, vi (1950), 187: 'Aber eine Abwendung von der mit dem Namen Israel bezeichneten Berufung dieses Volkes hat Paulus nie vertreten. Dadurch, daß er Abrahamskindschaft, Beschneidung, Volk Gottes überträgt, ist noch nicht gegeben und bewiesen, daß er auch den Namen überträgt, der das Bundesvolk von altersher kennzeichnet...die Folgerung [*sc.* from 1 Cor. 10: 18], daß sich daraus ein "Israel nach dem Geist" = Kirche ergeben müsse, wäre eine Überforderung des Textes.'

Romans particularly, that Paul is sufficiently concerned for the conversion of Israel that such a transposition is unlikely. The prayer is called for by the possibility of misunderstanding Paul's intention in the letter proper. When he reads it again and adds his own conclusion he clarifies his statements about the problem of circumcision and asserts the centrality of Christ's cross for all believers, but to prevent the Galatians from moving from this position to a new Christian exclusiveness and sectarianism, he adds his prayer for mercy on God's faithful people.[1] A paraphrase might run: 'May God give peace to all who will walk according to this criterion, and mercy also to his faithful people Israel.'[2]

THE CIRCUMCISERS IN GALATIA
AND PAUL'S OPPOSITION

The first part of the autograph-summary requires similar attention to detail, for there is some vagueness about the number of groups mentioned. This is complicated by a textual variation in 6: 13: περιτεμνόμενοι or περιτετμημένοι.[3] Elsewhere in the letter, the perfect of the verb is not used; there is one aorist (2: 3), and four presents (5: 2, 3; 6: 12, 13). Two of these latter cases describe circumcising an uncircumcised person and point, therefore, to the results of a judaizing mission.[4] The perfect would, presumably, refer to Jewish opponents. Neither internal arguments nor the textual support are sufficient to establish beyond doubt the correct reading in 6: 13.[5] It can be argued either way. The problem is, first, whether the persons are resident in Galatia or outsiders; and, secondly, how the

---

[1] Cf. Ramsay, *Historical Commentary*, p. 471: '...then are added the more gracious words, "and on the Israel of God"...'; also 'This paragraph is the crowning proof that it is a mistake to read indignation as the chief feature of this letter...' (471 f.).

[2] It is difficult to get exactly the right sense in English: 'also' is not quite right, but 'even' is too strong.

[3] Present participle: ℵ A C D K P al Mcion f vg syr^p,h sah arm *et al.* Perfect participle: 𝔓⁴⁶ B 𝕶 (F G) al d g go bo eth *et al.* Were it not for 𝔓⁴⁶ the evidence would be decisively in favour of present participle.

[4] See Burton, *ICC*, p. 353.

[5] It is hypothetically possible that the perfect, as the more difficult reading, was altered to present, either under the influence of Gal. 5: 2 or through a failure, after the Galatian situation had changed, to remember that Jews were actively engaged in the difficulty there.

solution to this problem affects the question of the relationship of the Church and Israel.[1]

To determine whether these 'troublers' are inside or outside the Galatian community we list the following possibilities:

(a) *peritemnomenoi* (present passive participle). The most natural meaning is Galatian Christians, probably originally God-fearers, who are allowing themselves to be circumcised; but though they submit to the rite, as Gentiles they are unable to keep the whole Law. To accept one requirement of the Law is illogical.[2] Are these, however, the same persons as the subjects of the 3rd person plural verbs of 12 and 13*b*? If they are, the encouragement to circumcision is from inside the Christian community.[3] If they are not, οὐδὲ...φυλάσσουσιν is parenthetical, and *vv.* 12 and 13*b* do not affect the interpretation of *v.* 13*a*.[4]

(b) *peritemnomenoi* (present passive participle). A subtle alteration of the sense could have this apply to some in the Church who had previously moved so far towards Judaism that they had become full proselytes by accepting circumcision. The present tense would distinguish them from Jews circumcised from birth.[5] These proselytes, having become part of Israel, would not (as Christians?) be able to keep the Law. In the nature of the case, these must almost certainly be identified with the subject of *vv.* 12 and 13*b*.[6] A variation of this is

---

[1] The letter is so polemically oriented that the evidence is weighted before we begin. The objects of the polemic, whose identity is uncertain, represent in one form or another a group which is half-way between the Church and Israel (either Jews who are almost Christians, or Christians who are almost Jews). The group (if it be a group) represents a border situation between the two. Galatians yields its secrets on this question only with much prying. A further complication is that *Israēl* is a *hap. leg.* in Gal., and there we have had to resort to other considerations to establish its meaning.

[2] Cf. Moule, *Idiom*, p. 107: '...for not even the very ones who get circumcised keep the Law...'

[3] See Munck, *Paul*, ch. 4; Schoeps, *Paul*, p. 65; Ellicott, *in loc.*; E. Hirsch in *ZNW*, xxix (1930), 192–7; A. Oepke, *ThHNT* (1937), p. 121; G. Kittel in *ZNW*, xxx (1931), 148.

[4] No one is strongly in favour of this.

[5] The aorist might have been expected, except that in the LXX it is generally used to indicate circumcision from birth.

[6] It would be completely extraneous were they not. Both Lightfoot, *McM* (6th edition, 1880) and Oepke, *ThHNT*, *in loc.*, allow for this, but neither rests his exegesis upon it.

suggested by W. Michaelis: on the first journey Paul and Barnabas preached circumcision, and 6: 13 alludes to these early converts, one of whom is particularly troubling the Church.[1]

(c) *peritemnomenoi* (present middle participle). Those who are going around circumcising (with no reference to the time of their own circumcision) are not themselves capable of keeping the Law.[2] This retains the commonly accepted reading, and gives it a polemical force, but denies the possibility of deciding whether they are from inside or outside.[3] By maintaining a timeless present view, the complexities of the situation are avoided.[4]

(d) *peritetmēmenoi* (perfect passive participle).[5] Jews, circumcised from birth, cannot themselves keep the Law. (i) But could non-Christian Jews be the subjects of *v.* 12: 'They are forcing you to be circumcised, only in order that they should not be persecuted for the cross of Christ'? It is conceivable that Jews might be conducting a counter-mission among proselytes and God-fearers, or that they are persecutors, but hardly that they are themselves persecuted, and that 'for Christ's cross'. It is more likely that one should construe *v.* 13*a* as a parenthetic addition, predicated upon the mention of a Jewish persecution in *v.* 12. (ii) It would be better to interpret this as Christian Jews, who would be identified with the subjects of the verbs in

---

[1] *ZNW*, xxx (1931), 83–9; based largely upon ἔτι in 5: 11. S. Belkin, *JBL*, LIV (1935), 41–60, makes some good points against this, but not decisive in the face of the ἔτι.

[2] This is possible grammatically, though there is no lexicographical evidence that περιτέμνω has a distinctive middle voice, unless it is permissive (cf. Bl–D/Funk, 314, 317; Robertson, *Grammar*, pp. 808 f.). It is difficult to see why such a form should be chosen.

[3] It also overlooks the parallel in 5: 2 f. where, of necessity, περιτεμνό-μενος = ἐὰν περιτέμνησθε. In practice, those who maintain this view do not generally hold that they are from inside.

[4] See Burton, *ICC*, p. 273 on 5.2. We may list as proponents of this view: H. N. Ridderbos, *NLC*; G. S. Duncan, *MNTC* (1934); W. M. Ramsay, *Historical Com.*; Lightfoot, *McM*; Lagrange, *EtBib*; P. Bonnard, *CNT*; H. Schlier, *KEK* (12th edition, 1962); O. Holtzmann, in *ZNW*, xxx (1931), 176–83 in opposition to Hirsch, as noted above; H. A. A. Kennedy, *ExT*, XXII (1910–11), 419–20. Oepke, *ThHNT*, also allows for this view.

[5] As a perfect middle participle it would be unintelligible, and need not be considered; the middle, if possible at all, would have to carry something of a timeless force.

the context. That they do not keep the Law themselves would be a particularly damaging criticism calculated to undercut their position. Verse 13*a* would be polemical and not merely explanatory.[1]

These possibilities, all legitimate, indicate the necessity of determining the relationship of *v.* 13*a* to the rest. If it is parenthetic it has a theological or apologetic purpose, and not a polemical force; circumcised people, whoever they are, cannot keep the Law, so it is illogical for you to rely on this rite; you need not, you must not, submit to it.[2] Against its being parenthetic are the following: (i) the most natural antecedent of φυλάσσουσιν and the other verbs is ὅσοι; (ii) γάρ is logically dependent on the immediately preceding context; (iii) though οὐδὲ γάρ does not demand a concluding statement,[3] when ἀλλά follows closely it is likely to be a part of the train of thought;[4] (iv) not only a preceding, but also a following change of subject should have to be posited on the parenthetic interpretation, with a full stop after φυλάσσουσιν; (v) *v.* 13*b* being independent of *v.* 13*a* would be an unnecessary duplication of *v.* 12. But if *v.* 13*a* is not parenthetic, *v.* 12 says: they want to circumcise you to avoid persecution because of Christ's cross— a negative consideration of some force; and *v.* 13 says: although they cannot keep the Law, as I understand it, still they want to circumcise you to show their good intentions to those who matter in Judaism—a positive consideration of equal weight.[5]

Unfortunately we cannot establish an airtight case, but the hypothesis that *v.* 13*a* is not parenthetic makes the most sense of the sentences. If so, on the basis of the above analysis there is a choice between *peritemnomenoi* = those who, having submitted

---

[1] Ellicott appears to lean towards such a solution, though he rejects it on grounds of insufficient textual evidence. Burton, *ICC, in loc.*, cites Meyer as reading the perfect, without describing his view more fully.

[2] On the logic of Galatians, see T. W. Manson, *BJRL*, xxiv (1940), 59–80.

[3] Bl–D/Funk, 445. 1, 452.3.

[4] That is, boasting in the flesh, which they would be able to do if they encouraged circumcision, is a part of their attempt to keep the Law.

[5] On this generally, see Munck, *Paul*, pp. 87 ff. (and his criticisms there of Sieffert and Holtzmann); Schoeps, *Paul*, p. 65; W. D. Davies, *Christian Origins* (London, 1962), p. 194 (being a reprint of a review in *NTS*, ii (1955), 60–72).

to circumcision, are now urging it upon others,[1] and *peritet-mēmenoi* = some with a Jewish background who are urging circumcision.[2]

The early part of ch. 5 is a close parallel to the above, and is, therefore, important to this inquiry.[3] The immediate point of contact is the statement in 5: 3: μαρτύρομαι δὲ πάλιν παντὶ ἀνθρώπῳ περιτεμνομένῳ ὅτι ὀφειλέτης ἐστὶν ὅλον τὸν νόμον ποιῆσαι.[4] In 5: 2 f. *ean peritemnēsthe* and *peritemnomenos* must refer to the man undergoing circumcision and, as we have seen, if *peritemnomenoi* be the correct reading in 6: 13 it almost certainly has the same connotation. The assertions that it is necessary for a *peritemnomenos* to keep the Law (5: 3) and that circumcisers do not keep the Law (6: 13) are intended to cut the ground from under the opponents.[5] If you get circumcised you put yourself under an obligation to keep the whole Law, yet even the enthusiastic ritualists do not achieve the standard they set. Who are these ritualists? We may infer from 5: 2 that those who are urging circumcision are doing it on the grounds that it will be an advantage to undergo the rite. Far from being an advantage, it is merely an 'obstruction'.[6] Galatians 5: 12 hints at identification. The sarcasm of this offensive remark, 'one of the

[1] These would be people circumcised as Christians very recently (*a*), or those circumcised into Christianity by preachers who still hold to the need for it, or those who once were circumcised as Jewish proselytes (*b*).

[2] These could be Jewish Christians (*d*), either from inside or outside, but more likely the latter.

[3] It is convenient for commentators generally to divide the letter at the end of 5: 1, but this should not obscure the unity of the argument from ch. 4 into ch. 5. We shall maintain that foreshadowings of the problem dealt with in 5: 2–12 are to be found in 4: 17 ff.

[4] Another point of close contact is the repetition of οὔτε (γὰρ) περιτομή τι ἰσχύει (ἐστιν), οὔτε ἀκροβυστία (5: 6; 6: 15).

[5] F. R. Crownfield maintains ('The singular problem of the dual Galatians', *JBL*, LXIV, 1945, 491 ff.) that this problem is very important. Building upon the work of Ropes, *HTSt*, XIV (1929), he concludes that the 'two fronts' of these critics are really one group, syncretists who misunderstand Paul's message in two opposite ways. Their leaders are early converts to Christianity, connected with Jerusalem, who may have a connection with mystery cults. They accuse Paul of giving in to the Judaistic party and of keeping the full light from them.

[6] τίς ὑμᾶς ἐνέκοψεν; (5.7), cf. ὁ δὲ ταράσσων ὑμᾶς (5: 10). The singular, and ὅστις ἐὰν ᾖ, are generalizations, *contra* Hirsch, *ZNW*, XXIX (1930), 192–7, who says it is a Gentile Christian friend of Paul's.

bitterest and coarsest expressions in all his letters',[1] is applicable to either Jewish or Gentile opponents. To say this of Jews by birth is not meaningless; but it is far more relevant to the occasion if it is addressed to some who, having submitted willingly to the knife as adults, should, in Paul's opinion, have gone the whole way and become emasculated. There would then be irony coupled with sarcasm: they would be excluded from the fellowship of Temple worship which they seem to be so earnestly courting. This may tip the scales in favour of the opponents being Gentiles, and at the same time in favour of *peritemnomenoi* in 6: 13 as the correct reading. It must be seen how well this stands up in the rest of the letter.

Accepting this as a hypothesis, 5: 11 appears at first sight to be a reference to Paul's earlier Christian activity, when he actually did circumcise some in Galatia. Amongst these circumcised Gentile Christians are some who oppose his new stand on the matter.[2] This presents a compact argument (5: 2–12), where the details fit well together. This cannot be ruled out, but there is no corroborative evidence of a radical shift in Paul's practice.[3] Another view which would satisfy the passage is that it is a reference to his views before his conversion: he used to hold that it was necessary to be circumcised to become a member of God's people, now he no longer does. The weakness of this is that it has little relevance to the local problem, unless Paul had been a Jewish missionary previously.[4] Even then it would not be strictly relevant except as a mark of how much his message had changed as a result of Christ's coming. Usually it is taken as an exercise in logic, with *eti* used in two ways: in 11 *a* chronologically, and in 11 *b* as a logical inference.[5]

---

[1] Duncan, *MNTC*, p. 161. See the article ἀποκόπτω by Stählin, *TDNT*, III, 852 ff.   [2] So, basically, Michaelis, *ZNW*, xxx (1931), 83–9.

[3] J. H. Ropes, 'The Singular Problem of the Epistle to the Galatians', *HTSt*, xiv (1929), tries (following Lütgert, and cf. later Schmithals) to find a group of πνευματικοί in Galatia. In 5: 2 ff. Paul opposes judaizers, but in 5: 11 he turns upon the perfectionists, as if to say: there is the demonstration that I am no longer preaching circumcision. Cf. also the review by J. M. Creed, *JTS*, xxxi (1930), 421 ff.

[4] Schoeps, *Paul*, pp. 168, 219, citing E. Barnikol, *Die vor- und früh-christliche Zeit des Paulus* (Kiel, 1929), pp. 18 ff.

[5] So, e.g., Bauer/A–G, *s.v.*; Burton, *ICC*, p. 287. Duncan, *MNTC*, para-phrases this position well: 'They began by persecuting me for not demanding

There is a congruence between 5: 11 and 6: 12—in both persecution is predicated upon one's view of circumcision, and the offence of the cross of Christ is reduced to nothing if one preaches circumcision—in spite of the fact that in 5: 11 it is Paul who is being persecuted and in 6: 12 it is the Gentiles in Galatia. This means that in 5: 2 ff. the 'disturbers' are inside the Church as the expression in 5: 9 presupposes ('a little leaven leavens the whole batch'). The 'persecutors', who seem to be a second group, are an outside factor in the situation. Paul is confronted not with persecution from inside the Church in Galatia but with dissembling, which is spurred on by a desire to avoid persecution. In 5: 11, if the apodosis refers to Jewish persecution we may reconstruct the sense as follows:[1] in Galatia there are circumcised Gentile Christians,[2] who are encouraging other Gentiles to become circumcised also, as a way of avoiding persecution from the Jews. They justify this position, which is psychologically quite understandable, as a necessity in order to be full Christians, and perhaps they cite Paul in their support.[3] The real reason is a deep-seated desire to continue the relationship with Jews that came only as the result of a courageous decision. Paul writes back emphatically:[4]

But if *I* am still preaching circumcision, as you are, why do you suppose I am being persecuted while you enjoy peaceful relations with the Jews? No! I don't want Gentiles to be circumcised—this is why I am meeting such opposition. Those people who have been

that Gentile converts should be circumcised. Now they insinuate that at heart I recognize the necessity of circumcision, and sometimes enforce it. They cannot have it both ways. If they themselves believe that I do preach circumcision, why do they go on persecuting me for not preaching it?' (160.) The difficulty with this is Paul's reason for condensing such an important part of his argument to such a cryptic length. The precise meaning of the remark in the context is not clear.

[1] Cf. K. Lake, *The Earlier Epistles of Paul* (London, 1930), ch. 2, particularly pp. 36 ff.; on Jewish persecution generally, see E. Stauffer, *NT Theology* (London, 1955), ch. 47; Selwyn, *NTS Bul.* 1 (1950) on 1 Peter; Moule, *Birth*, ch. 7.

[2] When they were circumcised is impossible to determine; it could be before, on, or after their conversion to Christianity.

[3] Though possibly only in the passive sense: 'Your beloved Paul is circumcised, why should he want to hold us back from this same mark of distinction; let us all be circumcised.'

[4] Ἐγὼ δέ, ἀδελφοί... The emphasis is on ἐγώ and not on ἔτι.

circumcised and are urging it on others should go all the way and be castrated. That would put an end to the trouble.

The discussion of the Law preceding this is aimed directly at these people and any tempted to agree with them (οἱ ὑπὸ νόμον θέλοντες εἶναι, 4: 21). Its main point, certain to be offensive to Jews and Jewish Christians, develops the need for freedom from having to assume the mantle of Judaism; it is not a polemic directed against those who by birth are under that mantle.

Preceding this again in 4: 17 f. is another in the series of 'troubling' passages.[1] The attention bestowed is οὐ καλῶς; this can imply nothing else but the encouragement of circumcision.[2] The sense is reasonably clear, except for the phrase ἀλλὰ ἐκκλεῖσαι ὑμᾶς.[3] It is not impossible as a side issue, but the context does not suggest that 'exclusiveness' of a group is under consideration. More likely is the metaphorical use of ἐκκλείω,[4] with reference to Paul's immediately preceding question: 'Have I become your enemy because I tell you the truth?'[5] 'These people who are zealously cultivating you have unworthy motives,[6] they want[7] to prevent you (sc. seeing the truth[8] of the gospel about circumcision) so that you will emulate them (sc. in undergoing that rite). It is good to be zealously cultivated...for a good cause—and that good cause is to be not under the Law but to be free.'[9]

With this in mind, we turn to chs. 1 and 2. The 'troublers' are introduced in 1: 7: οἱ ταράσσοντες ὑμᾶς καὶ θέλοντες μετα-

---

[1] The antecedent of the 3rd person plural is so far back (3: 10 (?) or 3: 1) as to be not relevant. It must be supposed that the readers could easily supply it.

[2] This does not hold the centre of the stage here; the context is Law and Jewish observance generally (3: 1 ff., 23 ff.; esp. 4: 10 f.).

[3] See Moule, *Idiom*, pp. 25 f.; and contrast F. R. M. Hitchcock, *JTS*, XL (1939), 149–51: = 'to hatch you'.

[4] Cf. Liddell–Scott, *s.v.* = 'hinder, prevent'. Rom. 3: 27, the only other NT instance, also could have this metaphorical sense.

[5] 5: 7 is a close parallel then.

[6] Cf. Moule, *Idiom*, p. 26, for translation.

[7] The use of θέλω in Gal. in every case is *in malam partem* (1: 7; 4: 9, 17, 21; 6: 12, 13).

[8] Ellicott, *in loc.*, refers to Chrysostom's supplying τῆς τελείας γνώσεως, though he himself does not accept it.

[9] Note how compulsion to circumcision, truth, and freedom are closely allied in 2: 3 ff.

στρέψαι τὸ εὐαγγέλιον τοῦ χριστοῦ.[1] This follows the allusion in 1:6 to the ones who are departing from Christ to another gospel, i.e. it is a reasonable inference that the troublers are Galatians.[2] Compulsion to circumcise is introduced in 2:3,[3] as an activity of 'false brethren' who want to bring Christians into bondage.[4] If, as Paul implies, these men are in Jerusalem and perhaps have some close connection with οἱ δοκοῦντες (στῦλοι εἶναι), there is in that city a centre of judaizing activity. The principle at stake is the need for circumcision in the missionary situation, as vv. 7–10 illustrate. Paul claims the great weight of this meeting for his side of the dispute;[5] he is the missionary to the Gentiles, he need not demand circumcision. Whatever may have happened to Titus, it has no bearing on the gospel, except to show that circumcision is not required.[6] The council entrusted Paul with the primary responsibility for the gospel to the Gentiles, while Peter was given the sphere of the circumcision.[7] The general picture, then, which Paul portrays

[1] On this and 2:1 ff. cf. W. M. Ramsay, *Exp.* 5th Ser., II (1895), 103–18.

[2] Note the vague introduction, εἰ μή τινές εἰσιν κτλ. This should be sharpened if they are outsiders.

[3] ἠναγκάσθη περιτμηθῆναι; there are close parallels in Josephus, *Life*, 23: τούτους περιτέμνεσθαι τῶν 'Ιουδαίων ἀναγκαζόντων; cf. *Ant.* 13.9.1 (re Idumeans) and 13.11.3 (re Itureans).

[4] Schmithals, 'Die Häretiker in Galatien', *ZNW*, XLVII (1956), 25 ff., claims, perhaps rightly, that these are Jews. Dix, *Jew and Greek*, p. 36, independently comes to the same position; he sharply distinguishes between them and the leaders. In any event, Paul says that he resisted them for the Galatians' sake (2:5). On vv. 3–5 cf. T. W. Manson, *BJRL*, XXIV (1940), 66 f., who holds that they describe a later event. This is also advocated by Dom B. Orchard in *BJRL*, XXVIII (1944), 154–74; *JTS*, XLIII (1942), 173–7; *CBQ*, VII (1945), 377–97. He identifies Gal. 2:1–2, 6–10 with the visit in Acts 11, and Gal. 2:3–5 with Acts 15. On the problem of vv. 4–5 he proposes to supply for the missing subject and object: 'because of false brethren... *the liberty of the Gentiles is now in danger*'.

[5] Whichever one it be; it seems likeliest that it is a reference to Acts 11, rather than Acts 15 or an intermediate one (about Acts 13) which Manson postulates, as in the note above.

[6] Paul is clearly embarrassed by the incident, but even if Titus were circumcised, Paul regards it as an occasional incident. See D. W. B. Robinson, 'The Circumcision of Titus, and Paul's Liberty' (*Aus. Bib. Rev.* XII (1964), 24–42). He ties together ἔτι in 5:11 and the circumcision of Titus in the context of a legitimate exercise of Paul's liberty.

[7] Paul must be here oversimplifying. Any division cannot be so simple, for a large percentage of the constituency of the Diaspora synagogues was ἔθνη.

is agreement between him and the recognized apostles. Another group living in Jerusalem,[1] whose relationship to the apostles is not discussed, because, perhaps, it is too tricky a subject, is anxious to have Paul toe the mark on circumcision. Thus far, *pseudadelphoi* is the only group name for them.

The next section is more difficult, but one or two things are reasonably clear. There is a group called οἱ ἐκ περιτομῆς, behind whom lies ultimately the authority of James.[2] The relationship to them of τινὰς ἀπὸ 'Ιακώβου,[3] and the official nature of this latter group, is in doubt.[4] The people from James have affinities in Antioch with οἱ λοιποὶ 'Ιουδαῖοι, though it seems reasonably certain that the two cannot be equated.[5] On the contrary, the 'rest of the Jews' who 'played a part'[6] with

[1] So C. K. Barrett, 'Paul and the "Pillar" Apostles', in *Studia Paulina in hon. J. de Zwaan* (Haarlem, 1953), p. 1 n. 1.

[2] This group need not be a 'circumcising' party, so much as a group arising out of Judaism, though its position may be the same in either case. W. Schmithals, *Paulus und Jakobus* (*FRLANT*, LXXXV, Göttingen, 1963, ET London, 1965) wrestles with this passage (pp. 51 ff.). He concludes that οἱ ἐκ περιτομῆς are Jews, because if the subject of ἦλθον were the same as the object of the sentence, a simple unmistakable αὐτούς only would be necessary (p. 54). Cf. also Bo Reicke, in *Studia Paulina*, pp. 172 ff.; Dix, *Jew and Greek*, pp. 42 ff. The criticism of this view is, first, the strangeness of calling Jews those ἐκ περιτομῆς (οἱ περιτετμημένοι or some other word would be better); secondly, the contrast implied between οἱ ἐκ περιτομῆς and οἱ λοιποὶ 'Ιουδαῖοι (see below); thirdly, it sounds too much like an attempt to absolve James completely.

[3] The readings of 𝔓⁴⁶, τινα and ἦλθεν, together with συνήσθιον, are difficult to harmonize internally, let alone to account for them. Robinson, *Aus. Bib. Rev.* XII (1964), 24–42, accepts τινα but as a neuter plural, not a masculine singular, and suggests that the meaning is 'some things from James', i.e. the Decrees. If so, the main difference between Peter and Paul is the application of the decrees to themselves, not to the Gentiles. By adopting the decrees, Peter forced Gentiles to adopt them.

[4] G. Kittel, 'Die Stellung des Jakobus zu Judentum und Heidenchristentum', *ZNW*, XXX (1931), 145–57; esp. pp. 151 f.: the meaning is clear, table fellowship with uncircumcised people is impossible.

[5] This is apparent from the juxtaposition of οἱ ἐκ περιτομῆς and οἱ λοιποὶ 'Ιουδαῖοι, when in the latter case an emphatic 'they' is all that would be required were it the same group. Schmithals does not consider this, but uses the same argument for the earlier pair.

[6] συνυποκρίνομαι; cf. MM, *s.v.*: 'the other Jews pretended to agree with Peter though they really did not'. It was a marriage of convenience only. This accounts for the use of ὑπόκρισις, without resorting to expressions like 'inconsistency', as do the mediating attempts.

Peter are outsiders to the more restricted Messianic part of the Jewish community in Antioch.[1] Under this combined weight—Antiochean Jewish Christians, Jerusalem Christians from James and Antiochean Jews—even Barnabas' hand is forced.[2] In the undifferentiated conditions which must have obtained in the earliest period, it is quite conceivable that Jews[3] would act locally with strict Jewish Christians to embarrass less rigid members of the community.[4]

It is no argument against this view of 'the rest of the Jews' that Paul addresses Peter as *Ioudaios* in 2: 14.[5] This is analogous to calling Titus *Hellēn* (2: 3), and derives from the nature of the argument, where racial origin is essential to the meaning. The point of his confrontation with Peter (2: 14) is the contrast between his own practice (being Jewish in origin he lives not strictly but in fellowship with Gentiles)[6] and the implication of his action (which is to compel Gentiles to live like Jews).[7] The argument does not yet depend on the fact that Peter was a Christian, but only on the illogicality of his action at the most basic level. His Christianity is brought into play in the next

[1] Ἰουδαῖος is never used of Jewish Christians, though Rom. 2: 28 f. comes close. See P. Bonnard's attempted justification of the use of the word here, *CNT*, pp. 50 f.

[2] Peter gave way under the force of the men from James alone; cf. Bonnard, *CNT*, p. 50. For a different view see Munck, *Paul*, pp. 106 ff.; Schmithals, *Paulus*.

[3] Bo Reicke's description of the forces at work in persecution is generally convincing, but does not allow enough for local variations (*Studia Paulina*).

[4] The *pseudadelphoi* may also be unconverted Jews trying to embarrass Christians. Cf. Schoeps, *Paul*, p. 63, for a balanced statement on groupings; the inference is that they are not yet solidified.

[5] On 2: 14 see Schmithals, *Paulus*, pp. 56 ff.; he takes the ὑπόκρισις to be *Inkonsequenz*—it was a sincere drawing away and not apostasy. H. Schlier, *KEK* (1962), pp. 86 f. is similar.

[6] As the Galatians read it, this might have a special effect upon Gentile judaizers; even Jews by birth must not judaize. The reference to Gentile influences is intended to divide Peter from the other party, perhaps against his will. It is a debating trick. Munck (*Paul*, p. 125)—'If you, as an *am haaretz*, observe the law so badly...'—misses the mark since the question of common people is not to the fore.

[7] This is the broader form of the earlier problem in 2: 3. By his action (if not consciously) Peter lends his support to the *pseudadelphoi*. Ἀναγκ. Ἰουδ. sounds suspiciously like a catchword which was mooted in Gentile Christian circles, though it is not susceptible of proof.

verses. The emphatic ἡμεῖς (2: 15) associates Peter and Paul together in a common position:[1] we, though Jews by birth, have recognized that a man cannot be justified by the Law, but has to be justified by putting his trust in Jesus, as we have now done. In the Galatian situation this becomes an argument *a fortiori*;[2] how foolish it is for you Gentiles by birth (ἁμαρτωλοί) to try to supplement your trust in Jesus by a reliance upon the Law as well.[3]

The rest of the letter develops this material in chapter 2 in the manner of a preacher who begins with a dramatic illustration which sharpens the focus on the details and application of the subject under consideration; 2: 15–21 is a transition passage in which the attention shades off from Peter and moves imperceptibly over to Galatia, so that in 3: 1 Paul can come right out into the open: ὦ ἀνόητοι Γαλάται, τίς ὑμᾶς ἐβάσκανεν;[4] To what extent, however, do the three historical incidents in chs. 1–2 illustrate the picture we have tentatively drawn of the Galatian relationships? How much have these in common, and what are the specific points of contact?[5] In Jerusalem, the opposition is not precisely identified: probably it is from extreme Jewish Christians, but there is no way of establishing the

[1] It is unclear whether Paul intends to say that he is still addressing Peter at Antioch, or is reflecting on the incident for the Galatians' benefit.

[2] Bonnard, *CNT*, p. 52, citing Calvin.

[3] Paul goes on to say: 'If, seeking to be justified by faith in Christ, we should be reckoned (by others) to be sinners because we associate with Gentiles, then has Christ become an agent of sin? Not at all. For listen, Peter, if I should build up the requirement of obedience to the Law, I stand judged (by my inadequate Christology); for, being crucified with Christ, I have died to the Law in order to live for God. Any other basis for life frustrates the grace of God, for if righteousness can come by the Law, Christ died needlessly.' For a different view, see C. F. D. Moule, *ExT*, LVI (1944–5), 223 (and cf. *Idiom*, p. 196): μὴ γένοιτο belongs to an objector, and ἄρα is to be accented ἄρα. For another view similar to that proposed here, cf. Schmithals, *Paulus*, pp. 62 f. There is general agreement that the 1st person singular is directed towards Peter: if I adopted your point of view, this is where I (you) would be.

[4] Cf. 5: 7; 4: 17; 5: 10, 12.

[5] See M. J. Lagrange, 'Les Judaïsants de l'épître aux Galates' (*RB*, XIV, 1917, 138–67): 'Les judéo-chrétiens de Jérusalem ne sont pas les judaïsants de Galatie. Ces derniers étaient des zélateurs...les judaïsants pharisiens' (p. 164).

relationship between them and the 'Pillars'.[1] In Antioch the opposition is from Jewish Christians from Jerusalem, together with the support (?) of the rest of the Jewish community.[2] In Galatia, the opposition is primarily from Gentile Christians[3] (who may have been circumcised as proselytes) encouraged by the intimidations of Jews.[4] Should we revise our scheme to allow for a Jewish Christian intrusion into the Galatian situation? This is possible, though it does not seem necessary to postulate that extreme Jewish Christians went to Galatia to stir up trouble, on the analogy of Antioch.[5] There is a danger of reading more into the account than is warranted; and in the absence of clear evidence of outsiders in Galatia, we do well to maintain a *non liquet*. It seems better to work from the theory that the Galatian controversy is an internal problem.[6]

The application of these examples to Galatia is as follows. Since, in Jerusalem, Titus (a Gentile) was not *compelled* to be circumcised, you must not allow anyone to compel you to be circumcised (2: 3 ff.; cf. 5: 2 ff.; 6: 12 ff.). False brethren in Jerusalem were responsible for this attempt, working from inside the Christian community; so also you must beware of those who are encouraging this from inside your own community (2: 4; cf. 4: 17; 5: 8; 6: 12 f.). Their purpose is to entangle you Gentiles in the shackles of the law, but you must resist (2: 4; cf. 4: 3; 4: 8 ff.; 5: 9; 6: 13). Just as in Antioch some Jerusalem Christians prevented table fellowship between Jewish and Gentile Christians, it may be that Jewish Christians in Galatia have similar scruples; thus they encourage Gentiles to be circumcised to remove all bars to fellowship (2: 12 f.; cf. 4: 17 f.; 5: 8; 5: 12, ironically; 6: 13). The motivating factor in

[1] See Burton, *ICC, in loc.*: the latter urged Paul to circumcise Titus, but under Paul's insistence finally gave way to him. This leads Burton later (p. 104) to claim that the Antiochean problem is very different from that in Jerusalem.

[2] Cf. Michaelis, 'Judaistische Heidenchristen', *ZNW*, xxx (1931), 83–9.

[3] If 2: 15–21 is the transition passage it confirms this view, for it presupposes an application to Gentiles.

[4] If Antioch is an illustration for the Galatian situation, the significance of the 'rest of the Jews' is very great, for it has an almost polemic character in 2: 13.

[5] If so, Paul is, in ch. 2, trying to turn back the assault by attacking its strongest point, Peter and the Jerusalem Church and its work in Antioch.

[6] So also Dix, *Jew and Greek*, p. 42.

Antioch was fear of Jewish Christians; similarly Gentile Christians in Galatia (the main proponents of circumcision) are also acting from fear for their own security, for to be cut off from Jewish Christians would put them in a no-man's-land (2: 12; cf. 6: 12).[1] In Antioch *hoi loipoi Ioudaioi* abetted the disputants by pretending to be impressed by their course of action, whereas in Galatia Jews enter the picture more negatively, threatening persecution if converts to Messianism are not circumcised (2: 13; cf. 6: 12 *b*).

Briefly, then, this view proposes taking into account all the groups present in an early Christian community. The reconstruction suggests that no absolute break is yet made between Jews and Christians, though many of the things said in the letter are offensive to Jews and may encourage a break. Non-Christian Jews stand by as interested observers, threatening reprisals if Gentiles do not become circumcised. They bring pressure to bear upon their Jewish Christian friends to stop eating with uncircumcised Gentiles.[2] Among the Jewish group are some Gentiles who, perhaps formerly, have become circumcised, and who are the most natural avenue for encouraging fellow Gentiles to submit to the rite. They are in a most precarious position. Having made the decision to take the irremediable step to be circumcised, they tend to become staunch advocates of its necessity: 'I did it, so must you.' Consequently it is at this point that Paul attacks. The danger is great; an important principle is at stake—the efficacy of Christ's atonement. If he is sufficient, then there is no more circumcision or uncircumcision.

OLD AND NEW IN GALATIANS IN
RELATION TO ISRAEL

The proposed reconstruction of the group relationships in Galatia demands a relatively early date for the letter. When the

---

[1] By being able to boast in others' flesh (6: 13) they would at once solidify relationships with Jewish Christians, and mollify Jews who were tempted to take severe measures.

[2] Possibly for the good motive of plastering over cracks in the monotheistic ranks in the area? It is not impossible that pressure is also brought to bear through a knowledge of the position of the mother Church on this matter. In the absence of direct evidence we cannot say.

language is taken at its face value positions are less rigidly defined than is usually assumed. The situation in Galatia (and elsewhere) created *ad hoc* allegiances and varieties of groupings. If an early Christian community in an area like south Galatia could have had Gentile Christians, circumcised Gentiles, and Jewish Christians, and if it is possible that in the formative period there was still contact on the right wing with Jews, then adjacent pairs of these empirically identifiable groups could conceivably join together for common action or to defend a common position.[1] Under the influence of local circumstances, which at any time play an important role but especially in the formative years before positions are hardened, various situations might arise which would result from time to time in different combinations. There is considerable interaction, almost in the nature of a chain reaction, in Galatia. If so, it is somewhat incorrect to inquire into the relationship of the Church and Israel in Galatia without more exact definition.[2]

Nevertheless, in spite of having suggested a fluid situation in early Christianity, we must go on to assert the self-conscious identity of those who were Christians. They had much in common, in spite of the tensions resulting from the different backgrounds of the members; the things which they shared marked them off from non-Christian Jews.[3] What were the

[1] That is, Gentiles and circumcised Gentiles; or, circumcised Gentiles and Jewish Christians; or, Jewish Christians and Jews. Or further, all those circumcised could make common cause against the uncircumcised; or all those who see in Jesus the Messiah and the Saviour could unite against those who rejected this identification.

[2] The danger of incorrect methodology is shown by Dahl, *Volk Gottes*, where he first discusses the Church in Paul, and the name Israel, etc., and then reads all this back into particular passages. In Gal. he finds 'Das nachchristliche Judentum steht also für Paulus mit dem Heidentum auf einer Stufe, nur vor Christus war Israel das Volk Gottes gewesen!' (p. 127). He has a tendency to speak too much of the 'new' or 'true' Israel, and Israel *kata sarka*, when these expressions are theological formulations of a particular theory which is not defined in the material itself.

[3] One can assert this for the early period only after noting the variety. One of the results of a study of Jewish Christianity is an emphasis upon the tensions in the early Church. From the right wing, the Jews were loath to let their Jewish brethren separate off because of their Messianic belief. Pressure was brought to bear to retain a hold on them. From the left wing, the Gentiles needed Jewish Christians not only for early leadership and knowledge of the OT, but also in order to legitimate their inclusion in the

characteristics that separated the Messianic community from the rest of the Jewish community? In the first place, and of primary interest to the group in Galatia, they maintained (or should have maintained) that the Law was no longer valid for those who had accepted the atoning death of Jesus of Nazareth as an act of God's grace. This carried with it and in fact presupposed that Gentiles who also had trusted in Jesus did not need to come under the shadow of the Law by being circumcised. Entry into a covenant relationship with God was not now a matter of ritual circumcision and proselyte incorporation into Judaism. Bondage to the Law, with its implications for membership in God's people, was done away with.[1] This description of things let go is probably what Paul had in mind when, in defence of his apostolic office, he speaks of his zeal for Judaism in terms which imply he no longer has such zeal (1: 13 f.).

He has let go much, on the grounds that it had no abiding value, but was useful only before the end-time comes.[2] The time of promise sloughs off things of no consequence. But how much is to be retained of the old? It is important to notice that in this letter he does not assert the 'newness'[3] of the covenant (one of the things retained). In 3: 15 ff. he lays all the emphasis on the *one* covenant, a covenant which contains within itself the promise of good things to come. The fact that Law intruded does not annul the covenant (3: 17 f.). The original scope of God's purpose is not altered by the more limited scope of the interval under the Law; in Christ the promise is fulfilled in those who believe in him (3: 22). This is modified a little in

People of God. The line of demarcation can be drawn in two places, depending on the standpoint of the observer. When looking at things from a Christian point of view, it will always be drawn according to trust in Jesus rather than ties of race. It is necessary to talk of the Church's identity, as recognizably different from Judaism, but only after one has noted and accepted the ambivalence of the mediating group.

[1] E.g. 2: 3; 5: 2 ff.; 6: 12 ff. on circumcision; 2: 16 ff.; 2: 19; 3: 10 ff.; 3: 19 (the Law was added); 3: 24 (the Law was a tutor); 3: 25; 4: 21 ff.; 5: 14; 6: 13 on the Law; 4: 3; 4: 8 ff. on bondage.

[2] This conception of the 'end' is not present in Gal., the term used is the time of 'promise' (itself significant). The transitoriness of this time is discussed in Gal. Cf. Dahl's emphasis on the 'Endzeit' (*Volk Gottes*, pp. 212 ff.).

[3] καινός only once in Gal. (6: 15) of the new creation.

4: 24, with mention of two covenants, but again 'newness' is absent. There is a sharp contrast: servant/free; present Jerusalem/Jerusalem above, etc. But this contrast, like the discussion of the Law, illustrates primarily the contrast between bondage and freedom in the Spirit (note especially 5: 1). The two covenants of which Paul speaks are concurrent and can be identified in the original situation.[1] The second is latent in the first and, though it required the coming of Christ to bring it into prominence, it is not 'new' in the sense that it is divorced from the old or even that it picks up where the old left off. This is consistent with the way Paul uses 'sons of Abraham' (3: 6 ff.), a status which is taken over into the end-time. The complete fulfilment of the original promise is possible now through its universal application; Gentiles are included as sons of Abraham as God intended (3: 7). This can now be effected by being 'of Christ' (3: 29). But Abraham had two sons, two kinds of children (4: 22), and these two characterize two ways of life. Now, in this time, the one kind of sonship can be granted both to those who come out from under the Law (4: 5) and to those who approach it without having had this bondage (4: 21 ff.). Freedom is possible for all through Christ (5: 1).

Much is new. The source of everything new is Jesus Christ, the gift of God's grace, and the means is the atonement he has effected.[2] This is absolutely vital to Paul's doctrine of the relationship of Christians to Judaism. An inadequate Christology leads to a denial of the proper relationship (2: 21 and 6: 14). New things are associated intimately with Christ: baptism into Christ (3: 27); the Spirit is given because we are made sons (righteous) through Christ (4: 6; 5: 5, 18; cf. 6: 16); there are no distinctions because Christ annuls them all (3: 28; 5: 6; 6: 15). The most obvious result of these new things is that Christians become free (5: 1, 13), because they are set free from Law and directed by the Spirit. This results in a new ethic (5: 14 ff.; 6: 1 ff.; 6: 16) for new creatures.[3]

The pattern is significant. Paul takes over some things

---

[1] An important point made by G. Klein, 'Individualgeschichte und Weltgeschichte bei Paulus', *EvTh*, xxiv, 3 (1964), 126–65 (on p. 161).

[2] 1: 4; 1: 11 ff. (cf. 1: 13 ff.; 1: 23 ff.); 2: 16 ff.; 3: 1 ff.; 3: 13; 4: 4; 5: 1; 6: 14.

[3] As noted the only instance of καινός or its derivatives.

(covenant and sonship especially), but what is taken over is not transposed.[1] There is a difference between this letter and later ones. In Galatians the emphasis is upon the universalism that is latent within the old form. His remarks are directed at either the old things which are of no more value (Law, specifically circumcision, and the bondage which it brings) or the new things which are the result of Jesus' coming to the world (Spirit, and the freedom which he brings). The sharp antithesis is reserved for past characteristics *versus* the newly introduced or recovered, not for a new entity succeeding the old. That is to say, the main point is the correct interpretation of the old in the light of the new events. In the Galatian letter there is no attempt to document a take-over of the old attributes by the new entity which has been called into being.

Paul's doctrine of the Christian community in Galatians is largely dependent on the promise inherent in the call to Abraham: the universalizing of the people of God accomplished through Christ's death. Admission to the people of God is now possible to all on terms which are the same for each without distinction. No more do Law and circumcision enter the picture. But, and this must be emphasized, it is admission to the old entity, or what the old entity was really meant to be, and not to a new successor to it. The Church is aware of its own identity through the two factors noted above—it recognizes what must be left behind from the old, and it recognizes the implications of what has happened in Jesus. But the new is the ratification of the promises inherent in the old. Those who see the force of the new things enter into eschatological peace. However, God is continuing to work out his purpose before the end comes. He does not forget his people of the first covenant; they must hear the good news about the way that covenant has finally realized its full meaning, so that God may show mercy to them. The Church is the agent by which this will be done,

---

[1] There is confirmation of this and of the method adopted in the fact that the Pauline summary of 6: 11–18 deals firmly with what is let go (6: 13) and with what is new (6: 16), especially with the ground of the changes which are introduced (6: 14)—even with the fact that the gospel is universally applicable and there are no distinctions (6: 15). But he does not concern himself with elements of transposition or take-over. This is not yet an important factor in Christian apologetic because the separation has not yet been concluded.

because it is the community of those who recognize the importance of Jesus' death.

It is perfectly consistent for Paul to refer to Judaism, associated with the old transient things, in derogatory terms. It is also consistent to wish God's blessing upon Israel, the faithful within Judaism whom God will assuredly save. The Church as God's instrument does not aim to become a rival of Israel. The Church is a part of God's people, but not yet his only people. The Church has not transferred all Israel's attributes to itself because it has no need to—it is itself incorporated into Israel, or rather all its members, whether Jew or Gentile, are members of the people of God, even though many within Judaism might deny this.

ESCHATOLOGICAL HINDERING IN THESSALONICA

From Thessalonica on to Corinth, from which he writes 1 Thessalonians, Paul has had a time of almost unrelieved opposition by the local synagogues. This antipathy, forcing him to move on from place to place before he had completed an adequate presentation of the gospel, is reflected in 1 Thessalonians 2: 14 ff., an integral part of a εὐχαριστῶ period. Recent studies have expanded upon the work of P. Schubert and have defined some aspects of it more accurately, but his judgment still stands: the *eucharistō* period of 1 Thessalonians is a single tripartite section which concludes only towards the end of chapter 3.[1] This underlines the unity within the train of thought, a unity found in Paul's recollection of the way the

[1] P. Schubert, *The Form and Function of the Pauline Thanksgivings* (*ZNW*, Beih. 20, Berlin, 1939); but see T. Y. Mullins, 'Petition as a literary Form', *NT*, v (1962), 46–54; J. T. Sanders, 'The Transition from Opening Epistolary Thanksgiving to Body in the Letters of the Pauline Corpus', *JBL*, LXXXI (1962), 348–62; T. Y. Mullins, 'Disclosure, a literary form in the *NT*', *NT*, VII (1964), 44–50 (a partial correction of Sanders); cf. also J. M. Robinson, *BZNW*, xxx (*Haenchen Festschrift*), 194 ff., on the importance of the Jewish *berachā*; and for a different view of the structure of 1 Thess. see K. Thieme, in *Abraham Unser Vater* (Leiden, 1963), pp. 450 ff. While none of these draws the conclusion, it seems obvious that in both 1 and 2 Thess. there is only one thanksgiving period, admittedly rather complex in each case, but stylistically and formally indivisible. The *eucharistō* periods end at 1 Thess. 3: 13 and at 2 Thess. 3: 5. Moreover, the often-repeated charge (cf. Schubert) that 2 Thess. is less personal and less intimate than 1 Thess. because its thanksgiving is less elaborate falls to the ground.

gospel was received in Thessalonica and the results of that reception.[1] The thanksgiving at 2: 13 and its opposite (however that be defined) in 2: 14 ff. arise from reflections on the differing receptions of the word.[2]

There are two reasons for giving thanks for the Thessalonians: 'because...you received not word of man but...word of God', and the independent assertion, 'for you became imitators of the Judean churches'.[3] The section is practically motivated, though it moves beyond the purely pastoral in its development and becomes almost polemic. It is shaped as five indictments against the Jews, the last of which varies the close parallelism of the other four by its different introduction, length, form, and separate subordinate clause (ἵνα σωθῶσιν). It begins with a reference to the successful proclamation of the gospel, and ends with an accusation about hindering that proclamation. The final εἰς τό clause expresses the result of their action;[4] the judgment which follows is the direct result of their hindering God's word.

Dr E. Bammel has demonstrated the eschatological nature of the events presupposed by this section and of the conclusion to

[1] *Contra* K.-G. Eckart ('Der zweite echte Brief des Apostels Pls an die Thessalonicher', *ZTK*, LVIII, 1961, 30–44) who finds a second letter in I Thess. Cf. criticism by W. G. Kümmel, 'Das literarische und geschichtliche Problem des I Thess.' in *Neotestamentica et Patristica (Cullmann Freundesgabe, NT Sup.* VI, Leiden, 1962), pp. 213 ff.

[2] Cf. Rom. 1: 8, 14–16; I Cor. 1: 6; Phil. 1: 5 f.; Col. 1: 5 f.; I Thess. 1: 5 ff.; 2 Thess. 1: 3; cf. 2: 14; Eph. 1: 13 in the *eulogētos* period; 2: 1 ff. in the *eucharistō* period. In Gal. 1: 6 ff. the positive reception is being vitiated by their succumbing to another gospel, and therefore, as Schubert emphasizes, there is little to give thanks for.

[3] This is the last of the series of 10 uses of γίνομαι; there is a regular alternation from 1st person plural to 2nd person plural between I Thess. 1: 5 and 2: 14 ff., the 1st person plural always dealing with the way the gospel reached the Thessalonians and the 2nd person plural with the way that word was received. Here it has reference to the way the gospel was received, and what follows is an expansion of this idea. On I Thess. 2: 14 ff., but received too late for inclusion, is O. Michel, 'Fragen zu I Thess. 2: 14–16: Antijüdische polemik bei Paulus', in *Antijudaismus im NT? Exegetische und systematische Beiträge*, hrsg. W. Eckert, N. P. Levinson, M. Stöhr (München, 1967), pp. 50–9.

[4] The clause can be either purpose or result, but in Paul is usually purpose: see Moulton/Turner, p. 143; cf. Moule, *Idiom*, p. 141 (re 2 Cor. 8: 6) for a Pauline example of εἰς τό being strictly consecutive.

the section in 2: 16.[1] He has tried to show that Paul interprets the expulsion of the Jews (and Christians) from Rome as a sign that 'die Ereignisse die ganze apokalyptische Maschinerie wieder in Bewegung setzen' (p. 301).[2] The ὀργή is thus something present (p. 308) but still eschatologically conceived;[3] it follows directly, in Paul's opinion, from hindering the mission work and not from the execution of Jesus (pp. 307 f.).

Paul's activity among the Gentiles is, however, only one aspect of the accusation against Jewish opposition, albeit the one which generates this section. The structure of the clauses dependent upon ὑπὸ τῶν 'Ιουδαίων[4] breaks into two parts; the first (v. 15a, b; related to v. 14b) notes the actual incidents of which they are guilty, and the second (vv. 15c, d, and 16a) the attitude which lies behind these events.[5] In each there is a progression of ideas: persecution of (a) the Lord Jesus, (b) prophets,[6] (c) us; contrary to (a) God, (b) all men,[7] (c) us. The two important charges are the most general ones: 'you have suffered from your fellow-countrymen' (the thing about which

[1] 'Judenverfolgung und Naherwartung, zur Eschatologie des 1 Th', *ZTK*, LVI (1959), 294–315. The events are persecution of Christians, Gentile mission, and persecution of the persecutors, *ibid.* p. 312.

[2] P. 300, 'die Christen werden hier, wie noch lange Zeit später, das Schicksal der Juden geteilt haben', cf. p. 306. Kümmel, 'Das literarische', pp. 220 f., criticizes Bammel for reading too much importance into such an event. For other attempts to show the incidents lying behind ἔφθασεν see B. W. Bacon, *Exp.*, Ser. 8, xxiv (1922), 356–76; S. E. Johnson, *ATR*, xxxiii (1941), 173–6; and discussion in B. Rigaux, *EtBib* (1956) *in loc.*

[3] Elsewhere in 1 Thess. ὀργή is eschatological and set over against salvation in Jesus Christ, which is deliverance from wrath; e.g. 1: 9 f.; because of Paul's preaching they turned and are now waiting for Jesus; cf. also 5: 9. See Stählin, *TWNT*, v, 433, 439 f.; on 1: 9 f. see J. Munck, *NTS*, ix (1963), 95–110.

[4] Used only here in the letter; it could mean specifically Judeans.

[5] The attempt to show dependence one way or the other between 1 Thess. 2 and Matt. 23 pars. is doomed to failure. However, it is worth pointing out the similarity between Matt.'s first Woe and Paul's concluding charge, and Matt.'s last Woe and Paul's first charge. See J. P. Brown, *NTS*, x (1963), 27–48; J. A. T. Robinson, *Jesus and His Coming* (London, 1957), ch. 5; J. B. Orchard, *Bib*, xix (1938), 19–42; C. H. Dodd, *ExT*, LVIII (1946–7), 293–8.

[6] See H.-J. Schoeps, *Die jüdischen Prophetenmorde* (*SBU*, II, Uppsala, 1943).

[7] See Dibelius, *HNT* (3rd edition, 1937), Exk; however, the charge is not theoretical hatred of men, but rather practical opposition.

the Thessalonians are most concerned);[1] and the prevention of the gospel (the thing about which Paul is most exercised). The wrath which is about to fall[2] will be a result of all these things, but the full measure of sin is seen in the fact that they are trying to hold back eschatological events by restraining Paul himself.[3]

Basic to Paul's understanding of the missionary presentation of the word is that it will be received both gladly and spitefully.[4] There is a ready-made opposition to the gospel in the places which should be the first to accept, because many Jews are afraid of disturbing the *status quo*. They reject the gospel themselves, but even more devastating is their attempt to prevent others from hearing—for it is this which, as it seems to the synagogues, will create difficulties. An integral part of Paul's preaching was the invalidity of circumcision; to preach this in the very place which, while attracting Gentiles because of a strong and ethical monotheism, held them off by a demand for circumcision, was a revolutionary step. The words ἵνα σωθῶσιν carry a great weight of meaning. A changed relationship to the Gentiles on the basis of Messianic speculation was difficult for Jews to accept.

[1] On imitation see D. M. Stanley, *Bib*, xl (1959), 859–77; cf. the incredible exegesis of B. Gerhardsson, *Memory and Manuscript* (*ASNU*, xxii, Uppsala, 1961), pp. 274, 293. On fellow-countrymen, Rigaux, *EtBib* (1956) and Milligan, *McM* (1908), *in loc.*, are correct in taking this as local rather than racial; cf. Haenchen on Acts in *KEK* (1961), pp. 452 f.

[2] ἔφθασεν: the point is the certainty of the judgment, rather than the time. The expectation of a near (and final) event makes the exact nuance of the word less important.

[3] Note ἐνέκοψεν ἡμᾶς ὁ σατανᾶς (2: 18), with which most commentators identify ὁ πειράζων (3: 5); so Masson, *CNT* (1957); Rigaux, *EtBib*; Dibelius, *HNT*; Findlay, *CGT* (1904); Morris, *TNTC* (1956) and *NLC* (1959), *in loc.*; W. M. Ramsay, *St Paul*, p. 231, conjectures that ἐνέκοψεν refers to an 'impassable chasm between Paul and the Thessalonians' put there by the authorities (namely, preventing Paul from coming back). More likely is it that any hindering is prompted by Jews. Paul describes in 1 Thess. 2: 1–5 the characteristics of his opponents. This is not apologetic but attack. F. Zimmer, in *Theologische Studien für B. Weiss* (Göttingen, 1897), pp. 248–73, handles this section carefully, applying it all to Gentiles, not Jews; but he relies too much upon συμφυλέται as Gentiles. The apology proper follows in 2: 9–12, where Paul characterizes his own behaviour in positive terms.

[4] Cf. the closely parallel 1 Thess. 1: 5–8, esp. *v.* 6, ἐν θλίψει πολλῇ μετὰ χαρᾶς κτλ, which prepares for 2: 1 ff.

This does not mean, however, that in writing 1 Thessalonians Paul has arrived at the position where he holds to the priority of the Gentile mission.[1] The missionary obligation is universal, a position developed in Galatians in a basic way without prejudice to the relative priorities of the two aspects of mission. It is for all, on terms which permit everyone to come in the state in which he is found. The hindrance to this task in Thessalonica (contrary to that in Galatia) is not on a point of practice but, apparently, a point of principle; and it results not in covert encouragement to circumcise but in overt persecution to ensure that the Gentiles should not hear the gospel. But both Jews and God-fearers (possibly also pagans) did hear and did accept. There is no hint in Thessalonians about the relationship between these groups in the community.[2] Nor is there much about the relationship of Jews to Christians, nor the Church to Israel. Some Jews are condemned and Christians praised for their respective receptions of the word; the one will experience judgment and the other blessing, but there is no suggestion that either all Israel[3] is rejected or the Church has become Israel.[4] In fact there is less in the way of transposition from one to the other in Thessalonians than in Galatians, possibly as a result of the need for defence and apologetic in the latter, which is missing here; but perhaps also because, as Dr Bammel's hypothesis might suggest, events have happened in the interval which cause Paul to concentrate upon the nearness of the end.

There is a section in 2 Thessalonians (2: 10 ff., 13 ff.) reminiscent of 1 Thessalonians 2: 13 ff. This also falls in a *eucharistō* period, 2: 13 ff. being the second part of what we

[1] See Bammel, *ZTK*, LVI (1959), 313, who cites the relevant literature for a distinction between the ideas behind Rom. 11 and 1 Thess. 2.

[2] Because of the absence of any reference to Jewish or Gentile Christians, one must reject Harnack's hypothesis (followed by Lake, *Earlier Epistles*) about the destination of 1 Thess. (to Gentiles) and 2 Thess. (to Jewish Christians).

[3] It is worth underlining that it is *Ioudaioi* which is used of the persecutors, not *Israēl*.

[4] Dahl's comment is wishful thinking (*Volk Gottes*, p. 211): '...die Gemeinde ist durch Kultus, Geschichte, Eschatologie, und Ethos konstituiert. Aber dieser "Kirchenbegriff" ist radikal verchristlicht, die Existenz der Gemeinde ist ausschließlich durch den geschichtlichen, gegenwärtigen und kommenden Christus bestimmt. Der Gedanke, die Gemeinde sei das "Israel Gottes" steht im Hintergrund, wird aber nirgends betont.'

have maintained is a single period.[1] In this section, one of the main ideas is that those who afflict Christians will be afflicted (2: 11 f., cf. 1: 6 f.).[2] When describing these persons, he seems to have in mind the Jewish opponents whom he met in Thessalonica, and perhaps elsewhere;[3] the apocalyptic instruction in 2 Thessalonians may be viewed as a fuller explanation, and possibly a correction, of the time of the *orgē* (1 Thess. 2: 16). In 2: 10 f. these opponents are identified by the first plural substantive in this section (τοῖς ἀπολλυμένοις),[4] their judgment following because having heard the gospel they did not accept it (cf. 1: 5–9). This recollection of the Thessalonian situation causes Paul to give thanks again for

[1] The bibliography that lies behind this conclusion is listed on p. 102 n. 1. The exhortation of 2: 1 ('Ερωτῶμεν δὲ ὑμᾶς κτλ) flows out of the preceding section (ὑπὲρ τῆς παρουσίας, 2: 1; cf. 1: 7, 10). The negative aspects of judgment arise out of thanks for the positive reception of the word as in 1 Thess. 2: 13 ff. The apocalyptically oriented section (2: 3 ff.) follows a practical piece of advice in 2: 1 f. and concludes with a recollection of the negative reception of the word in 2: 10 ff., together with the judgment which will fall on such obtuseness. This again leads directly into a renewed thanksgiving (2: 13 ff.). But this is not yet the final conclusion of the *eucharistō* period, for another mild exhortation is included, still as a part of the same section, in which prayer is requested on Paul's behalf that he may overcome his opponents, after which comes the concluding *berachā* before the introduction of the exhortatory ('petition') section in 3: 6 ff. This is a complex structure stylistically, but its unity is found in precisely the same factor that gave unity to the tripartite *eucharistō* period in 1 Thess.: thanksgiving for faithful reception of the gospel and recollection of refusal to hear, with reflections on the opposition to which this leads. The eschatological section is not central to the letter, but a part of the instruction necessary in the pastoral situation with which he is faced. It both rises out of, and flows into, a consideration of the Thessalonians' own situation.

[2] On retribution see F. V. Filson, *St Paul's Conception of Recompense* (*UNT*, xxi, Leipzig, 1931).

[3] Paul modifies the allusion to Isa. 66: 4, 15 with τοῖς μὴ ὑπακούουσιν τῷ εὐαγγελίῳ τοῦ κυρίου ἡμῶν ᾿Ιησοῦ (1: 8; cf. 2: 10; 2: 12). Masson, *CNT*, p. 87, thinks the omission of ἔθνη from the Jeremiah allusion (10: 25) in 1: 8 generalizes it; but it could equally well be construed as an attempt to make the Jer. citation conform to the recalcitrant Jew allusion of Isa. 66: 1–4.

[4] Many of the characteristics of 2 Thess. 2: 9–12 are an echo of those in 1 Thess. 2: 3–5, where these seemed to be features of Jewish opposition. See commentators, and also W. Bousset, *The Antichrist Legend, a Chapter in Christian and Jewish Folklore* (London, 1896), pp. 22, 133.

the Thessalonian Christians (2: 13). As in 1 Thessalonians 2: 13 ff., he contrasts the two possibilities when the gospel is preached.[1]

If Paul's preaching in Thessalonica is the background of ch. 1 and of 2: 10 ff. the Thessalonians would have read this letter in the light of their recent acceptance of the gospel and the persecution which has since flared up again.[2] It is likely that some of the allusions in 2: 3 ff. will gain meaning from a reference to such events and to the eschatological expectations which these engendered. Syntactically τοῖς ἀπολλυμένοις is an integral part of the second half of the apocalyptic section, going back to ἡ παρουσία (v. 9) and ultimately to the verb (καὶ τότε ἀποκαλυφθήσεται ὁ ἄνομος). Verses 11 f. have direct links not only with v. 10b,[3] but also with what precedes in vv. 8 ff.[4] Further, this description of the Thessalonian situation has a parallel preceding it. The section 7b – 10 is closely related to vv. 6–7a.[5] There is yet another earlier parallel in vv. 3b ff., where the key words ἀποκαλυφθῇ ὁ ἄνθρωπος τῆς ἀνομίας (with a number of dependent clauses partially paralleling vv. 9 f.) reappear.[6] But

---

[1] Those who accept are an ἀπαρχή, the correct reading in 2: 13. Rigaux, *EtBib*, p. 65, rejects this reading, possibly because he wants to reject Harnack's theory that these are Jewish Christians; but this is not necessary. Dibelius, *HNT*, *in loc.*, takes this to be an '. . . Ehrentitel Israels. . ., den sich die Christen angeeignet hätten. . .'.

[2] On the hypothesis that 2 Thess. is actually the second letter and not the first; *per contra*, T. W. Manson, *BJRL*, xxxv (1953), 428 ff.

[3] αὐτοῖς/τοῖς ἀπολλυμένοις; εἰς τὸ πιστεῦσαι αὐτούς/εἰς τὸ σωθῆναι αὐτούς; οἱ μὴ πιστεύσαντες τῇ ἀληθείᾳ/τὴν ἀγάπην τῆς ἀληθείας οὐκ ἐδέξαντο.

[4] The three specific features of those referred to in vv. 10bff.: ἐνέργεια πλάνης, τὸ ψεῦδος, ἡ ἀδικία are almost exactly paralleled in vv. 9 f.: κατ' ἐνέργειαν τοῦ σατανᾶ (for σατανᾶς cf. 1 Thess. 2: 18); καὶ τέρασιν ψεύδους καὶ ἐν πάσῃ ἀπάτῃ ἀδικίας. Note that ἐνεργέω is used in 1 Thess. 2: 13 of the working of the word; cf. Bertram, *TWNT*, ii, 650 f.

[5] Apart from κατέχον/κατέχων, note also ἀποκαλυφθῆναι/ἀποκαλυφθήσεται; τὸ μυστήριον τῆς ἀνομίας/ὁ ἄνομος; νῦν. . .ἐν τῷ αὐτοῦ καιρῷ. . . ἤδη/μόνον. . .ἄρτι ἕως. . .καὶ τότε; ἐνεργεῖται/ἐνέργειαν τοῦ σατανᾶ, and for 'mystery', cf. ἐν πάσῃ δυνάμει καὶ σημείοις καὶ τέρασιν ψεύδους. As well as these verbal parallels, all the subjects of 6–7a are impersonals, whereas the subjects of vv. 7f. are all personals.

[6] For a hesitant attempt to detail the parallels, see N. Freese, *TSK*, xciii (1920–1), 73–7; *per contra*, B. Rigaux, *L'Antéchrist et l'opposition au royaume messianique dans l'Ancien et le Nouveau Testament* (Paris, 1932), pp. 299 f. and *EtBib*, pp. 665 f.

in 3*b* f. ἡ ἀποστασία is found precisely in the place of τὸ κατέχον.[1]

3*b* ὅτι ἐὰν μὴ ἔλθῃ ἡ ἀποστασία πρῶτον
    καὶ ἀποκαλυφθῇ ὁ ἄνθρωπος τῆς ἀνομίας κτλ.
6   καὶ νῦν τὸ κατέχον οἴδατε,
    εἰς τὸ ἀποκαλυφθῆναι αὐτὸν ἐν τῷ αὐτοῦ καιρῷ·
7   τὸ γὰρ μυστήριον ἤδη ἐνεργεῖται τῆς ἀνομίας.
    μόνον ὁ κατέχων ἄρτι ἕως ἐκ μέσου γένηται
8   καὶ τότε ἀποκαλυφθήσεται ὁ ἄνομος (ὃν ὁ Κ.Ι.....παρουσίας
    αὐτοῦ)
9   οὗ ἐστὶν ἡ παρουσία κατ᾽ ἐνέργειαν τοῦ σατανᾶ κτλ.
11 καὶ διὰ τοῦτο πέμπει αὐτοῖς ὁ θεὸς ἐνέργειαν πλάνης κτλ.
12 ἵνα κριθῶσιν πάντες οἱ μὴ πιστεύσαντες τῇ ἀληθείᾳ κτλ.

With *apostasia* at the beginning of the eschatological section we are brought into close connection with Paul's thanks for the reception of the word and the refusal on the part of some. We propose interpreting *apostasia* of the general Jewish failure to receive the gospel; i.e. refusal becomes a form of relinquishing faith in what God is doing (in Jesus Christ), and so technically can become *apostasia*.[2] This kind of failure is the necessary prelude to all the more apocalypticized conceptions which follow. These apocalyptic events will not be discussed here; it will be sufficient to observe that, if there is any validity in the parallelism between *apostasia* and *katechon*,[3] the latter is used *in malam partem* of restraining or holding back something as in 1 Thessalonians 2: 13 ff., 18.[4] There remains a puzzle in Paul's description of all these events;[5] but behind it all is a practical

[1] P. Andriessen, *Bijdragen*, XXI (1960), 20–30, not available, but summarized in *IZBG*, IX (1961–2), 735.

[2] Cf. StrBill *ad loc.*, for the Jewish background. Apostasy, which follows (the first) and precedes the (second) coming of the Lord, is departure from God and his *Torah*. It is, as Paul sees it, simply believing the lie and not accepting the truth.

[3] For *katechon* see O. Betz, *NTS*, IX (1962–3), 276–91; O. Cullmann, *RHPR*, XVI (1936), 210–45; Munck, *Paul*, pp. 36 ff.; Buzy, *RScR*, XXIV (1934), 402–31; J. Schmid, *TQ*, CXXIX (1949), 323–43; V. Hartl, *ZKT*, XLV (1921), 455–75; M. Brunec, *VD*, XXXV (1957), 3–33.

[4] Cf. Freese, *TSK*, XCIII (1920–1), 73–7; Frame, *ICC* (1912), pp. 259 ff. (citing Döllinger and Schaefer).

[5] Not much clarified by the close resemblance to Matt. 23–4 pars. There is a circular series: 1 Thess. 2, Matt. 23, Matt. 24, 2 Thess. 2, 1 Thess. 2. For the synoptic question see J. A. T. Robinson, *Jesus and his Coming*, ch. 5;

application. The καὶ νῦν οἴδατε refers, on this view, to a presently observable phenomenon of hindrance, a 'mystery of lawlessness'[1] which is already at work (v. 6), it is the work of Satan (v. 9), the working of a lie (v. 11) which some in Thessalonica prefer to believe in place of the truth of the gospel.

In warning them in this way Paul is saying that this obtuseness is an event prior to the return of Christ, and something understandable because experienced through Jewish unbelief.[2] Nevertheless it is only a preliminary to the more dramatic personal manifestation of wickedness, still to follow,[3] which ultimately is related to Satan. He hinders by creating the present apostasy in those who, not believing, actively oppose Paul.

The necessary correction for the Thessalonians is that, on the basis of his first letter, they thought the end was about to come because of this Jewish apostasy and the activity of Satan presupposed by it.[4] In fact, Paul holds that it is necessary that there be first the apostasy, and then a great personal appearance of the Lawless One, and then Jesus shall come to destroy them. They had forgotten this teaching.[5]

Taken together, 1 and 2 Thessalonians portray Paul's denunciation of unbelieving Israel. Care must be taken not to abstract this from its context of sharp refusal to accept the gospel, coupled with a violent hindering of the spread of the gospel to the Gentiles. There is no trace of the idea that because of this opposition Israel is let go and the Gentiles will become

G. R. Beasley-Murray, *Jesus and the Future*, pp. 58 f., 76, 232 ff.; E. Cothenet, *RScR*, XLII (1954), 5–39; J. B. Orchard, *Bib*, XIX (1938), 19–42; C. H. Dodd, *JRomSt*, XXXVII (1947), 47–54; Rigaux, *Bib*, XL (1959), 675–83; J. P. Brown, *NTS*, X (1963), 27–48.

[1] *Contra* E. E. Schneider, *TZ*, XIX (1963), 113–25; cf. P. H. Furfey, *CBQ*, VIII (1946), 179–91.

[2] Others who see a variety of Jewish references here are Bousset, *Antichrist*; E. Cothenet, *RScR*, XLII (1954), 5–39; B. B. Warfield, *Biblical and Theological Studies* (Philadelphia, repr. 1952), p. 473; R. Mackintosh, *Exp*, 7th Ser., II (1906), 427–32.

[3] On ἐκ μέσου γένηται, see Freese, *TSK*, XCIII (1920–1), 73–72; E. E. Lofstrom, *ExT*, XXVIII (1916–17), 379 f.; H. W. Fulford, *ExT*, XXIII (1911–12), 40 f.

[4] A similar point of view is suggested by the title 'La incredulidad de Israel y los impedimentos del Anticristo según 2 Th 6–7 [*sic*]', by J. M. González Ruiz, in *Estudios Bíblicos*, X (1951); not available to me.

[5] Cf. 2: 5, a parenthetical remark of great importance, to be attached to *vv.* 1–4.

the heirs of salvation—only an acute awareness of the shortness of the time left, of the folly of disbelief, and of the apostasy, which this refusal constitutes, heralding the end. It is not yet possible to deduce from a general Jewish failure to respond that the Church has taken over the attributes of Israel. This is not even in the background in 1 or 2 Thessalonians. The time is too short to worry about such matters, sufficient is it to state that God loves and has chosen and called the members of the Thessalonian Church, through Paul's gospel, to be a first-fruit in this time just before the end.

PHILIPPIANS: THE BEGINNING OF
THE TRANSPOSITIONS

There are affinities between Thessalonians and Philippians: the absence of 'apostle' from the greeting, the rarity of OT quotations, and the harshness of the language (Phil. 3: 3 ff.,[1] cf. 1: 28).[2] The passages in which we are interested gain from a comparison with Galatians also (particularly κατατομή, cf. Gal. 5: 12), and the descriptions bear fruitful comparison with the later descriptions of the opponents in 2 Corinthians. In spite of these contacts however, the identity of the persons referred to in Philippians 3 is not sure.[3] Part of the difficulty is connected with the question of the unity of the letter: while acknowledging the force of the shift in 3: 1–2, we are inclined to accept the hypothesis that it is a single letter.[4] Another

---

[1] See D. Guthrie, *NT Introduction, Pauline Epistles* (London, 1961), p. 152 n. 1. Cf. also E. Schweizer, 'Der zweite Thessalonicherbrief ein Philipperbrief', *TZ*, 1 (1945), 90–105; pp. 286–9; *per contra*, W. Michaelis, *ibid.* pp. 282–6.

[2] See G. Bornkamm, *Neotestamentica et Patristica*, pp. 192 ff., esp. p. 198: 'Wahrscheinlicher ist, daß die Philipper ähnlich wie die Thessalonicher von Juden oder Heiden bedrängt sind (vgl. 1 Th 2.14 ff.) und Paulus darum hier [*sc.* 1.28] wie da von einer Solidarität im Leiden sprechen kann.'

[3] From the newer literature, see: W. Schmithals, *ZTK*, LIV (1957), 297–341; and *ZNW*, LI (1960), 225–54; H. Köster, *NTS*, VIII (1961–2), 317–32; and *RGG*, III, 17–21; B. D. Rahtjen, *NTS*, VI (1959–60), 167–73; *per contra*, B. S. Mackay, *NTS*, VII (1960–1), 161–70; V. Furnish, *NTS*, X (1963–4), 80–8; A. F. J. Klijn, *NT*, VII (1965), 278–84.

[4] The claim to be able to isolate three separate letters, and to identify the theology and *Sitz im Leben* of each is a piece of critical subterfuge (Schmithals, *ZNW*, LI (1960), esp. pp. 230–5). In Phil. the material is too

difficulty, apart from whether the two allusions in ch. 3 (2 ff. and 18 ff.) are to the same persons, is the identity of those in 1: 12 ff. T. W. Manson has shown decisively that 1: 12–17 refers to Paul's troubles in Corinth—his arrest, defence before Gallio, and acquittal—which gives the Corinthians boldness in speaking, even though (as 1 Corinthians 1–4 demonstrates) there may be mixed motives there.[1] The prison reference is, therefore, irrelevant for the Philippian situation.

However, 1: 27 ff., addressed to the Philippians, is important because of its introduction of οἱ ἀντικείμενοι,[2] coupled with ἀπώλεια (cf. also 3: 19), within an exhortation to remain firm in the gospel. This mention of opposition in Philippi relates the fuller treatment in ch. 3 to the rest of the letter, even though there is no way to identify the opponents in ch. 1.

We should not try to find in 2: 12–18 a reference to opposition; this is a general statement, applicable to almost any Christian community. Nor in 2: 21, a reference to immature Christians of whom Paul had thought better, is there any implication that these are opponents.[3]

This takes us to the main point of interest, ch. 3.[4] In interpreting this chapter too much stress is usually laid on the assumption that this is an internal problem in Philippi. The triple βλέπετε (v. 2), the very general εἴ τις δοκεῖ (v. 4), and πολλοὶ γὰρ περιπατοῦσιν need indicate no more than an incipient incitement to abandon Christ. It is not necessarily a present problem. Recourse to Paul's ignorance of the situation,

diverse to fit any neat scheme of collation, such as Bornkamm's theory of a 'formal rule' of compilation (as above, and *NTS*, viii (1961–2), 258–64).

[1] *BJRL*, xxiii (1939), 182–200. Phil. is written early in the Ephesian ministry, before 1 and 2 Cor.; there is no need to assume a prison milieu, *contra* G. S. Duncan, *St Paul's Ephesian Ministry* (London, 1929).

[2] Paul's uses of this word are all early: Gal. 5: 17; 1 Cor. 16: 9; 2 Thess. 2: 4; cf. 1 Tim. 1: 10; 5: 14.

[3] This verse is more difficult to understand when placed in Ephesus; see commentators, esp. J. H. Michael, *MNTC* (1928); P. Bonnard, *CNT* (1963); F. W. Beare, *BNTC* (1959). K. Barth, *The Epistle to the Philippians* (London, 1962) and W. Michaelis, *ThHNT*, i, refer to the similarity with 2: 4. R. P. Martin, *TNTC* (1959), takes it as a reference to the world generally, not to fellow-Christians.

[4] The suggestion of Furnish, *NTS*, x (1963–4), 80–8, is ingenious: Paul was at the point of closing the letter but decides to write the same things as Timothy and Epaphroditus were going to say personally.

and hence inability to be specific, does not meet the case.[1] He has in mind a specific problem but one that the Philippians have not yet experienced. An external attack upon the Christian community is the most likely threat. To eliminate the possibility of Jewish opposition by a deduction from Acts that there was no synagogue in Philippi goes considerably beyond the evidence.

There can be little doubt that the expected opposition is going to urge circumcision; βλέπετε τὴν κατατομήν.[2] ἡμεῖς γάρ ἐσμεν ἡ περιτομή (vv. 2 f.). The confidence (vv. 3 b–4), on which Paul expands in v. 5, is 'in flesh', and his own claim to greater confidence begins with 'circumcised the eighth day'. The autobiographical information (vv. 5 f.) could be directed at any of the possible opponents; Jews, Jewish Christians, or even Gentile proselytes circumcised later in life.[3] Our criteria for determining who these may be are circumscribed by Paul's experiences to date: by the opposition found in Galatia,[4] Philippi, Thessalonica, Beroea, Athens, Corinth and (recently) in Ephesus. Thus far, Jewish Christians have not played a particularly large part, except in Galatia where we found proselytes to be the main factor in a very fluid situation. We would suggest that the likeliest source of trouble in Philippi is Jews,[5] perhaps especially from Thessalonica.

'Dog' is an insulting epithet, to whomever it is applied;[6] in a Jewish framework, it conjures up 'die Unwissenden, die

[1] οὓς πολλάκις ἔλεγον ὑμῖν (3: 18) destroys such an expedient; this will refer not to previous letters but to his original stay with them, and warnings based upon his experience in Galatia.

[2] H. Köster, TWNT, viii, 109 ff., demonstrates the ironical use of the word, and approvingly quotes Beare, 'Paul denies this title to Jews and replaces it with a jeering title of his own coinage...' (BNTC, p. 104).

[3] Beare, BNTC, p. 106; Barth, Philippians, p. 96: 'particularly zealous fresh-baked Jews'.

[4] Gal. 5: 12 is vital: 'I wish those who trouble you would castrate themselves', cf. 6: 11 ff.

[5] Cf. N. A. Dahl, Volk Gottes, p. 235. E. Lohmeyer, KEK (8th edition 1930), pp. 124 ff., emphasizes the element of persecution (cf. 1: 29 f.). It does not materially affect the main point if these are Jewish Christians, much the same exegesis applies in either case, so long as they be Jewish in origin.

[6] H. Köster, NTS, viii (1961–2), 317 ff.; the aim is not to describe but to insult. Michel rightly points to the difference between Matt. 7: 6 and Phil. 3: 2 (TWNT, iii, 1102).

Gottlosen und die Nichtisraeliten'.[1] This is matched by the irony in *katatomē/peritomē*; the one who thinks he has the mark of circumcision actually has changed it into mutilation. 'Evil-workers' is unspecific, it could be applied to a whole range of people. The three together, if directed towards Jews, are heavy with irony; those who think they are clean, and do good, and are inborn members of God's people have converted these features into the opposite through their opposition to the gospel. Paul's description of himself parades features which his opponents might not all share as members of the Diaspora or as proselytes. The trilogy with which he closes could not be matched by one of them. In their eyes this might have set Paul apart from them, but in fact what now sets him apart is his abandonment of all confidence in these in order to gain a righteousness which they, and the Law, could not give (*v.* 9; cf. *v.* 6).

The middle part of ch. 3 has been pressed into service by those who develop a theory about a gnostic strain in the opponents.[2] We need not go into this except to agree that, if there is gnosticism behind the opposition, this part has a polemical purpose; however, gnosticism need not be present to understand this satisfactorily.

Paul returns to the expected opposition in 18 ff.: πολλοὶ γὰρ περιπατοῦσιν is related to 3: 2 ff. and to the opponents of 1: 27 ff.[3] There is an ellipsis here; the reader expects an adverbial phrase which is lacking. Paul breaks off the thought to remind them of his discussion about this problem of Jewish unbelief which he recalls with tears.[4] As long as they remain

[1] StrBill *ad loc.*; cf. Barth, *Philippians*, p. 93 (with reference to Jewish Christians) '…preached ceremonial cleanness. Like the lash of a whip comes Paul's term: dogs!—unclean *precisely* in your cleanness.' This is supported by J. Jeremias on Pap.Ox. 5 840 in *Con Neot* 11 (Lund, 1947, *Fridrichsen Festschrift*), pp. 104 f., where it is combined with χοῖροι and means simply 'unclean'.

[2] From different points of view Köster, *NTS*, VIII (1961–2), 317 ff., and Schmithals, *ZTK*, V (1957), 297–341; *per contra* Klijn, *NT*, VII (1965), 278–84.

[3] Few who interpret 3: 2 f. as Jews take 3: 18 ff. in the same way. There is no inherent necessity for these to be the same groups but, other things being equal, it seems likely. E.g. Lohmeyer speaks of 3: 18 ff. as *lapsi* (*KEK*, pp. 153, 156); for a criticism see Bonnard, *CNT*, pp. 70 f.

[4] Lohmeyer, *KEK*, pp. 152 f., thinks Jewish agitators would not merit Paul's tears, but this is absurd; cf. Rom. 9: 1 f.

enemies of the cross of Christ their end will be destruction (v. 18).[1] If all this refers to Jewish opponents, perhaps it is not so 'fanciful' to take 'their God is the belly' as an allusion to Jewish food laws, and 'they glory in their shame' as an allusion to circumcision.[2]

To interpret this as a threat means that the two self-identifications in 3: 3 (ἡμεῖς γάρ ἐσμεν ἡ περιτομή) and 3: 20 (ἡμῶν γὰρ τὸ πολίτευμα ἐν οὐρανοῖς ὑπάρχει)[3] are preventive measures. The best defence against incorrect demands by Jewish opposition is to assert beforehand whatever will undermine their attraction. Philippians 3: 3 gets underneath an incitement to adopt the marks of Judaism; there is no need, for we, who know God through Jesus Christ, are the circumcision.[4] Similarly, 3: 20 is a defence against a claim that Christians must validate their faith by external participation in cultic Israel, for their 'community'[5] is characterized by heavenly and not earthly things.[6] The stress is laid not on 'special rules', but on the different features of the two communities and the saving significance of Jesus Christ. There is a strongly individual eschatological note in 3: 20 f. (cf. 4: 5) which modifies the community consciousness of v. 20.[7] Generally though, Paul has asserted two principles as over against Judaism: Christians are the circumcision and they belong to a heavenly community. Here is an advance upon

[1] Cf. 1: 28; 1 Thess. 2: 14 ff.; 2 Thess. 2: 11 f. As in Gal. 5: 11 Paul relates persecution (and opposition) to a double offence: failure to preach circumcision, and the cross. In Phil. 3 the twin foci of circumcision (vv. 2 f.) and the cross (vv. 7 ff.) are present. There is nothing inconsistent in predicating opposition by Jews upon the cross (e.g. Rom. 11: 28).

[2] Contra M. R. Vincent, ICC (1897) in loc. Important to this is Hab. 2: 16 (LXX); cf. the whole of Hos. 4, esp. v. 7; Prov. 26: 11; and Ecclus. 4: 21. See Bultmann, TDNT, I, 189 ff. Others refer to the nakedness of circumcision; cf. Mic. 1: 11; Nah. 3: 5.

[3] Note the additional link to 1: 27 through the verbal form πολιτεύεσθε. Literature in Bauer/A–G, s.v.

[4] There is a difference between the functional modifiers here (λατρεύοντες, καυχώμενοι, πεποιθότες) and the qualitative limitations in the similar discussion in Rom. 2: 25 ff.

[5] A. N. Sherwin-White, Roman Society, pp. 184 f.

[6] The contrast heavenly/earthly underlies 3: 3 also: spirit/flesh.

[7] σῶμα here refers to the individual, not the corporate entity; Bauer/A–G, s.v. 1 b; cf. J. A. T. Robinson, The Body (SBT, v, London, 1952, repr. 1961), pp. 30-2, 78-80. See N. Flanagan, CBQ, xviii (1956), 8-9, for parallels between this and 2: 6-11.

anything reached before, and it is a direct result of continued Jewish failure to believe and consequent opposition to the gospel.

Both statements are christologically grounded. In the one case, just as Jesus Christ has been abased and then exalted, we shall have our lowly bodies transformed when he returns from his place of exaltation. In the second, we replace our confidence in fleshly things (circumcision) with a boasting in Jesus Christ. For this reason, even now we share in the heavenly community and in the earthly 'circumcised' community.

This latter statement has a cultic context: οἱ πνεύματι [θεοῦ] λατρεύοντες.[1] Paul uses sacrificial language figuratively in a number of different applications: their generosity is a sacrifice (4: 18; 2: 30);[2] the one who conveys it is a priest (2: 25); their faith is a sacrificial service (2: 17); he himself is a libation (2: 16 f.);[3] the community in Philippi offers a genuine service (*pneumati*, 3: 3). This last thought could be combined with allusions to the Philippians' gifts to suggest that the community is an *ersatz* Temple; but if so, the community's cultic service is primarily the act of giving to Paul. The cultic language does not apply directly to the community's self-understanding and does not seem to have extensive ramifications for its self-awareness.[4]

[1] For cultic language see 2: 17; 2: 30 (re Epaphroditus, *v.* 25); 4: 18 concerning the gift brought by Epaphroditus. K. Weiss, 'Paulus—Priester der christlichen Kultgemeinde', *TLZ*, LXXIX (1954), 355–64, builds a case for Paul as a priest who offers a sacrifice, consisting of the Gentiles, to God. The Christian community itself is a Temple—a *Kultstätte*—in which God is present through his Spirit. He takes this to be very objective language, not just a spiritualizing, but rather a 'heils- oder endgeschichtliche Verwirklichung des Kultus'. This is overdrawn, particularly in its emphasis on Paul alone. Weiss has to overlook the references in 2: 25, 30 to Epaphroditus, and misapply 'your faith' of 2: 17 (cf. 4: 18).

[2] K. Staab, *RNT* (1959), p. 189: 'Mit diesem der sakralen Sprache entnommenen Ausdruck gibt er ihr eine höhere Bedeutung als die einer bloß karitativen Unterstützung; sie wird zu einer gottesdienstlichen Handlung...'

[3] This is usually taken (with Weiss, above; Michaelis, *ThHNT*, p. 49) as a reference to Paul as a priest. Michel, *TWNT*, VII, 529 ff., prefers this sense (see for a full bibliography). This interpretation for Phil. 2: 17 is dependent upon the exegesis of Rom. 15: 16.

[4] See C. F. D. Moule, *Worship in the NT* (London, 1961), pp. 83 ff.; and especially W. D. Davies, *Paul and Rabbinic Judaism* (London, 1962, 2nd edition), p. 259, on Paul's hesitancy in using sacrificial motifs.

The language is occasional and does not imply that Christianity is a new *Kultgemeinde*. Paul uses cultic language in a Christian context as a preventive measure, but he does not fully portray Christianity as the replacement of the old temple services.[1] The cultic overtones are subordinate to the thanks Paul gives for this gift; it is a sacrifice partly, no doubt, because of their straitened circumstances. He himself is a libation poured out in addition to it.[2]

These three hesitant transpositions, more hesitant in the case of the cult than the other two, indicate the direction Paul's mind is taking. In the case of *politeuma* (a clearly collective word but one which gives way in *v.* 21 to an individual eschatological hope), Christians have not taken over the status of Israel itself, for Israel is not a *politeuma* in any sense of the term; rather, Christians are using the analogy of the Jewish *politeuma* in a foreign city to show that theirs is not an earthly but a heavenly citizenship. As with *leitourgia* it is an analogical relationship and not an exclusive transposition. The third, *peritomē*, is still farther along the way, and its use in Philippians represents an advance on the use of the word in Galatians. There it was necessary, because of the situation, to denigrate the thing itself, and the normative statement was, 'circumcision is nothing, nor is uncircumcision'; but in Philippians Paul is preparing the little community for an attack that has not come yet. For that, the best defence is not to say that it does not matter, but to claim that Christians already have it and are the *peritomē*.

THE 'NEW COVENANT' DISCUSSION
IN CORINTHIANS

The exact identity of Paul's opponents remains veiled to some extent in the Corinthian correspondence also. However, it is

[1] For a brief analysis of the development, H.-D. Wendland, *RGG*, III, cols. 1647–51.

[2] Vincent, *ICC* (1897), *in loc.*; Lightfoot, *McM* (2nd edition, 1869), p. 117; Heinzelmann, *NTD* (1955) followed by Bonnard, *CNT* (1950), *in loc.* The metaphor is a mixed one, the Philippians are both sacrifice and priests; so H. C. G. Moule, *CGT* (1897), p. 49; *per contra*, M. Jones, *WC* (1912), p. 40.

clear that his opposition is Jewish in origin,[1] and that it originates in Palestine.[2] The closest point of agreement with Galatians is found in 2 Corinthians 3,[3] and specifically in the association of covenant, promise, Law, spirit and freedom.[4] When Paul discussed the two covenants in Galatians, he interpreted these as concurrent. In 1 and 2 Corinthians this is not the case. In 1 Corinthians 11: 25 he refers to the new covenant made in the blood of Jesus Christ. Where Galatians showed how the old itself was to be interpreted in the light of Christ, 1 and 2 Corinthians deal with the interpretation of the old references to the new. The new covenant of Jeremiah 38: 31 (LXX) is to be taken with the universal implications developed in the Abraham discussion of Galatians (2 Corinthians 3: 6). The mark of this new covenant is that it is not written (for that would be Law) but that it is of the Spirit[5]—life-giving as opposed to killing. Moreover this is something which happens in men's hearts, not on stone.[6] The activity of the Spirit constitutes all the recommendation Paul needs.

Ἡ καινὴ διαθήκη[7] is a term descriptive of the end-time

[1] 2 Cor. 11: 22; cf. W. Schmithals, *Die Gnosis in Korinth, eine Untersuchung zu den Korintherbriefen* (*FRLANT*, LXVI, Göttingen, 1956), pp. 35 f.; cf. G. Friedrich, 'Die Gegner des Paulus in 2 Kor', *Michel Festschrift*, pp. 181 ff.; D. Georgi, *Die Gegner des Paulus in 2 Kor* (*WMANT*, XI, Neukirchen-Vluyen, 1964).

[2] It is possible that Ἑβραῖοι could refer to Diaspora Jews speaking Hebrew as well as Greek (see C. F. D. Moule, *ExT*, LXX (1958–9), 100 ff.); cf. Gutbrod, *TWNT*, III, 392 ff.; Lietzmann, *HNT* (1949), Exk. p. 150, and Kümmel's note, p. 211; T. W. Manson, *BJRL*, XXVI (1941), 101–20 (either under the direct leadership, or in the name, of Peter); Munck, *Paul*, pp. 184 ff. (not judaizers, just some individual Jewish Christians who came at a bad moment).

[3] Cf. Karl Prümm, *Bib*, XXXI (1950), 27–72, 'Gal. und 2 Kor.—ein lehrgehaltlicher Vergleich'.

[4] See Karl Prümm, *Diakonia Pneumatos, der zweite Kor. als Zugang zur apostolischen Botschaft: Auslegung und Theologie*, II, 1. Teil (Rome, 1960), 188 ff.

[5] See Schrenk, *TDNT*, I, 764 ff.; B. Cohen, *HTR*, XLVII (1954), 197 ff.

[6] The new covenant language is not central; it comes from the recollection of Ezek. 11: 19; 36: 28 which has suggested the parallel in Jer. 38: 33, which in turn calls to mind the new covenant.

[7] See W. C. van Unnik, 'La conception paulinienne de la nouvelle alliance', *Recherches Bibliques*, V, ed. A. Descamps (Bruges, 1960), pp. 109 ff. esp. 122 ff.; cf. E. Käsemann, *Leib und Leib Christi*, BHTh, IX (Tübingen, 1933), p. 177.

(i.e. time of promise of Galatians)[1] in which anyone can receive Christ's gift in a way recognizable by others (3: 2 f.). But where before the *diathēkē* is a result of God's dealing with Abraham, and the argument about the two *diathēkai* is based on the analogy of his children, here the two *diathēkai* stem from God's dealing with Moses. This thought complements the contrast written/Spirit which, though similar to the contrast law/freedom in Galatians, differs in the end result. The Moses typology does not allow a dual possibility in concurrent terms as did the Abraham typology, it permits only a single application which must pass away before a second can take its place.[2] Under Moses there is a single people which has been constituted already as 'children of Israel' (3: 7), with nothing else standing beside it as is the case with Abraham and his children. 1 and 2 Corinthians, therefore, deal more fully with the theological implications of the intrusion of the Law considered in Galatians. In so far as it was an old and written covenant, it had to pass away under the influence of the new which was from the Spirit.[3] That is, one of the new things which Christ brings is the replacement of written Law and with it circumcision. But by treating *this* as the covenant, given under Moses rather than Abraham, the emphasis has shifted, intentionally or otherwise, from fulfilment of promise to supersession.[4]

[1] Ἐπαγγελία, only in Cor. at 2 Cor. 1: 20; 7: 1; in neither case analogous to Gal.'s usage; cf. Schniewind/Friedrich, *TDNT*, II, 582 ff.

[2] See C. K. Barrett, *From First Adam to Last: A Study in Pauline Theology* (Hewett Lectures for 1961, London, 1962), ch. 2 on Abraham, ch. 3 on Moses; cf. E. E. Ellis, *Paul's Use of the OT* (Einburgh, 1957), esp. pp. 128 ff.

[3] In the NT the term ἡ παλαιὰ διαθήκη appears only here, and is approached in Heb. 8: 13. If H. W. Montefiore's view of Heb. (*BNTC*, 1964) is correct, Apollos would have been the first to suggest the term and his use influenced that of Paul; this contrast, which now supersedes the bondage/promise contrast, became normative because of the (probably) strongly typological interpretation of Apollos.

[4] Cf. J. Jocz, *A Theology of Election: Israel and the Church* (London, 1958), pp. 116 ff.: 'The "new" covenant is therefore not a different covenant, but the original covenant established once and for all' (p. 117). Jocz does not allow sufficiently for the shift we have described. Dahl, *Volk Gottes*, p. 283, hints at this same point when he claims that Paul's exegesis and his understanding of the Church correspond: a *pneumatische* exegesis of the OT leads to an interpretation of the Church as *Israēl kata pneuma*.

Arising out of Paul's claim to be διάκονος καινῆς διαθήκης, 3: 7–11 builds on the contrast of the two *diakoniai*, in which the glory of the one is superior to the glory of the other.[1] The inferiority of the Mosaic glory depends upon two facts: it is destined to fade away, and the people could not properly utilize it.[2] These are developed further in 3: 11–18: Moses' veil[3] prevented the children of Israel from looking on τὸ τέλος τοῦ καταργουμένου, which is not just Moses' visual glory, but the glory which the old covenant possessed (3: 14). Paul takes us by degrees from the new back to the old, but he comes back to the present time, full circle. The application of the discussion is that the 'same veil' is still effectively over the old covenant itself (3: 14) and over those who listen to it being read (3: 15).[4] Understanding was hardened in the old times and is so today.[5] The veil is only taken away in Christ; Jews are still able to turn to the Lord to have the veil lifted (3: 16).

The *diakoniai* of Paul and Moses are discussed in the Corinthian situation because they focus the issues in Paul's struggle with his opponents (4: 1 ff.; cf. 3: 1 ff.). The one side argues that the Mosaic *diakonia* cannot be abolished; Paul argues not only that it can, but that it must because it gives no one freedom or confidence.[6] The relationship of one people to another is a secondary question to that of practice. The people of the old covenant, both historically and in the contemporary synagogue, are veiled from a true understanding of God. Those who turn to God in Jesus have that veil removed and obtain confidence (freedom) from acknowledging the Lordship of the Spirit. The new covenant in this passage is a characteristic of

---

[1] 3: 8: πῶς οὐχὶ μᾶλλον ἡ διακονία τοῦ πνεύματος ἔσται ἐν δόξῃ;, cf. 3: 9–11.

[2] The addition of τὴν καταργουμένην (3: 7) is an anticipation of 3: 11, 13.

[3] See W. C. van Unnik, *NT*, VI (1963), 153–69. 'To uncover the face (or head)' is an Aramaic idiom equivalent to 'boldness' = παρρησία. Hence the logic is consistent through to the end of *v.* 18.

[4] Van Unnik, *ibid.* p. 164, has detailed the parallelism of this passage, both horizontal and vertical, when set out with *vv.* 13 and 14 in one column and 15 and 16 in a second.

[5] Van Unnik, *ibid.*, refers to Isa. 29: 10 as the link in the ideas of veiling and hardening.

[6] One step farther back, the section represents a defence of Paul's apostleship, and its effectiveness in bringing men into union with God.

the new end-time predicated upon the work of Christ;[1] it is not, however, a new entity but rather a new operation of the Spirit which replaces the old things which are let go. Paul is saying: Christ is the end of the Law. We may remark that in this passage no specific identifying titles or attributes are applied to Christians.[2]

The treatment of Moses and the eschatological link between the former time and the end-time unite 2 Corinthians 3 and 1 Corinthians 10.[3] The same midrashic character is obvious in both, although the underlying analogy is different.[4] Both are anchored in a practical situation, where instruction is needed on a basic aspect of Christian life: in 2 Corinthians 3 the problem is the validity of the Law, in 1 Corinthians 10 the efficacy of sacraments and holiness.[5]

The warning in 1 Corinthians 10 is sufficiently clear to require little discussion. The people had every protection that might be expected to keep them from falling (10: 1 ff.), yet they still fell (10: 5, 8, 10, 12). Likewise the Christian (ὁ δοκῶν ἑστάναι),[6] in spite of having received blessing from God, must take care lest he also fall. God provides a way of overcoming, but it must be grasped (10: 12 f.). This leads to the application of the example: participation in idols is antipathetic to union with Christ (10: 16 f.; cf. 10: 7). Now it is in this context that Paul

[1] So H.-D. Wendland, *NTD* (7th edition, 1954), p. 155. '"Neu" ist ein eschatologisch heilsgeschichtlich zu verstehendes Adjektiv, d.h., es bezeichnet Ereignisse der endzeitlichen Vollendung...und deren gegenwärtig beginnende Erscheinung, die mit Christus gegeben ist.'

[2] In this section 3: 1 – 4: 6 Christians are distinguished primarily by practice and not by distinctive titles. This is identical to our observation that in Gal., especially 6: 16, Christians are identified functionally, whereas Israel retains its distinguishing title.

[3] 10: 11; cf. L. Cerfaux, *The Church in the Theology of St Paul* (New York, 1959), pp. 95 ff.

[4] See W. D. Davies, *Paul*, pp. 105, 107; E. E. Ellis, ' A Note on 1 Corinthians 10: 4', *JBL*, LXXVI (1957), 53–6. Note especially 1 Cor. 10: 6 (τύποι; cf. 10: 11, τυπικῶς) and 2 Cor. 3: 8 ff. (πῶς οὐχὶ μᾶλλον;, cf. 3: 13, οὐ καθάπερ), and 3: 14, ἄχρι γὰρ τῆς σήμερον.

[5] For 1 Cor. 10 see Barrett, *First Adam*, pp. 47 ff.: means not 'type', but 'warning example'. For the relevance of both sections to the Lord's Supper see E. Käsemann, *Essays on NT Themes* (*SBT*, XLI, London, 1964), pp. 108–35.

[6] It is difficult to be sure whether there is a nuance in this expression which might identify the opponents; see commentators.

introduces the phrase: βλέπετε τὸν Ἰσραὴλ κατὰ σάρκα,[1] from which follows a statement about being sharers in the altar. The train of thought is complicated by textual variations: *v.* 19*c* is to be omitted, and τὰ ἔθνη is to be added in *v.* 20 as the subject of θύουσιν.[2] On the basis of this text *vv.* 18–19*b* form a parenthesis to forestall an objection or an incorrect deduction.[3] The main point comes only in *v.* 20 with ἀλλ' ὅτι: my point is not that Jews who share in the altar are idolaters, but rather that Gentiles who sacrifice to demons *and not to God*[4] have fellowship with demons. *Israēl kata sarka* is a synonym for *Ioudaioi* and means simply Israel with all its customs, especially those customs which are past and gone because of Christ's sacrifice.[5] There is a derogatory tone in the phrase because the particular thing noted no longer has any effect; but it is still used *in bonam* and not *in malam partem*.

These are the only examples of *Israēl* in 1 and 2 Corinthians; *Ioudaios* is found more often. In 1 Corinthinas 9: 19 ff. the meaning of *Ioudaios* is not necessarily equivalent to 'being under law'.[6] It seems to mean instead a Jew who is not particularly scrupulous about his observance, whereas the next phrase represents the one who is scrupulous. Though Paul can say in *v.* 20*b* 'not being myself under law', he does not say 'not being a Jew' in *v.* 20*a*, just as he does not say 'not being weak' in

[1] 10: 18; to this point nothing has been said of the relationship between the Church and Israel, except for a possible inference from ἐγράφη δὲ πρὸς νουθεσίαν ἡμῶν (10: 11). Basically the argument is analogical.

[2] See K. W. Clark, *de Zwaan Festschrift*, pp. 59 f. The authorities are: 𝔓[46] 𝔖 𝔎 lat sy co. Could it have been omitted by Marcion to make the rest apply to Israel, and therefore to show how degenerate it was?

[3] See Lietzmann, *HNT, in loc.*: 'Ehe Pls nun die Folgerung zieht, schützt er sich durch eine Zwischenfrage gegen Mißverständnisse.' The Corinthians' letter to Paul, which asked about idols (8: 1 ff.), might have made some allusion to Jewish practice; Paul tries to correct a misconception about it: namely, Jews are not on this account idol-worshippers, only Gentiles are (cf. S. Aalen, 'Das Abendmahl als Opfermahl', *NT*, VI, 1963, 128 ff.).

[4] Καὶ οὐ θεῷ is an important distinction between *Israēl kata sarka* and *ta ethnē*.

[5] The theory that *Israēl kata sarka* demands a correlative *Israēl kata pneuma* = *tou theou* cannot be accepted. Many things which take *kata sarka* do not have a correlative *kata pneuma*.

[6] As C. H. Dodd maintains, 'ΕΝΝΟΜΟΣ ΧΡΙΣΤΟΥ', *de Zwaan Festschrift*, pp. 96–110; similarly, Gutbrod, *TWNT*, III, 383.

v. 22.[1] In 1: 22 ff. there are three instances of *Ioudaios*, contrasted once with *Hellēn*,[2] once with *ethnē*, and once linked with *Hellēn*. The Jew and the Greek, starting from radically different presuppositions, both have the same choice: either to accept or reject the cross of Christ. Equality of status is found in the more difficult 1 Corinthians 10: 32 ff., the conclusion to the argument on 'freedom' which began in 6: 12, to which Paul has reverted a number of times. Absolute freedom must be qualified by always seeking the good of the other person, with the example again that of eating food offered to idols. Whatever is done must be for the glory of God, and for saving some (10: 31, 33; cf. 9: 22).[3] Consideration for God and other persons, both Christians (10: 24, 29) and non-Christians (10: 33), underlies the saying in 10: 32 where the groups[4] to whom no offence is to be given are as widely based as possible—Christians[5] and non-Christians, whether Jews or Gentiles.[6] The Church does not represent so much a *tertium genus* over against Jews and Gentiles[7] as a third group, distinguishable from the rest of Jews and Gentiles, that might take offence at an individual's behaviour. As 1: 24 (cf. 12: 13) shows, the Church itself is composed of, and called out from (οἱ κλητοί), *Ioudaioi* and *Hellēnes*; it cannot be contrasted starkly with them.

When substantiating a similar proposition in ch. 6: 12 f., Paul concludes on the theme of Christians as a Temple

---

[1] The structure of this group of four is not clear. It is tempting to find some form of chiasmus based on the two μὴ ὤν phrases, and the use of ἐγενόμην in 1 and 4. But the groups behind the phrases cannot be ordered into a logical sequence in agreement with this, unless we identify ἀσθενεῖς with Jews (as e.g. J. Héring, *CNT*, 1948, *in loc.*) and οἱ ὑπὸ νόμον with Gentiles = proselytes (as e.g. in the Galatian situation).

[2] Cf. StrBill III, 27 ff., at Rom. 1: 14.

[3] On Paul's 'opportunism', see the excellent article by H. Chadwick, 'All Things to All Men', *NTS*, 1 (1954–5), 261–75; he does not stress sufficiently the ἵνα clause as the purpose of Paul's theory. The concern is identical to 1 Thess. 2: 16, except in positive terms.

[4] Dahl (*Volk Gottes*), takes this to be the one clear example of a *tertium genus* in Paul.

[5] Robertson and Plummer, *ICC* (2nd edition, 1914), *in loc.*, suggest 'the weak brethren who have needless scruples'.

[6] Cf. 9.20 f.; see Ellicott (1887), p. 197: '...to the οἱ ἔξω...and to the οἱ ἔσω they were to be alike ἀπρόσκοποι'.

[7] Later this gradually developed, but when first introduced in *Kerygma Petri* it was still a third way of worshipping.

(1 Corinthians 6: 19).[1] The motive for ethics is twofold, says Paul: Christians are united with Christ,[2] and indwelt by the Holy Spirit.[3] The same idea was expressed earlier in almost identical terms,[4] and is found also in the harsh passage incorporated in 2 Corinthians 6: 14 ff.[5] These references are all individually applied to the ethical dilemmas facing the Christian living in a pagan world; naos is not yet a metaphor readily applicable to the whole community as such.[6] The Spirit lives within each member of the community enabling him to overcome temptation (cf. 1 Corinthians 10), to be free of Law (cf. 2 Corinthians 3), and to live a life directed towards the glory of God and the winning of others. This is a stage prior to the identification of the new community with the Temple of God.[7] This happened only later.[8]

Another demonstration of the individual application of motifs taken over and reapplied is καινὴ κτίσις in 2 Corinthians 5: 17.[9] As in Galatians 6: 16, the 'new creation' is the man for whom

[1] See B. Gärtner, *The Temple and the Community in Qumran and the NT* (*SNTS Mono. Ser.* 1, Cambridge, 1965), esp. pp. 49 ff.; H. Wenschkewitz, *Die Spiritualisierung der Kultusbegriffe, Tempel, Priester und Opfer in NT* (Leipzig, 1932); and M. Fraeyman, *La Spiritualisation de l'idée du temple dans les épîtres pauliniennes* (*EphTheolLov*, XXXIII, 1947, 378–412).

[2] 6: 15: 'Do you not know that our bodies are members of Christ?'

[3] 6: 19: 'Do you not know that your body is a temple of the Holy Spirit in you?'

[4] 3: 16: 'Do you not know that you are a temple of God and the Spirit of God lives in you?'

[5] 6: 16: 'We are a temple of the living God.'

[6] Gärtner, by starting from 2 Cor. 6: 16, thinks he can demonstrate this, though he has trouble with 1 Cor. 3: 16. Dahl, *Volk Gottes*, p. 222, recognizes the difficulty of taking 1 Cor. 6: 19 collectively, but does so on the basis of the next verse! He claims that in 2 Cor. 6: 14 ff. naos theou = laos theou. Neither recognizes that in 1 Cor. 6: 19; 3: 16 naos is an indefinite singular.

[7] Michel, *TWNT*, IV, esp. pp. 490 f., is aware of the development, though he does not go far enough.

[8] *Contra* Gärtner, *Temple*, who makes the NT uniform; cf. p. 99: 'The bond which binds together Qumran and the NT is undoubtedly the intense self-consciousness of the two communities represented; both considered themselves to have been set up in opposition to the temple of the old covenant and its cultus; both believed themselves to have replaced the old temple, for in both the community was the temple.' Cf. also pp. 139 f. on the relation of this to Christology.

[9] For the Jewish background, StrBill at John 3: 3 (II, 421.2).

all things have become new through an acknowledgment of the significance of the life, death and resurrection of Jesus; as a result, the old things have passed away.[1] This last phrase is a reference to personal attitudes, presuppositions and beliefs, and not to things of the old covenant directly. However, while emphasizing in the above the individualism of these transpositions and applications, we should not like to overstress this at the expense of all community consciousness.[2] Especially in Corinth, surrounded by numerous temptations, there would be a clear awareness that they formed a community of believers in Christ. The community was founded upon the eschatological character of the Christ-event, and was commissioned to be a saving entity. The two characteristics have both an individual and a corporate face, but the corporate importance of Christians is not yet to the fore. That it is growing in importance can be seen by the concern for purity within the community, and by the concern for the proper use of gifts in worship, both problems arising under the impact of local circumstances. It is not yet intimately related to the problem of Israel and the need for a self-understanding over against it. For the moment it is necessary to deal with things primarily at an individual level. Christians are a new creation and a temple of the Holy Spirit; they are those in whom can be observed the deadness of the Law and the newness of the things (freedom especially) which Christ brings.

The Corinthian letters, consequently, do not deal much with the relationship between the Church and Israel, and only slightly more with Christians' relation with Jews and with Gentiles. The midrashic treatment of the Old Testament shows how it may be used by Christians, but the *midrashim* are not the basis for a complete transposition of attributes from Israel to

---

[1] Cf. Delling, art. ἄρχω, *TDNT*, I, 487: 'Paul is first thinking of the attitude of contemporaries to the earthly Jesus, then of his own Pharisaic piety'; and P. E. Hughes, *NLC* (1962), *ad loc.*, '...while the new is so different from the old that the latter can be said to have passed away, yet there is a radical continuity between them, so that it is also possible to say that the old has become new'.

[2] The corporate character is seen especially in the idea of the 'body', though not everywhere does 'body' have a corporate sense; see J. A. T. Robinson, *The Body* (*SBT*, v, London repr. 1961); cf. J. J. Meuzelaar, *Der Leib des Messias* (Assen, 1961), especially pp. 15, 20 ff.

the Church, as happened later. In particular, the phrase *Israēl kata sarka* does not call forth an antithetical *Israēl kata pneuma* (or *tou theou*), it is merely illustrative. Other corporate titles are related either directly to Christ or to the activity of the Spirit, but not yet transposed from Israel as if the Church had superseded it. There is an advance upon the position reached in Galatians, particularly with respect to *diathēkē*, but the implied relationship of Christianity to Judaism is one of creative contact rather than unrelated opposition. It is only in Romans that the question of the relationship is discussed thoroughly.

ROMANS: PAUL'S INTERPRETATION OF GOD'S PURPOSE

There is a growing consensus that Romans must be interpreted in the light of Paul's missionary situation;[1] in particular, Romans 9–11 are best understood as reflections on what God is doing in Paul's missionary work. Whatever the underlying structure of the letter,[2] it is clear that the last paragraph of Romans 11 marks a pause. It concludes a discussion of practical historical realities (chs. 9–11),[3] which in turn builds upon a statement based upon theoretical and theological first principles (chs. 1–4). In spite of Paul's attempted reconciliation of contrary data (it is God's will to save Jews; yet Jews do not accept as readily as Gentiles)[4] he is not confident

[1] T. W. Manson, *BJRL*, xxxi (1948), 140 ff.; J. Munck, *Paul*, ch. 7; G. Schrenk in *Studien zu Paulus* (*ATANT*, xxvi, Zurich, 1954), pp. 81–106; E. Trocmé, *NTS*, vii (1960–1), 148–53. G. Lindeskog thinks this is too one-sided, *SvExArs*, xxvi (1961), 57–92, see p. 62. More recently, see M. Jack Suggs, 'The Word is Near You', in *Christian History and Interpretation: Studies presented to John Knox*, ed. W. R. Farmer, C. F. D. Moule, R. R. Niebuhr (Cambridge, 1967), pp. 289–312.

[2] See the perceptive article by J. Dupont, *RB*, lxii (1955), 365–98, and his full survey and criticisms, to which should be added K. Prümm, *ZKT*, lxxii (1950), 333–49. Two problems are the Gentile/Jewish transition in chs. 1–2 (see F. Flückiger, *TZ*, x, 1954, 154–8, who puts the break between 1.31 and 1.32) and the place of ch. 5, which is the key to the problem of the structure (thus Dupont).

[3] *Contra* those who sum up Rom. 9–11 under a weighty theological heading and those who find no consistency in the argument (e.g. G. B. Caird, *ExT*, lxviii, 1957, 324–7; L. Cerfaux, *Church*, pp. 49–54).

[4] On the problem generally, A. Charue, *L'incrédulité des juifs dans le NT* (Louvain, 1929).

that he has found the final solution (11: 34: 'Who has known the mind of the Lord?'). At best it is a well-thought-out trial run.[1] Convincing support for this approach to Romans comes from the intermediate conclusion of 11: 28–32. This very carefully structured[2] concluding period directs the reader away from election and retribution towards gospel and mercy.

28a κατὰ μὲν τὸ εὐαγγέλιον   κατὰ δὲ τὴν ἐκλογὴν   28b
    ἐχθροὶ δι' ὑμᾶς   ἀγαπητοὶ διὰ τοὺς πατέρας·
29   ἀμεταμέλητα[3] γὰρ   29
                τὰ χαρίσματα
  καὶ ἡ κλῆσις τοῦ θεοῦ.
30 ὥσπερ γὰρ ὑμεῖς   οὕτως καὶ οὗτοι   31
ποτε ἠπειθήσατε τῷ θεῷ   νῦν ἠπείθησαν τῷ ὑμετέρῳ ἐλέει
νῦν δὲ ἠλεήθητε τῇ τούτων   ἵνα καὶ αὐτοὶ νῦν ἐλεηθῶσιν.
  ἀπειθείᾳ
32   συνέκλεισεν γὰρ ὁ θεὸς   32
  τοὺς πάντας εἰς ἀπείθειαν
  ἵνα τοὺς πάντας ἐλεήσῃ.

If conclusions isolate the main features of the preceding section, 11: 28–32 is an important guide to the basic intention of Paul.[4] This is no simple *heilsgeschichtliche* scheme,[5] but a complex interaction between two entities—one with a special relationship to God, the other far from him. The positions of these two become inextricably related by God's action, so that both might benefit by his mercy.[6] This mercy can be shown in

---

[1] Cf. Dinkler, *JR*, xxxvi (1956), 12: 11: 33–6 'lay bare the fundamental insecurity of human thought about God's wisdom...If one treats this doxological conclusion of Rom. ch. 9–11 as a liturgical annex, one does not recognize that Paul, in fact, relativizes his previously given "mystery"...'

[2] Barrett, *BNTC* (1957), p. 224; cf. on *vv.* 30–1, M. Dibelius, 'Vier Worte des Röm.' (*SBU*, iii, Uppsala, 1944), pp. 3–17.

[3] C. Spicq, *RB*, lxvii (1960), 210–19.

[4] *A priori* this is likely; Gal. shows this in a particular instance.

[5] G. Klein, 'Römer 4 und die Idee der Heilsgeschichte', *EvTh*, xxiii (1963), 424–47, indicates that Rom. 4 is not a *locus classicus* for *Heilsgeschichte*, but rather a denial of such a scheme. What follows here supports his contention. See also E. Schweizer, *NTS*, viii (1961), 1–11, esp. p. 3; L. Goppelt, *Interp*, xxi (1967), 315–26.

[6] Instrumental datives, O. Michel, *KEK* (12th edition, 1963), p. 284 n. 2; M.-J. Lagrange, *EtBib* (1950), p. 288.

different ways (εὐαγγέλιον, ἐκλογή)[1] but it has the single aim of embracing all. While there is a neat parallelism between the two columns, it originates with a consideration of Judaism, which is looked at from two points of view: on the one hand enemies, on the other the beloved (v. 28). The concentration on Judaism gives way to an interest in both Jews and Gentiles through the mention of 'you' as the purpose behind the enmity. The original concern for one group, which is enemy and beloved alike, is transferred into a concern for 'all' which comprehends both 'you' and 'them'.

'You' are Gentile Christians,[2] and 'they' are Israel discussed in 11: 25–7.[3] These verses introduce the periodic formula of 11: 28 ff. and explain the allusions.[4] Verse 31 is explanatory of the 'mystery'[5] of v. 25 ('partial hardness (πώρωσις) has come upon Israel'), and v. 30 is the equivalent of the last part of v. 25 ('until the full number (πλήρωμα) of the Gentiles enters'). Romans 11: 25–6 are not a precise parallel to 11: 28 ff., only the basis of it, so that 'all Israel will be saved'[6] does not correspond to 'all' in 11: 32. It is a reversal of the negative statement about 'hardness upon Israel' which immediately precedes it.

The *pesher* citations of 11: 26 f. are applied directly to unbelieving Israel.[7] There can be no other explanation for Paul's breaking off his quotation of Isa. 59: 20 f.[8] just at the point

[1] See Schrenk, *TWNT*, IV, 181 ff.; cf. Herntrich/Schrenk, art. λεῖμμα, *TWNT*, IV, 198 ff. Schrenk's view that ἐκλογή is used quite differently in 11: 28 and 9: 11; 11: 5, 7 must be corrected.

[2] T. Fahy makes an unconvincing case for Jewish Christians; *IrTQ*, XXVI (1959), 182–91; cf. N. Krieger, *NT*, III (1959), 146–8.

[3] Cf. the exegesis of E. Peterson under the title 'Die Kirche aus Juden und Heiden' in *Theologische Traktate* (München, 1951), pp. 239–92.

[4] C. Müller, *Gottes Gerechtigkeit und Gottes Volk* (*FRLANT*, LXXXVI, Göttingen, 1964), pp. 38–43, points out the similarity to Rev. 11.

[5] 'Mystery' is often overemphasized; e.g. H. Schlier, 'Das Mysterium Israels' in *Die Zeit der Kirche* (Freiburg, 1956), pp. 232–44; G. Molin, 'Mysterion Israel', *Jud*, X (1954), 231–43.

[6] Gutbrod rightly notices that it is not πάντες οἱ 'Ιουδαῖοι but πᾶς 'Ισραήλ; *TWNT*, III, 389 f. W. Vischer, *Jud*, VI (1950), 81–132, attempts to show that πᾶς 'Ισραήλ is every Jew.

[7] E. E. Ellis, *Paul's Use of the OT*, p. 123 n. 5; p. 140; cf. B. Lindars, *NT Apologetic* (London, 1961), pp. 245, 257.

[8] It is misleading to refer to Jer. 38: 33 f. for 11: 27a; it is exactly Isa. 59: 21a; *contra* Dodd, *MNTC* (1932), *in loc.*

where it becomes explicitly applicable to Christians.[1] He replaces this with a recollection of Isaiah 27: 9 about forgiveness of Jacob's sins.[2] Jacob, as often in Isaiah, stands for the mainstream of the people of God, a synonym for Israel.[3] The variation between Israel in 11: 25 f. and Jacob in 11: 26 has no theological importance.

There is a clear and close relationship between 11: 25 ff. and the metaphor of the olive tree.[4] The transition to this section (beginning in *v.* 16*b*) from what precedes is less clear,[5] but once made the whole section from *v.* 11 on through has the single aim of demonstrating that there is hope for unbelieving Israel, and that the Gentile part of the Church has not taken over the place of Israel. The obvious feature of the olive tree figure, sometimes overlooked, is that a pruned Israel retains its place in God's activity; where Gentiles graciously have been grafted in, on condition of continuing faithfulness (*v.* 22), it is unnatural. The wild and the cultivated grow together in one tree only contrary to nature (*v.* 24). This cuts out all ground of Gentile boasting (*vv.* 18 ff.),[6] but at the same time makes Gentiles partakers (συγκοινωνός, *v.* 17) of the root of the tree. In that fact lies God's 'goodness'. His 'severity' to those who have not listened is conditional also, and will turn into goodness if they give up their unbelief.

This metaphor is the basis for 11: 25 ff. in that it demonstrates the conditional nature of God's attitude to both Jews and Gentiles. The olive tree example arises out of the need to explain

[1] τὸ πνεῦμα τὸ ἐμόν, ὅ ἐστιν ἐπὶ σοί κτλ.

[2] *Iakōb* ties the two passages closely together in Isa., particularly with respect to God's future gracious purpose of taking away sin. Odeberg (*TWNT*, III, 191 f.) misses the point of the quotation.

[3] Cf. Isa. 27: 6; 10: 20 f.; 14: 1; 29: 22 f.; 41: 8 ff.; but not in the later instances in 58: 11, 14; 59: 20; 65: 9. On the subject generally see G. A. Danell, *Studies in the Name Israel in the OT* (Uppsala, 1946).

[4] W. M. Ramsay, *Exp*, 6th ser. XI (1905), 16–34, 152–60; M. M. Bourke, *A Study of the Metaphor of the Olive Tree in Rom.* 11 (Washington, 1947).

[5] There is an obvious parallelism between 16*a* and 16*b*, but it is not certain what, in the preceding verses, is referred to as ἀπαρχήν—probably with Barrett, *BNTC* (1957) *in loc.* it is 'some of them' of *v.* 14, which then corresponds to 'election' (*v.* 7) and 'remnant' (*v.* 5). Most take ἀπαρχήν of the Patriarchs, on the analogy of *v.* 28, but the connection is tenuous; cf. Maurer, *TWNT*, VI, 985 ff.

[6] Not an 'enthusiastisches Pneumatikertum'; Michel, *KEK*, p. 277.

statements which parallel those of 11: 25 ff. Jews did not stumble in order to fall (11: 11); their transgression has meant in Paul's experience that salvation has thereby been possible for Gentiles (11: 11, 12, 15).[1] Gentile acceptance also has a purpose—to make Israel jealous (παραζηλόω, 11: 11, 14)[2] so that Paul will save some.[3] This section employs a circular argument as in 11: 25 f. and 11: 28 ff.: beginning with Jews and their antipathy it moves on to Gentiles and their acceptance, and then back to Jews and their ultimate ingrafting.[4] The Church has no existence apart from Israel and has no separate identity.[5] It exists as an interim measure until the fullness of Israel (v. 12, τὸ πλήρωμα αὐτῶν; v. 15, ἡ πρόσλημψις) is brought in and grafted on (v. 23). Only then will the olive tree be full and ripe. The thought is distinctly Israel-centric.[6]

The argument we have traced from the conclusion backwards begins at 10: 14, a verse that sets the tone clearly on the note of apostolic proclamation. The argument has a counterpart in 9: 6–10: 13,[7] dealing with the background of the present situation. It culminates in the conclusion of 10: 12–13: 'There is no distinction between Jew and Greek…all who call on the name of the Lord will be saved.'[8] The division of Romans 9–11 into two sections (rather than the usual three) concentrates attention upon the practical matters of whom God calls, how he calls and what that call's effect is.

The moving introduction in 9: 1–5 presents a full list of

[1] Sanday–Headlam, *ICC* (1895), p. 321.

[2] The antecedent of 11: 11*b* clearly is not the immediately adjacent 'Gentiles', but the subject of 11*a*.

[3] See J. Munck, *Christus und Israel* (*Acta Jutlandica* 28.3, Aarhus, 1956), pp. 91 ff.; and K. F. Nickle, *The Collection: A Study in Paul's Strategy* (*SBT*, XLVIII, London, 1966), esp. pp. 134 ff.

[4] Cf. Althaus, *NTD* (9th edition, 1959), p. 96: 'Der jetzige Fall ist nicht Ende, sondern Durchgang, nicht Ziel sondern Mittel.'

[5] See G. E. Ladd, 'Israel and the Church', *EQ*, XXXVI (1964), 206–13; J. van der Ploeg, *The Church and Israel* (London, 1956); H. H. Graham, 'Continuity and Discontinuity in the Thought of Paul', *ATR*, XXXVIII (1956), 137–46.

[6] Munck, *Christus*, p. 92.

[7] 9: 1–5 being an introductory statement.

[8] These two propositions, argued in these one and a half chapters largely from the OT, are the basis of Paul's work. Note their close relationship to the theme in 1: 16–17, additional reason for the division we propose.

attributes belonging to Israel.[1] In the following explanation two courses were possible: either to apply the prerogatives one by one to Christians and to them alone, or else to show how, while these prerogatives are opened up to include others, they retain their basic application to Israel.[2] In following this latter course Paul indicates his respect for 'Israelites' by refusing to set out a Christian take-over.

The unexpressed presupposition of the extended list of attributes is that, in spite of the advantages they confer, they have not helped to lead Israel to Christ. This does not mean that God's word is ineffectual,[3] rather the assumption lying behind any expectation of full acceptance is false,[4] for not every Jew is really a part of Israel.[5] In this statement, the first Israel refers to the Patriarch and the second to the progeny, as the following sentences show.[6] In both historical instances, Isaac and Jacob, sonship to God is reckoned[7] (λογίζεται εἰς σπέρμα) not according to physical descent but according to promise. Some commentators introduce the notion of a 'dual Israel'—an 'eschatological' and a 'natural'.[8] That Paul is drawing a

---

[1] Lietzmann, *HNT* (4th edition, 1933), p. 89: 'Die persönlich gehaltene und von höchster Wärme erfüllte Einführung 9. 1–5 lehrt, daß auch hier ein eminent praktisches Interesse...'

[2] Ἰσραηλῖται remains untouched; for υἱοθεσία see Gal. 4: 5; Rom. 8: 15; for δόξα 2 Cor. 3: 9 ff.; for διαθῆκαι 2 Cor. 3: 6, 14; Gal. 4: 24; for νομοθεσία and the problem connected with it, Gal. 3: 13 ff.; for λατρεία Phil. 3: 3; for ἐπαγγελίαι Gal. 3: 14 ff.; 2 Cor. 7: 1; for πατέρες 1 Cor. 10: 1. L. Cerfaux, 'Le privilège d'Israël selon s. Paul', *Recueil L. Cerfaux*, II (Gembloux, 1954), 339 ff., esp. pp. 340 f., points out that in this enumeration attention is focused on the Patriarchs and away from the Law; this is consistent with what we have observed of Paul's theology.

[3] For οὐχ οἷον δὲ ὅτι see Bauer/A–G, *s.v.* οἷος; Bl–D/Funk 304, 480.5 take it as an ellipsis of λέγω. Moulton/Turner, pp. 295, 300, take it as an ellipsis of εἰμί.

[4] See Michel, *KEK*, p. 231, for a discussion of the logical connection.

[5] οὐ γὰρ πάντες οἱ ἐξ Ἰσραήλ, οὗτοι Ἰσραήλ (9: 6).

[6] Gutbrod, *TWNT*, III, 386, cf. p. 390; Kugelman, 'Hebrew, Israelite, Jew in the NT', *Bridge*, I (1955), 204–24. Paul begins with the Patriarch who gives the name to the people, and then proceeds to show how, in his descendants, there is a process of selection always at work, a selection which is a constituent aspect of God's purpose.

[7] Cf. Müller, *Gerechtigkeit*, pp. 28 f., 90 ff.

[8] Especially E. Dinkler, 'Prädestination bei Pls' in *Festschrift für G. Dehn* (Neukirchen, 1957), pp. 81–102; *idem*, 'The Historical and Eschatological

distinction between the total and a godly part of Judaism is clear;[1] but is it sufficiently accurate to call the latter 'eschatological' Israel?[2] The term can be filled with almost any content one desires; in this instance one is allowed to posit that the Church has filled the eschatological expectation, and therefore *is* Israel.[3] Undoubtedly the Church fulfils certain expectations concerning the end-times, and there are some theological reasons for identifying the Church with Israel. But to distinguish *a priori* between natural and eschatological Israel is to prejudge the whole question. Paul's thought is moving entirely in the realm of historical realities in ch. 9: it has always been true throughout God's dealings with men that not all of the chosen people are an integral part of the People of God.[4] God does not respect doctrinaire orders of priority. He is free and sovereign; where he maintains a historical continuity it is a mark of his loving-kindness.[5]

Sovereignty is the theme of the next section (9: 14–

Israel in Rom. 9–11; a Contribution to the Problem of Predestination and Individual Responsibility', *JR*, xxxvi (1956), 109–27. Müller and others follow him. Dinkler's thesis falls when it is observed that there is a distinction between the terminology of Rom. 1–4 and 9–11 with respect to Israel, and that this affects the interpretation of 'Israel' in 9–11.

[1] What Davies, *Paul*, p. 78, refers to as Paul's 'rediscovering the meaning of the term "Israel"'; cf. all ch. 4.

[2] Cf. Bultmann, *Theology*, i, 53 f., 96 f.

[3] Cerfaux, *Recueil*, p. 355: the promises pass by the historic people and rest on those who follow Christ. Historic Israel is a 'fidéicommissaire du testament et un dépositaire de la promesse'. Contrast Müller, *Gerechtigkeit*, p. 91: 'Die Unterscheidung der beiden Arten 'Ισραήλ bzw. σπέρμα dient hier nicht wie Gal 4 den Aufweis, daß das "wahre" Gottesvolk sind, sondern der Erhellung dessen, daß das Gottesvolk Israel allein im Willen Gottes seine Existenz hat.'

[4] Dinkler thinks that there is a decisive contradiction between 9: 6–13 and 11: 1–32: in ch. 9 the problem is solved by reinterpreting 'Israel'; in ch. 11 the same problem is answered by the role of the continuing historical Israel. If, however, our view of 9: 6 is correct, then both form a single solution to a single problem: God saves all those who are truly Israelites, even those who do not yet acknowledge Jesus as Lord. Paul is using 'Israel' soteriologically, but still continuous with the 'biological–historical concatenation'.

[5] Müller, *Gerechtigkeit*, p. 93, would say, of the 'eschatologischen Neuschöpfung Israels als Volk Gottes'; cf. Michel, *KEK*, p. 232 n. 3: 'Die Geschichte Israels ist eine Geschichte der göttlichen Erwählung und Verwerfung.'

29).[1] He epitomizes this thought in two ways: first, by the contrast wrath/glory which parallels the goodness/severity contrast or 11: 28, and secondly, by the notion that his sovereignty extends to both Gentiles and Jews.[2] The Jewish people alone were the subject of the previous section, which demonstrated the negative proposition that God will not allow his action to be determined by blood relationships. The present section is the obverse of that, demonstrating the right of God to work with whom he pleases.

It is an important part of Paul's argument to introduce the scriptural proofs which substantiate both aspects of the problem. The one side is buttressed by an appeal to Hosea 2: 25 and 2: 1[3] with a shift of application from northern Israel to Gentiles.[4] Hosea 2: 1 immediately links with Isaiah 10: 22 f. through the clause about 'the number of the children of Israel' (Romans 9: 27). The verse is used not as a 'theory of rejection'[5] but to show that God calls from Jews as well: τὸ ὑπόλειμμα σωθήσεται. This is linked with a quotation from Isaiah 1: 9 where the descendants (σπέρμα) left in Israel are sufficient to distinguish them from Sodom and Gomorrah. The implication is that Israel is not being rejected like the others.[6]

Often overlooked by those who see 9: 25 ff. as a substantiation of the rejection of Israel is the fact that in 9: 30 ff. *Israēl* is still used *in bonam partem*. Israel was pursuing righteousness, but they did not attain what they sought (οὐκ ἔφθασεν). The reason was that they pursued it incorrectly and, accepting one presupposition, they stumbled when that was shown to be false.[7]

[1] See Müller, *Gerechtigkeit*, pp. 27 ff., esp. p. 32: 'Pls versteht also die gegenwärtige Situation Israels als Wirkung der Schöpfer*macht* und des Schöpferr*echts* Gottes an seinem Volk'; and all of ch. 5.

[2] *Ioudaios* only at 9: 24 and 10: 12 in chs. 9–11 (*passim* in 1–4); otherwise always *Israēl* in 9–11 (and never in 1–4). See von Rad/Kuhn/Gutbrod, *TWNT*, III, 356–94.

[3] See B. Lindars, *NT Apologetic*, pp. 242 f.; cf. Appendix B, below.

[4] F. F. Bruce, *TNTC* (1963), p. 196.

[5] *Contra* Lindars, *Apologetic*, pp. 242 f.; in both this and the next quotation God is showing mercy in not casting off all Israel; cf. F. Leenhardt, *Romans* (ET of *CNT*, London, 1961), pp. 260 f.

[6] Cf. C. H. Dodd, *MNTC*, p. 172.

[7] Müller, *Gerechtigkeit*, pp. 33 ff., demonstrates that 1 Pet. 2: 6–10 (see ch. 6, below) uses the idea of stumbling differently from Paul; the latter uses it soteriologically, the former ecclesiologically, and therefore 1 Pet. is forced into separating Israel and the Church more sharply than Paul.

Thus, while *Israël* had a zeal for God they were ignorant of the fact that Christ (God's righteousness) is the end of the Law.[1] Anyone, whether outside or under the Law, can inherit the benefits of Christ's work without coming under the requirements of the Law.

The new standing is accessible 'to everyone who believes' (10: 4; cf. 1: 16 where it stands over the whole letter), a notion which recurs throughout 9–11, especially at the conclusion to the first one and a half chapters in 10: 11–13.[2] In this first half, working from observations made during his preaching missions, Paul claims:

(1) his experience substantiates what he should already have known about God's action among men—God is totally free to call whom he likes;

(2) his experience reinforces the fact that never have all God's people responded wholeheartedly to his call—it has never been more than a portion of them;

(3) his practice is an expression of his concern that Jews be saved—he wants to make known to them that Jesus is God's righteousness;

(4) there is no longer any distinction between Jews and Gentiles in the people of God—the latter have been incorporated into the former.

With 10: 14 we move into a discussion of problems arising from these basic propositions.[3] Usually 10: 14–21 is taken to refer to complete Jewish failure to receive the gospel, but this can only be done by neglecting the conclusion of 10: 13 ('Everyone (Jew and Greek) who calls upon the name of the Lord...') and the logical connection of 10: 14 with that ('But how should men call upon him?'). The catena of quotations from Isaiah and Psalms and Deuteronomy stresses the need for a universally proclaimed gospel, because there is a universal possibility of acceptance and an equal status for all who do accept.[4] Preaching of the good news 'to all the earth...and to the ends of the

---

[1] On the logic see Leenhardt, *Romans*, pp. 265 f.

[2] In both this and the previous occurrence of *Ioudaios* Paul is recalling his formulation of chs. 1–4. Here it has a 'joyful sound' where earlier it had a 'grim sound' (Bruce, *TNTC*, p. 202).

[3] Cf. Sanday and Headlam, *ICC*, p. 294.

[4] See Munck, *Christus*, pp. 75 f., on the representative character of the reception.

world' (*v.* 18; Ps. 19: 5) is in accordance with God's purpose and fulfils the old expectation. Anyone within these bounds can hear and accept and come to trust in God. Tragically, however, not all believe. This is dealt with in two parts. In *v.* 20 Isaiah's 'bold' statement (Isaiah 65: 1) is confirmed by Paul's own experience: those who had no interest in God actually have found him (cf. 9: 30). Concerning Israel Paul finds (*v.* 21) that his experience substantiates what Isaiah maintained (Isaiah 65: 2): it is disobedient and not prepared to listen to God.[1] However, not only does God continue to hold out his hand but he is also gracious, as Paul discerns from Deuteronomy 32: 21 (Romans 10: 19), in that the very acceptance of the gospel by those 'not a people'[2] will provoke Israel to jealousy over the gospel.

There is no break in the argument when Paul inserts the rhetorical question that begins ch. 11.[3] The expletive μὴ γένοιτο is the natural outcome of the quotations and of the trend of the discussion.[4] It is fundamental to recognize that central to Paul's understanding of the then present position of the Jews is the fact that they have not been cast adrift. In what follows, God's mercy in not rejecting his people is dealt with in two ways.[5] There is, first, the remnant (λεῖμμα) which has already partici-

---

[1] This quotation from Isa. 65: 1–2 (LXX, with a reversal of the two main words and of the two clauses) originally applied to a single group. Paul, because of his own situation, and especially because of the use of *ethnē* in *v.* 1 and *laos* in *v.* 2, has driven apart the two verses so that the one applies to Gentiles and the other to Jews. This is an important (and neglected) aspect of Paul's use of the OT (see Appendix B).

[2] Note again *ethnos*.

[3] For the place of Paul himself in 11: 1 ff. see W. Vischer, 'Das Geheimnis Israels' (*Jud*, VI, 1950, 81–132), pp. 111 ff.

[4] F. Lovsky, *RHPR*, XLIII (1963), 32–47, says of 11: 1 ff.: 'C'est précisément parce que des chrétiens d'origine juive, peut-être, et des paganochrétiens, certainement, avaient élaboré une doctrine anti-juive du rejet avec des éléments puisés dans l'AT, que s. Paul a écrit son traité de mystère d'Israël...' (p. 41). This could well be true.

[5] Lindars, *Apologetic*, p. 241, claims that Paul 'transfers the distinction from believers and unbelievers within Judaism to the issue between Jews and Gentiles. The Jews are rejected totally, so that the remnant is the Gentiles.' This is not so. Note *kata tou Israēl* in 11: 2 and the mark of the similarity of situations in 11: 5 (οὕτως οὖν καὶ ἐν τῷ νῦν καιρῷ). The remnant is a Jewish remnant and, as Paul goes on to claim, the rest of Israel, far from being totally rejected, is only temporarily put to one side (11: 11 ff.).

pated in God's grace—it is 'chosen' (ἐκλογή, 11: 5, 7), and is a presently observable part of the people of God. There remains the wider-based Israel, which does not obtain what it looks for while the 'chosen' do. These (οἱ λοιποί) are hardened, but this is only a partial hardening, for the point of Israel's rejection of the gospel is that God's mercy might be shown to still more people.[1] The quotations in 11: 8–10 do not give the definitive word on the subject.[2] They are the OT background to the situation as it now exists before God again turns to his own people to save them. The character of chs. 9–11 is first practical (arising completely out of the missionary situation c. A.D. 45–55), and secondly hopeful. Israël carries a more restricted sense than the full number of all Jews; it is in this restricted sense that Paul speaks of salvation for 'all Israel' after their temporary hardening. That a number have already acknowledged Jesus as Lord augurs well, thinks Paul, for this hope. It is impossible to stress too much that over all of Romans 9–11 stands 9: 6b: 'not all descendants of Israel belong to Israel'.

Over Romans as a whole stands Paul's imaginative phrase: 'to everyone who believes, Jew first and also Greeks...the iustified by faith shall live' (Romans 1: 16–17). The priority of the Jew, to which Marcion objected,[3] is asserted at the very beginning of Romans, but is held in tension with the new universalism of the gospel. This temporal and historical priority[4] is seen not only in the election of Israel, in Jesus' own proclamation to his nation, in the injunction to the disciples, and in the original nucleus of Jewish Christians, but also in Paul's own practice of going always to the Jewish synagogue in each city he visited before taking up his responsibility to the Gentiles.[5]

---

[1] See B. W. Helfgott, *The Doctrine of Election in Tannaitic Literature* (New York, 1954), p. 4.

[2] Cf. Barrett, *BNTC*, p. 212; they 'led Paul a little astray from his point'.

[3] Marcion's omission of πρῶτον (with B G sa Ephr) is typical, see Lietzmann, *HNT*, p. 30; cf. Michaelis, *TWNT*, vi, 870.

[4] Cf. K. Barth, *Epistle to the Romans* (London, 1933), p. 40, on the distinction between precedence and priority. A. Nygren, *Commentary on Romans* (London, 1952), pp. 73 f., thinks πρῶτον and τε–καί seem to contradict each other. Michel, *KEK*, p. 53, refers to a 'heilsgeschichtliche Notwendigkeit'.　　　　　[5] Cf. Michel, *ibid.*

Paul first shows that the contrary of his thesis applies to both Gentiles and Jews:[1] Gentiles in 1: 18–31[2] and Jews in 1: 32 — 2: 5 (4?).[3] The most important feature in this opening accusation is the breaking down of the Jews' security. By stressing that they do the same things (1: 32; 2: 1; 2: 3), thus bringing judgment on themselves (2: 1) that demands repentance (2: 4), Paul effectively undercuts pride of position. This first skirmish with Judaism, concentrating as it does upon the similarity of all creation's culpability, shades off into a general summary of opposition to God (2: 5) which in the 'day of wrath' will be judged and rewarded. To the good will be given life, to the disobedient wrath (2: 7–8); in either case the judgment is for the Jew first and for the Greek, 'for with God there is no distinction of persons' (2: 11).

To Paul this is an absolutely vital point in his case[4] (a case which is completed only at Romans 11: 32). The next step is to set aside the obvious objection to his assertion of 'no distinctions'. This is done by demonstrating the differing ground of judgment for those who have a superior revelation and those who are lacking it (2: 11–16).[5] Once more the basis of Jewish security is whittled away, this time by heightening the demands.

---

[1] Note the repetition of ἀποκαλύπτεται in 1: 17, 18 with the contrast between δικαιοσύνη and ὀργή; see Michel, *KEK*, pp. 60 f.; Bornkamm, 'Die Offenbarung des Zornes Gottes: Röm. 1–3' in *Das Ende des Gesetzes* (*BEvTh*, xvi, München, 1952), pp. 9–33; and A. Schlatter, *Die Theologie der Apostel* (Stuttgart, 1922), pp. 263 f., 279 ff.

[2] It may be that 1: 32 belongs to 1: 18 ff. as a conclusion (so all comm.), but Flückiger's arguments (*TZ*, x, 1954, 154–8) are cogent, in spite of the difficulty with οἵτινες and the lack of an adversative. Certainly it fits well with the following διό, and is precisely parallel to 2: 3 f. It is just the δικαίωμα which the Gentiles do not know (though they may be able to keep some of the δικαιώματα, 2: 14; so Schrenk, *TDNT*, iii, 221).

[3] Lietzmann, *HNT*, pp. 37 ff.; H. Schlier, 'Von den Juden: Röm 2.1–29' in *Die Zeit der Kirche* (Freiburg, 1956), pp. 38–47; G. Bornkamm, *BEvTh*, xvi, 26 f.

[4] Michel, *KEK*, p. 73: 'Wichtiger als die Polemik ist aber, daß Paulus in unserem Abschnitt die Gleichheit der menschlichen Situation vor dem Gericht Gottes verkündigt.'

[5] M. Barth, *SJT*, viii (1955), 288–96, holds that all of 1: 18 – 2: 16 is quite general with no reference to either Jews or Gentiles; this does not accord with 2: 9–11.

From 2: 17 attention focuses upon the Jew.[1] On the basis of his consideration of the Jews' obedience to God with their fuller knowledge, Paul makes the devastating accusation that 'because of you, God's name is blasphemed among the Gentiles' (2: 24, quoting Isaiah 52: 5).[2] All the things which set the Jew apart (2: 17–23) become a judgment to him and a cause of offence to others when misused. A *mehr lehrhaftthetisch* part of the argument begins in 2: 25,[3] building upon the concern for Gentiles expressed in 2: 24. The final proposition (2: 28 f.) takes into account both groups though it is framed entirely in terms of Judaism, just as the argument which leads up to it is predicated upon purely Jewish factors.[4] The point is that transgression of the law (obedience to which is necessary for circumcision's validity)[5] converts circumcision into uncircumcision. The converse Paul holds to be true also, that uncircumcision can be reckoned as circumcision on the grounds of obedience to the precepts of the Law.[6] The outward rite of circumcision is not significant, only one's relationship to the Law of God matters. What circumcision is thought to produce is actually available to the man who is not circumcised. Given this, Paul's conclusion follows logically (2: 28 f.): οὐ γὰρ ὁ ἐν τῷ φανερῷ 'Ιουδαῖός ἐστιν, οὐδὲ ἡ ἐν τῷ φανερῷ ἐν σαρκὶ περιτομή· ἀλλ' ὁ ἐν τῷ κρυπτῷ 'Ιουδαῖος, καὶ περιτομὴ καρδίας ἐν πνεύματι οὐ γράμματι. As with Philippians 3: 3 the application of the term *peritomē* to the Christian is a matter of function. There, the man who worships genuinely is reckoned circumcised; here, the one whose heart shows God's imprint *en pneumati* (cf. Philippians

[1] *Ioudaios* is restricted to chs. 1–3 (except for 9: 25 and 10: 12 in formulae borrowed from chs. 1–3), contrasted generally to *Hellēn* (which appears also at 10: 12). The restriction in terminology, with the exclusive use of *Israēl* in chs. 9–11, is a mark of the different levels of discussion in the two sections.

[2] B. Lindars, *NT Apologetic*, p. 22, deals with the shift in context.

[3] Michel, *KEK*, pp. 85 f.

[4] For the section as polemic, see Michel, *KEK*, pp. 90–3.

[5] See StrBill, IV, 1, 3 Exk. 'Das Beschneidungsgebot', sections 4 and 5 (pp. 31–40); S. B. Hoenig, 'Circumcision: the Covenant of Abraham', *JQR*, LIII (1962–3), 322–34.

[6] There may be a subtle distinction between the verbs γέγονεν and λογισθήσεται. For the latter, an important word in Paul's argumentation (Heidland, *TWNT*, IV, 287 f., neglects this instance), Rom. 9: 8 is a close parallel. See StrBill, III, 119 ff.; rabbinic Judaism would have rejected the logic of Paul's argument; so also Meyer, *TWNT*, VI, 82.

3: 3) *ou grammati* (cf. 2 Corinthians 3: 3, 6) is, by implication, circumcised, and therefore an inward Jew.[1] In each of the four clauses there is ellipsis: the reader must supply for the second half of each '(true) circumcision' and for the first half '(true) Jew', which, if an allowable term, must be equivalent to *Israēlitēs*, as in Romans 11: 1.[2] Instead of transposing the term 'circumcision' to Gentiles, Romans 2: 28 f. limits the advantages of circumcision, first by showing the need to keep the Law, then the effect of not keeping the Law, then the opening up of circumcision to those uncircumcised. The end result of this dual movement of closing down and opening up the category 'Israelite', under the guise of the term 'circumcision', is that the single criterion of belonging to God's people is now the receptivity of one's heart to the work of the Spirit.[3]

Paul determines once again to broach the question of the value of circumcision (3: 1),[4] recognizing as he does so that the unbelief of circumcised people is more of a problem than he has admitted in his polemical propositions at the end of ch. 2. He refuses to allow the logical inference from their unbelief that God's faithfulness has been frustrated; he rejects this with the same horror that he rejects similar questions in chs. 9–11 (3: 3, 5). Without having answered the question he repeats its substance and gives a cryptic answer (οὐ πάντως)[5] whose intention, compared with 3: 2 (πολὺ κατὰ πάντα τρόπον) seems to be: there is a great advantage but it is not an absolute

---

[1] All the parallels StrBill cite (III, 124 ff.) are late.

[2] So Lietzmann, *HNT*, p. 45, with a reference to John 1: 47. Cf Michel, *KEK*, p. 92: 'Für Pls ist der Begriff "Jude" eine theologische, nicht nur eine heilsgeschichtliche Größe.'

[3] The OT background is in Lev. 26: 41; Deut. 10: 16; 30: 6; Jer. 4: 4; 9: 25; Ezek. 44: 7, 9; also note Philo and Rabbinic literature cited in StrBill *in loc.*; and see also 1QS 5: 5; 1QH 11: 5. Jer. 9: 25 provides a stage on the way to the full universalizing of the idea; for not only are all the nations who are circumcised reckoned to be uncircumcised (including Judah!) but the whole house of Israel is uncircumcised in heart. Here Israel has become like the nations precisely in their failure to be receptive. Circumcision unratified by purity is worthless.

[4] On the structure, J. Jeremias, *de Zwaan Festschrift*, pp. 146 ff.; Michel, *KEK*, pp. 94 f.

[5] Cf. Moulton/Turner, p. 287; Moule, *Idiom*, p. 168; Bl–D/Funk, 433.2. In such a case the context will have to be decisive. Everything about the verse is in dispute: intention, text, voice, punctuation, translation. Bauer/ A–G gives a good summary, *s.v.* προέχω.

advantage.[1] This modification of the unrestricted claim at 3: 2 is followed by the very thing which makes the modification necessary: Jews and Greeks both are under the dominion of sin. This introduces a catena of double-edged quotations from the oracles of God (3: 2), directed towards the universality of man's condition, and also to the relative advantage of the Jew. They (οἱ ἐν τῷ νόμῳ, 3: 19) know what God desires and by that knowledge are convicted of sin (3: 20).[2]

The ground is well prepared for Paul's positive statement on justification by faith 'outside the law...to everyone who believes; for there is no distinction'.[3] Without detracting from the importance and creativity of this section, it must be noted that it is no more than a piece in the main puzzle with which Paul is struggling. It establishes the crucial points: (1) with respect to righteousness—it is the righteousness of God through faith in Jesus (3: 22); (2) with respect to men—they are made righteous freely by God's grace through the redemption which is in Christ Jesus (3: 24); and (3) with respect to time—it is happening now (3: 26; cf. 11: 5).[4] The primary purpose is to eliminate all ground for Jewish boasting (3: 27) by showing that the Jew's need is as great as the Gentile's. We have returned to the problem of the Jew and his similarity to the Gentile (3: 27–31).[5] Faith is essential if God is to justify either a man of the circumcision or of the uncircumcision.[6] The train of

---

[1] So also Michel, *KEK*, pp. 98 f.; Lietzmann, *HNT*, p. 47; C. H. Dodd, *MNTC, in loc.*, with reservations. Both C. K. Barrett, *BNTC*, pp. 66–9, and F. F. Bruce, *TNTC*, p. 97, accept the 'advantage' of 3: 1 as a presupposition of 3: 9, and have the latter deal with 'superiority' to the Gentiles, with the answer 'certainly not'.

[2] T. W. Manson, *On Paul and John*, p. 43: '...his special treatment by God merely aggravated his case'.

[3] The temporal advantage of the Jew is slipped in even here: 'though the Law and the prophets bear witness to it'; cf. Michel, *KEK*, p. 105 n. 1.

[4] See Leenhardt, *Romans*, pp. 98 f. Müller, *Gerechtigkeit*, pp. 110 ff., interprets this against the background of Jewish Christianity's insistence on an incorrect priority.

[5] It must be phrased this way, and not inverted (cf. 1: 18–2: 4).

[6] StrBill, iii, 185, sums up the synagogue's attitude: 'Gott ist der Gott aller Menschen, insofern er sie geschaffen hat und insofern sie vor seinem Richterstuhl stehen werden; Gott aber ist Israels Gott, insofern nur dieses Volk das Volk ist, das von Gott geliebt wird, und für die Seligkeit bestimmt ist.' G. Klein, *EvTh*, xxiii (1963), 424–47, on 3: 28 says: *anthrōpos* marks 'die theologische Indifferenzierung von Juden und Heiden zum ersten

thought began from the problem of Jewish privilege (3: 1, 9, 27) and some modification has been necessary as Paul has proceeded. Though asserting the absolute equality of Jew and Gentile with regard to the means of salvation in the present time, Paul retains the original tension arising from the historical advantage of the Jew (3: 2, 19 f., 31) by claiming in conclusion that law,[1] far from being useless (3: 3, 20, 31; contrast 7: 6) still remains effective.[2]

The account of Abraham and the reason for his importance to 'us' (cf. 4: 32 f.)[3] may have existed as an independent piece of exegesis. It is fastened on at 3: 21–31 because it illustrates the point of that section and shows how the Law has validity.[4] In this partially polemical chapter there is a recurrence of Paul's curtailment of the Jewish basis for security and self-sufficiency, his demonstration of the new universalism based here on an old act of God, and the specifically Christian application of all this. To this end he constructs a rabbinic *midrash* (*gezera shawa*) on the account of Abraham in Genesis 15: 6.[5] Romans 4: 1–8 posits that Abraham's justification is on the basis of faith; 4: 9–12 that his justification was without circumcision; 4: 13–17 that his justification was without the Law; and 4: 18–25 explains the consequences of believing in the history of Abraham. In *v.* 9 Paul picks up again the question of circumcision and uncircumcision,[6]

Mal in Röm'. In *vv.* 29 f. Jew and Gentile are particularizations of the category *anthrōpos*. These verses are an 'Entsakralisierung und Profanisierung' of Judaism (p. 428).

[1] Without the article. The exact sense of *nomos* is unsure here. Barrett widens it, Lietzmann narrows it to the OT.

[2] Michel, *KEK*, p. 112 (and n. 3) recalls Matt. 5: 17, and claims that Paul is nearer the Aramaic underlying that passage than Matt. He cites approvingly Schlatter's reference to common Rabbinic formulae.

[3] This is not yet a take-over of the OT scriptures for Christian use alone, though it is a step in this direction. See also Rom. 15: 4 and 2 Cor. 3: 15.

[4] So Jeremias, *de Zwaan Festschrift*, p. 150. See also Michel, *KEK*, p. 114; Lindars, *NT Apologetic*, p. 227; *per contra*, Barrett, *in loc.*

[5] Jeremias, *de Zwaan Festschrift*, pp. 149 ff. This device allows him to move on to Ps. 32: 1 f., where the same word (λογίζεσθαι) is used (Barrett, *From First Adam to Last*, pp. 32 f.), and so to demonstrate that the forgiveness of sins took place while Abraham was uncircumcised. Schweitzer, *Mysticism*, p. 208, refers to Gen. 15: 6 (and Hab. 2: 4) as 'Paul's brilliant discovery'.

[6] Lindar's observation that the question of time of Abraham's circumcision is not mentioned in Galatians, where circumcision is the chief problem, is tantalizing (*NT Apologetic*, pp. 228, 239).

and concludes that circumcision is a sign (σημεῖον), a seal (σφραγῖδα) of the righteousness which Abraham had in faith while still uncircumcised (*v.* 11). There is therefore a *dual* paternity latent in Abraham's case:[1] he is both father of all who believe while uncircumcised so that righteousness might be reckoned (λογισθῆναι) to them, and father of those of faith from the circumcision who walk in the steps of Abraham while he was uncircumcised (*v.* 12).[2] There is in Abraham's fatherhood a ramification which can only be seen later: his justification by faith before his circumcision when coupled with his later circumcision makes him uniquely a father of both circumcision and uncircumcision. Abraham—the only person who can tie together both uncircumcision and circumcision—is the natural focus of Paul's argument. By interpreting the Abraham account in such a way that his fatherhood of uncircumcised people has a temporal priority over his fatherhood of circumcised people, has Paul provided a basis for his theory that Gentiles must first be saved before the full number of Jews comes in? There seems to be no direct connection between this exegesis and the theory in Romans 11, but it may be a subconscious part of the background.

When Paul says in *v.* 16 that Abraham is the father of us all (cf. 4: 1), he is reiterating the equivalence of opportunity and of sonship. When he cites Genesis 17: 5 ('I have made you a father of many nations') he chooses a text which uses the general word *ethnē* to be consonant with this universality. In what follows, he forgoes the elaborate exegesis in Galatians about 'seed/seeds', although the results of that exegesis are presupposed in his conclusion to the chapter: 'righteousness will

---

[1] Just as there was a dual possibility of sonship with respect to the covenants in the treatment of Abraham in Gal., see above. E. Jacob, *RHPR*, XLII (1962), 148–56, rightly puts Abraham's function as father at the very centre. See also K. Berger, 'Abraham in den paulinischen Hauptbriefen', *MTZ*, XVII (1966), 47–89.

[2] L. Cerfaux, 'Abraham "père en circoncision" des gentils', *Recueil Lucien Cerfaux*, II (Gembloux, 1954), 333–8, thinks Paul is making Jewish Christians twice children of Abraham—by circumcision and justification—and suggests *peritomēs* is a genitive of relation = 'père en circoncision'. This misses the point of Paul's argument. Cerfaux stresses Abraham's fatherhood of Gentiles at the expense of Jews. For the problem of one or two groups in the latter half, see Michel, *KEK*, p. 120 n. 2; cf. Müller, *Gerechtigkeit*, p. 52 n. 20.

be reckoned to us who believe on the one who raised our Lord
Jesus from the dead'. The last three verses, with the emphasis
on 'us' and 'our', are an application from the conclusion in
v. 22 ('it was reckoned to him as righteousness') of a very
involved piece of exegesis.[1]

It is on the theme of Abraham that Paul reopens his discussion in ch. 9.[2] He considers his important conclusion from
the treatment in ch. 4 to be the negative, that not all Abraham's
children are reckoned as seed, but only those who are the fulfilment of the promise (9: 7–9; 4: 12, 14, 16). Where ch. 4 dealt
with the results of the case of Abraham for Jews and Gentiles,
ch. 9 handles the application of the principle of restriction of
Abraham's 'true' children. That is, *epangelia* is used differently
in the two chapters: in the one case it refers to the eschatological
promise, capable of fulfilment only in Jesus, to all nations; in
the other case to the immediate promise about Abraham's
children and the way it worked out historically. The two
strands are drawn together in the conclusion of this line of
thought in 9: 24 and in 10: 11 ff. It is as if there were an
objection to Paul's exegesis of Abraham's case: namely, that the
promise was actually fulfilled in Abraham's own children *kata
sarka*. Paul's answer to the objection is that not all Abraham's
children are really seed, nor is all Israel really Israel.

The chapters which fall in between (5–8) are marked by the
absence of ideas which apply to one group or the other. It is
almost all 'we' from 5: 1 on, with no special application to Jew
or Gentile. The general features of Christian experience appear
from the way (5: 12 ff.) Paul goes back past Abraham, the
latest point at which he can assert a close interrelationship
between Jews and Gentiles, to Adam the universal prototype.
Even a mention of Moses (5: 14) does not deflect him into a
discussion of particulars. When Law is introduced in 5: 20, it
is subordinate to the main concern; even 6: 14 is merely the
recital of a formula, not an integral part of a discussion of those

[1] Cf. Michel, *KEK*, p. 115: 'er erklärt, deutet, paraphrasiert den
Glaubensbegriff und stellt die typologische Beziehung zwischen AT und
urchristlichem Bekenntnis her'; cf. pp. 127 f.

[2] Chs. 2–4 are the theoretical basis of chs. 9–11 (a summary of historical
realities and present problems). One is inductive, the other deductive.
Chs. 9–11 must be read in the light of chs. 2–4 to understand the grounds
for Paul's opinion about what God is doing in his work.

who are under the Law. When he speaks (7: 1 ff.) 'to those who understand law',[1] attention is directed to the contrast between the old and new life (ἐν καινότητι πνεύματος καὶ οὐ παλαιότητι γράμματος, 7: 6; cf. 2: 29; 2 Cor. 3: 6) and the great gulf fixed between them (οὐδὲν ἄρα νῦν κατάκριμα τοῖς ἐν Χριστῷ ’Ιησοῦ, 8: 1). Chapter 8 develops more extensively the benefits of the man who is in Christ; e.g. he has received the Spirit as first-fruit (ἀπαρχήν) and waits for the redemption of the body that comes with the adoption as son (8: 23).[2] These four chapters are rich in christology and anthropology, and must be at the heart of any treatment of the Christian life, but they have little to say to the Church/Israel problem.

The same is true of the paraenetic chapters (12 ff.). It is possible that the reference to 'parts' in 12: 3 ff. builds upon the letter's treatment of Jews and Gentiles, but this is not made clear. It is just as likely that a multiplicity of individuals is in mind. The priestly imagery of 12: 1–2 is applied to Christians as individuals ('your bodies') and not to the Church as the 'body of Christ'. However, that there is a division of some kind within the Church in Rome is clear from passages that refer to Jewish Christian difficulties, especially in 14: 1–15: 6 (ὁ ἀσθενῶν is opposed to ὁ δυνατός, 15: 1).[3] These two groups who accuse one another (14: 3) are the same as those who should welcome one another (15: 7 ff.).[4] An important shift has taken

---

[1] This phrase need not refer to some Jewish group, or even to Judaism generally, though there may be an underlying polemical reference which does not come to the surface.

[2] Omit υἱοθεσίαν 𝔓46vid D G it Ambst; note the use of this and ἀπαρχήν in 9–11 with reference to Israel, as well as the use of the terminology of 8: 28 ff.

[3] Barrett, *BNTC*, p. 256, refers to 11: 13–24; 12: 3, 16 f.; and all of 14: 1–15: 13 as applying to Gentile Christian disparagement of the Jewish brethren. Michel is not so clear: he applies 'strong' to Pneumatics; 'weak' is a critical term used by them of the other groups, but he is reluctant to equate them with Jews or Gentiles until after 15: 8 (p. 358, cf. pp. 288 ff., 333 f.); cf. Lietzmann, *HNT*, pp. 118 f. Rom. 16: 17–20 cannot apply to the same group (cf. Schmithals, 'Die Irrlehrer von Röm. 16: 17–20', *NT*, XIII, 1959, 51–69). This is a different situation, and argues strongly for an Ephesian address for ch. 16.

[4] Because of the movement of thought this is more likely than an analogical relationship: divisions, 14: 1–15: 6; christological explanation of Gentile/Jew problem, 15: 7–13; return to Roman divisions, 15: 14 ff.; return to Gentile problem, 15: 16 ff. If the example were not applicable Paul would hardly have returned to the Roman problem.

place in the early Church: Jewish Christians are no longer pillars in the community, they are 'weak'.[1] This may be explained partly by Gentile numerical superiority and by their readiness to leave behind, in a way impossible for most Jews, things indifferent in Judaism. However, an admission of the 'weakness' of Jewish Christians does not suggest to Paul a revision of his estimate of the relationship of Jew and Gentile; he repeats his view (Rom. 11: 28 ff.) that historically the gospel came to the Jews, for Christ became a servant of circumcision (15: 8) in order that God might confirm his promises to the Patriarchs. Gentiles share this only through the great mercy of God (15: 9). The *haraz* which follows is strung on the key-word *ethnē*.[2] It is remarkable, and consistent with the whole tenor of Romans, that *laos* should be included in two quotations and presumed in one. In these cases *laos* retains its reference to the Jewish people, with whom the Gentiles shall rejoice.[3] It is not applied only to Gentiles, or even to the whole Church; there remains the same tension between the assertion of no distinctions and the acknowledgment of the different origins of the two constituent groups. Part of the purpose of these quotations, as with the olive tree metaphor in chapter 11, is to eliminate Gentile domination over Jewish Christians (cf. chapters 12 and 14).

The liturgical language, noted in 12: 1–2, reappears in 15: 15 ff. with reference to Paul's priestly service to the Gentiles.[4] In the exposition of this, Munck's conjecture about the secondary purpose of the collection for Jerusalem must carry some weight.[5] He holds that Paul anticipates a rather extensive Jewish acceptance of the gospel in Jerusalem, on the basis of

[1] See Michel, *KEK*, p. 358; cf. L. Goppelt, *Jesus*, pp. 127 ff.
[2] Cf. Ellis, *Paul*, p. 50; see Appendix B, below.
[3] Deut. 32: 43; Ps. 116: 1; Isa. 11: 10. Perhaps the introductory one (2 Sam. 22: 50 = Ps. 17: 50) means literally 'among the nations' to Paul. Barrett sees, rightly, that '7–13 are a summary which looks back to chs. 9–11 as well as to ch. 14' (*BNTC*, p. 273).
[4] λειτουργόν, ἱερουργοῦντα. See Munck, *Paul*, pp. 47 ff.: he takes the 'offering' to be a still future event, identical with the fullness of the Gentiles of 11: 25, and with 15: 18. Cf. Nickle, *Collection*, pp. 129 ff.
[5] *Paul*, ch. 10. We would reject his insistence on a Gentile address for Romans, and also his view of the eschatological nature of Paul's preaching (particularly with respect to 2 Thess. 2). Cf. J. Knox, *JBL*, LXXXIII (1964), 1–11.

the demonstration, by both the collection itself and the Gentiles who bring it with Paul, of a general Gentile acceptance of the same gospel. This fits in admirably with Paul's theory of the relationship between Israel and the Gentiles in Romans (cf. 15: 27).[1] In general terms, when Paul thinks of himself as a priest offering up the Gentiles, the purpose behind this is nothing else than the ultimate conversion of Israel. The representative selection of Gentiles taken with him to Jerusalem is a 'try-out' of the theory espoused in Romans 11: 25 ff.,[2] not necessarily assumed to have extensive eschatological ramifications, but just another facet of Paul's missionary enterprise. The main feature of this task expressed in Romans 15, however, remains the completion of the day-to-day task of preaching to the Gentiles.

To sum up: Paul begins with a phrase which becomes the touchstone of much of the letter: 'the Jew first and also the Greek'. The assumption of Jewish priority is held in tension with the other assumption of the phrase—universality. Jesus Christ renders soteriological distinctions invalid.[3] But a difficulty is posed by the fact that there is a distinction; Gentiles are more ready to turn to God through Jesus than are Jews. Thus there is a contradiction between the theoretical priority and the actual missionary situation. It is this that Paul sets out to resolve. We have discussed what we take to be his well-considered answer, and have suggested some reasons for his arriving at the shift in the actual priority of missionary response. In this, Paul takes Jesus' position on the question (mission to Jews and, through that, mission to the Gentiles) and pushes it as far as possible within the altered context of his own situation, so that it becomes: attempted mission to Jews, rejection, mission to Gentiles, rebound reaction by Jews leading to their acceptance. In this radical rethinking of missionary cause and effect Paul does not take the term *Israël* and fill it with a solely Christian content. There is yet hope for that portion of his

[1] As we saw Paul expects 'Israel' to be saved in the near future. He sees his success in the Gentile mission as leading to Jews' salvation.

[2] Munck, *Paul*, p. 304.

[3] We have noted at a few points a preference for 'soteriological' emphasis rather than 'ecclesiological'. For Paul the newness of Christianity is found primarily in its new soteriology rather than in its new ecclesiological arrangements. Later the emphasis becomes reversed.

people who love God and seek to do his will. These will follow in the footsteps of those (a remnant) who have already placed their trust in Jesus. By distinguishing between 'Judaism' and 'Israel', and by associating with Judaism the transient characteristics,[1] Paul resolves his dilemma.[2] 'Israel' is not applied to the Christian Church,[3] though all Christians become a part of Israel by virtue of their faith in Christ. In the same way 'circumcision' and 'seed' are not transposed to the Church although, again, Gentile Christians participate in them and can be reckoned as if they had them.

COLOSSIANS AND EPHESIANS: THE RELAXATION
OF HOPE

In this chapter we shall concentrate on the problem posed by Ephesians, especially by Ephesians 2: 11 ff., and refer to Colossians' parallels or differences only incidentally. The question of greatest interest is whether Ephesians 2: 11–22 represents a live or a dead situation. A common approach is to relate non-Pauline authorship of Ephesians to a totally Gentile address, and claim that the relationship of Jew and Gentile is a dead issue.[4] Even the hypothesis of Pauline authorship stumbles over alleged assumptions of the author in chapters 1–2 *vis-à-vis* a Gentile audience.[5] Both solutions have trouble with the relation between Jews and Christians which the letter suggests. The conundrum is exaggerated by Ephesians 2: 11–22 itself,

---

[1] Namely, circumcision, Law; seed is applied to either (in a different sense); note how σώзω/σωτηρία is applied only to 'Israel'.

[2] He has at the same time opened the way for the transposition of the name 'Israel' to Christianity. Because 'Israel' in 9–11 is given this hopeful character, separated from the abandoned features of Judaism, later writers could, with little difficulty, take it over completely, without considering the argument of chs. 9–11.

[3] See B. Reicke, *Jud*, XIV (1958), 106–14: 'Wenn wir Christen auf diese Weise aufhören die Kirche Jesu Christi als das wahre Israel zu betrachten, von dem die Propheten sprechen, dann haben wir unsere Gemeinschaft mit dem NT und mit der apostolischen Verkündigung in einem wichtigen Punkte abgebrochen' (p. 109).

[4] Failure to explain the purpose of this theory finally tips the scales for E. Percy in favour of Eph.'s genuineness (*Die Probleme der Kolosser- und Epheserbriefe* (Lund, 1946), p. 448).

[5] See H. Chadwick, 'Die Absicht des Eph.', *ZNW*, LI (1960), 145–53.

where there seems to be a conflict, with respect to the Church and Israel, between the theology of 2: 11–14, 16–22 (participation) and 2: 15 (*tertium genus*). The internal difficulties correspond to an external one—the relationship of Ephesians to Romans; for in the former there is nothing of the same hope for Israel's return as expressed in the latter, and we must ask whether this hope died, or was fulfilled already,[1] or was transformed thoroughly.[2]

The 1st person plural and 2nd person plural are unusually mixed in parts of Ephesians, especially in the first two chapters.[3] In 1: 1–10 the 1st person plural refers generally to the benefits accruing to all through Jesus Christ. It is quite natural in a blessing (*eulogētos* period) directed to God. Between 1: 11 and 2: 22 the alternation is more marked, and this corresponds to a marked degree with a discussion of the relationship of Jew and Gentile in the Church, a fact which has led some commentators to conclude that the use of personal pronouns might clarify the train of thought. The problem begins with the parallelism between 'in whom also we' (*v.* 11) and 'in whom also you' (*v.* 13).[4] If the 1st person plural, as before, carries a general significance based on Christian experience (for a sharp break at *v.* 10*b* is very artificial)[5] then the point lies in the application

---

[1] See P. Benoit, *Analecta Biblica*, XVII–XVIII, II (Rome, 1963), 57–77. He takes Eph. to be a synthesis between Col. and Rom., resolving the problem of Rom. 9–11 within a cosmic horizon. Cf. his essay in *Neutestamentliche Aufsätze. Festschrift für J. Schmid* (Regensburg, 1963), pp. 11–22.

[2] H. Chadwick says that in Rom. 9–11 'Paul sees Gentile Christianity as a parenthetic protestant movement to recall catholic Judaism to its true vocation...The limited vision of Rom 9–11...has become replaced by an altogether wider and more confident idea of a permanent world-wide Church, universal in its range.' ('Ephesians', in *Peake's Commentary*, para. 856*c*.)

[3] In ch. 3 the 2nd person plural is natural: the 1st person plural in *v.* 11 is a formula and in *v.* 12 a general and emphatic 'we all'. In the paraenetic section (chs. 4–6) the 2nd person plural again naturally dominates; the 1st person plural is always explainable.

[4] As often in the cases that follow, there are textual variants.

[5] It is incorrect to imagine that the 1st person plural of 1: 1–10 is predicated upon Jewish Christian privilege; *contra* D. W. B. Robinson, 'Who were the Saints?', *RefThR*, XXII (1963), 45–53, see p. 51. υἱοθεσία (*v.* 5) need not apply to Jewish privilege. Nor do *vv.* 10*b*–12 refer to Jewish Christians; προηλπικότας can have a temporal meaning, without denoting a special group: cf. Bultmann, *TDNT*, II, 534 f.

of these general 'we' statements to 'you' (*v.* 13) who have believed in a particular place. The shift from 1st person plural to 2nd person plural is occasioned by recollection of the Church's reception of the gospel[1] and not by a contrast between 'we' Jewish Christians and 'you' Gentile Christians.[2] Whatever the Church's composition, 'you' refers to the total Church, and *v.* 14, which returns again to the 1st person plural, concludes the whole hymn of praise with a general reference to the inheritance of all Christians, with no break from the 2nd person plural of *v.* 13.[3]

Thanksgiving for their acceptance of Jesus as Lord is clearly the reason for the shift to the 2nd person plural in *vv.* 15 ff. The natural 'you' in the thanksgiving proper is interrupted by the 1st person plural only at *v.* 17 (a near formula) and *v.* 19 (a necessary generalization to include all believers).[4]

As with 1: 10*b*–14, there is a general agreement among commentators that in 2: 1 the 2nd person plural refers to Gentiles, in 2: 3 the 1st person plural refers to Jews, and in 2: 5 the 1st person plural refers to both together.[5] Difficulties for this view are: (1) the absence of any expansion of the 1st person plural between *vv.* 3 and 5; (2) the presence of πάντες in *v.* 3 and its absence in *v.* 5; (3) the shift back to the 2nd person plural in *v.* 5 and *v.* 8. In *vv.* 5, 8 one would expect an inclusive 'we'

---

[1] It is usual in the thanksgiving to recall the reception by the church addressed; cf. esp. Thessalonians and Col. 1: 3–8. See R. A. Wilson, *Studia Evangelica*, II (*TU*, LXXXVII, Berlin, 1964), 676–80; cf. N. A. Dahl, *TZ*, VII (1951), 241–64.

[2] *Per contra* Abbott, *ICC* (1897), p. 21; Scott, *MNTC* (1930), p. 147; J. A. Robinson, *McM* (2nd edition, 1904), pp. 145 f.; H. Schlier, *Der Brief an die Eph* (Düsseldorf, 1957), pp. 66 ff.; Dibelius–Greeven, *HNT* (3rd edition, 1953), pp. 61 f.; Ellicott, *Eph*, pp. 16 f., hesitantly. Taking our view is Masson, *CNT* (1953), p. 146 n. 3 and 147, with Chadwick, *Peake's Commentary*, para. 859*a* hesitantly.

[3] There is a similar shift in Col. 1: 13 f. in somewhat the same context.

[4] This is more probable than that κληρονομία and ἄγιος (*v.* 18) and 'we' refer to Jewish Christians; *contra* Robinson, *RefThR*, XXII (1963), 45–63.

[5] As above; to the contrary only Ellicott and Masson, again. Note a similar, though not so difficult, shift in Col. 2: 13 f. Goodspeed has an imaginative solution (*The Meaning of Ephesians*, Chicago, 1933, p. 32) predicated upon a Gentile author assuming a Jewish mask which slips occasionally.

of general Christian experience.[1] When it is seen that 2: 1 is picking up, after the paean of praise at the end of chapter 1, the reference to the situation addressed, the 2nd person plural becomes a reference to the readers and the 1st person plural to all Christians.[2] There is no contrast between Jewish and Gentile Christians, for the statement in 2: 11 has not been made yet, but rather an application to a particular instance from general experience.[3] If this be correct, the 2nd person plural of *vv.* 5, 8 ('by grace you are saved') is an interjection with significance in the situation addressed,[4] and does not imply that only Gentiles need to be saved by grace! It sounds like a rejection of the tendency to claim that 'we have pulled ourselves up by our own boot-straps'.[5] Boasting is excluded (to use the language of Romans 3: 27),[6] by the fact that we are created by God in Christ Jesus. Is it just possible that there is a veiled refutation of the insinuation that the circumcised (perhaps particularly proselyte Christians) have a ground for boasting that others do not?[7] This would satisfy the probable Gentile background of 2: 2 and retain the particularist 'you' references, together with the general 'we' statements (*v.* 10).

Moreover, as one moves into 2: 11 ff., attention focuses immediately upon that ancient ground of privilege, circumcision.[8] The paragraph introduces for the first time a specifica-

---

[1] As, e.g., in 4: 7 ff.; 3: 11 f., 20. The tension between 'you' and 'we' is felt in *vv.* 7–8, but is noticeable also in *v.* 5, and between *vv.* 8 and 10. There is no evidence that then (as now) 'by grace you have been saved' was a formula into which the author naturally falls (cf. Acts 15: 11—'we').

[2] So Masson, *CNT*, pp. 157 f. especially p. 158 n. 7; 159 n. 6. He cites Oltramare, Haupt and Schlatter in his support.

[3] Accounting for πάντες in *v.* 3 and not in *v.* 5.

[4] This is an example of 'submerged polemic' (Chadwick's phrase, *Peake's Com.*, para. 858c); the parallel passage in Col. 2: 13 has a more natural use of 1st and 2nd persons plural; cf. Masson, *CNT*, p. 162, for the relationship.

[5] Hence the emphatic position of χάριτι. Commentators usually allow the neat distinction between 'you' and 'we' to fall into disuse in this section.

[6] Cf. also Phil. 3: 3 f.; 1 Cor. 1: 25 ff.; Gal. 6: 13 f.; see Bultmann, *TWNT*, III, 648–53.

[7] Schlier, *Eph.* p. 115, also relates *v.* 8 to judaizers.

[8] Cf. the parallel in Col 2: 11 ff. which seems to imply heretical teaching in Colossae (cf. Masson, *CNT Col*, 1950, pp. 125 f. and n. 4; and for the difficult conjunction of phrases, C. F. D. Moule, *CGTC*, 1957, pp. 94 ff.). Col. represents a stage in the taking over and 'spiritualizing' of circumcision.

tion of the addressees—ὑμεῖς τὰ ἔθνη ἐν σαρκί. This could either clarify all the previous references to the 2nd person plural[1] or, by virtue of its precision, be addressed to a portion within the Church.[2] The broader question concerns the relationship between Jews and Gentiles in the Church:[3] is the letter predicated upon Gentile supremacy and is the situation therefore a dead one, or does it reflect a living problem in the Church addressed? In 2: 11 ff. there are two instances of a 1st person plural, and in both cases (vv. 14, 18) it is equivalent to 'both', so that 'we' is not associated with Jewish Christian privilege, but with the submerging of any privilege in the unity.

The paragraph appears to protest too much if it is not written to discuss a living issue. There is a hint of tension between 'those called uncircumcision' and 'what is called the circumcision (made by hands in flesh)'.[4] Part of the object of this section is to eliminate grounds for Gentile boasting (cf. v. 9) by recalling their former condition of estrangement (vv. 12, 19).[5] Thorough as this was, now the Gentiles are drawn from a state of separation to one of 'nearness' by the preaching of the gospel. Near to what? Apparently they are near to Jews (peritomē, Israēl, diathēkē), for the thought moves to the fact that the dividing wall—i.e. between Jews and Gentiles[6]—is now broken. The enmity is destroyed by Christ (vv. 16, 14) on the

[1] Should we then have had πάντες ὑμεῖς τὰ ἔθνη?

[2] If so we might have expected ὑμεῖς ἐκ τῶν ἐθνῶν or τὰ παρ' ὑμῖν ἔθνη.

[3] See M. Barth, The Broken Wall (London, 1960), pp. 115–27; idem, 'Israel und die Kirche im Brief des Pls an die Eph', ThExHeute, LXXV (1959), pp. 3–47; idem, 'Conversion and Conversation—Israel and the Church in Paul's Epistle to the Eph', Interp, XVII (1963), 3–24.

[4] There is no ridicule here, but a designation of two groups within the early Church. The attempt to read scorn into 11 b derives from the view that, since the whole Church is Gentile, this reference is unnecessary and therefore sarcastic.

[5] Verse 12 is both a negative description of the Gentiles and a positive appreciation of the place of historic Israel; contra H. Sahlin, 'Die Beschneidung Christi', SBU, XII (Lund, 1950), pp. 5–22; Stig Hanson, The Unity of the Church in the NT: Colossians and Ephesians (ASNU, XIV, Uppsala, 1946), p. 142; see criticism in F. Mussner, Christus, das All und die Kirche (TrThSt, V, Trier, 1955), p. 78 n. 9.

[6] Contra H. Schlier, Christus und die Kirche in Eph (BHTh, VI, Tübingen, 1930), ch. 2.

ground of his abolishing the law of commandments (*v.* 15), enabling the two to be reconciled (*v.* 16). This reconciliation does not annul all differences. When 'near/far' appears again in *v.* 17 it is quite explicitly '*you* who were far off'.[1] However, 'the near ones' has no modifying personal pronoun; had all the 1st persons plural to this point referred to Jewish Christians, then 'we' would clearly be called for here, as a parallel to the other phrase to make the contrast effective. The omission is no doubt accounted for as a generalization,[2] but is this because the 'Jewish problem' has receded into the background or because there is still an awareness of the two constituent parts of the Church? If it be the latter, *v.* 18 follows on quite normally: ἔχομεν...οἱ ἀμφότεροι. Whether there is a specific and known problem being addressed, or merely an awareness of the possibility of Gentile ascendancy, the passage is directed towards keeping the proper perspective in a situation of tension between Gentiles and Jews.[3] In this sense Ephesians 2: 11 ff. (with the exception of *v.* 15) is very much in line with Romans 11,[4] except that there is no expression of a further hope for Jews and no expression of the temporary nature of the Gentile mission.[5] Gentiles must still be 'made near' to Israel to become partakers of the covenants and to overcome their estrangement. Having done so, they have become fellow-citizens.

The middle verses (14–18) of this paragraph form a unit

[1] The closest OT parallel is Isa. 57: 19; here, as in other cases, the author has taken what refers to two aspects of Israel and has separated them to apply to Jews and Gentiles within the Church. Cf. also Isa. 52: 1; Zech. 9: 9–16; Ps. 84: 9; and StrBill III, 585 ff.

[2] In our view neither 1st nor 2nd person plural would be satisfactory; 'we' would assert an incorrectly privileged position, 'you' would be incorrect or too ambiguous.

[3] See Chadwick, *ZNW*, LI (1960), 152 f.: Eph. is written with a specific situation in view, but it is general, and concerned with asserting Pauline authority over Gentile non-Pauline churches. So far as it goes, this is correct. He does not deal adequately with the question we raise.

[4] See Percy, *Probleme*, pp. 284 ff., 278, 446.

[5] It is therefore more similar, perhaps, to Rom. 15: 7 ff. where there is no expression of a theory, only a practical concern for Church relationships. Can these two omissions from Eph. be accounted for by the failure, subsequent to writing Rom., of the expected 'rebound reaction' by the Jews in Jerusalem as a result of Paul's trip? If so, he has abandoned his theory but not his presuppositions, and is here trying to work out a new formulation in cosmic terms. If so, Benoit, *Analecta*, is almost correct.

which can be isolated.[1] It is in these verses that emphasis falls heavily on a *oneness* that, at its most basic level, is the absence of enmity between Jew and Gentile because of the reconciliation wrought by Jesus. A new turn is taken in *v.* 15 where *oneness* between two groups is transformed into a new entity—εἰς ἕνα καινὸν ἄνθρωπον.[2] This phrase, suggestive of a *tertium genus* concept (though that is not explicit even here) apparently sets the Church over against both parts of mankind from which it derives its members. Up to this point, and indeed in the context, 'reconciliation' is either to bring together disparate elements on the human plane, or on the supernatural plane between God and man.[3] In 2: 15 the 'new man' has an ecclesiological reference to the Church itself;[4] it is not a statement about the transformed character and standing of the people in the Church, nor is it about Jesus himself.

Some difficulty seems to have been felt by the early scribes also, although it did not give rise to many textual variants.[5]

[1] See Dibelius–Greeven; they are an excursus on the present position of Gentile Christians (*HNT*, p. 69).

[2] κτίζω εἰς is infrequent and difficult; it appears always to connote purpose. This is a remote idea here. Ἄνθρωπος, of the Church or any precise group, is also difficult.

[3] E.g. 2: 10; as the next phrase shows, it has an ethical connotation, cf. 4: 18–24 with its contrast between the 'old' and 'new', where 'new man' is an allusion to Christ (cf. Gal. 3: 27; Rom. 13: 14; Col. 3: 9 f.; Rom. 5: 1–6, 14; 1 Cor. 15: 44 ff.). See H. Schlier, *Eph*, pp. 220 ff.; O. Cullmann, *The Christology of the NT* (London, 1963), pp. 166–81; Behm, *TWNT*, III, 450 ff.; Jeremias, *TDNT*, I, 366; S. F. B. Bedale, *Studies in Ephesians*, ed. F. L. Cross (London, 1956), p. 72. In 4: 13 εἰς ἄνδρα τέλειον may also be an oblique reference to Christ himself: so Schlier, *Eph*, p. 201; *idem, Christus*, p. 28; Dibelius–Greeven, *HNT*, follows this; E. Best, *One Body in Christ* (London, 1955), pp. 149, 151. A difficulty however is the use of ἀνήρ, see Oepke, *TDNT*, I, 360 ff.

[4] Some take both 4: 13 and 2: 15 as formulations dependent upon the identification of the Church with the Body of Christ, and therefore double-edged. This is possible, though difficult: ἐν αὐτῷ may in some way be appositive to εἰς ἕνα καινὸν ἄνθρωπον, so that there is in the latter a reference to Jesus' body; cf. W. D. Davies, *Paul*, pp. 56 f.; J. A. T. Robinson, *The Body*, ch. 2; Manson, *Paul and John*, p. 67. Difficulties for this are the κτίζω εἰς construction, the redundancy of ἐν αὐτῷ with εἰς...ἄνθρωπον, and the fact that 'one' refers here to 'making peace' and not to the One Man, Jesus. Cf. Col. 1: 20 ff.

[5] ℵ D G pm Mcion read ἑαυτῷ for αὐτῷ; F reads εἶναι for εἰς ἕνα; K reads καὶ μόνον for καινόν.

There is one, found in 𝔓⁴⁶ F G which read κοινόν for καινόν (either explained by, or dependent upon, the use of τὸ κοινόν as a technical term),[1] which shows that the scribes understood the verse ecclesiologically. A second suggestion of difficulty is that some scribes (notably of A and 𝔓⁴⁶) punctuate after ἕνα, and in A also after εἰρήνην.[2] This represents the opposite attempt, to give a christological significance to the phrase, although the resulting grammar is inexplicable. The same tendency is seen in a third factor—the common abbreviation of *nomina sacra*. Again 𝔓⁴⁶ and A (against ℵ) read A̅N̅O̅N̅,[3] perhaps reinforcing the christological reference in these manuscripts. These inconclusive data cannot be welded into a single satisfactory explanation but they illustrate two opposite attempts at interpretation of the passage: ecclesiological (ΚΟΙΝΟΣ ΑΝΘΡΩΠΟΣ) and christological (ΚΑΙΝΟΣ A̅N̅O̅Σ̅).

In the absence of sufficient textual grounds for emendation we must accept the present text and punctuation. This is a *hapax nooumenon* in the Pauline corpus, a 'border'—i.e. a concept which 'is actually to be found within the NT but which cannot be brought into a real consistency with the rest of the NT'.[4] The phrase 'into one new man' is an extension of the idea, which pervades this chapter, of unity from two parts of mankind.

The introduction of *anthrōpos* seems to be almost a slip at an unguarded moment, rather than a closely reasoned theological position.[5] He goes on from this verse to describe not a *tertium genus* but the way the two constituent parts of this new building are united by the Spirit. The momentary shift is consistent with the new emphasis upon the Church in Colossians and Ephesians. It is possible to hold that this is a legitimate advance, based upon the union of the concept 'no distinctions' and the 'body'

---

[1] Could κοινόν be the original reading? It is the more difficult; it could later have been changed under the influence of 4: 13; and later theological opinion would work for the change.

[2] 𝔓⁴⁶ has an additional letter α after εἰρήνην.

[3] The scribe of 𝔓⁴⁶ does not consistently abbreviate, and, where he does, it is not necessarily a *nomen sacrum* (e.g. 3: 5).

[4] W. G. Kümmel, *Man in the NT* (London, 1963), pp. 93 f., on Acts 17: 28 and 2 Pet. 1: 4.

[5] I.e. unless *anthrōpos* actually be intended to point to the Body of Christ, a position which involves more difficulties than it solves.

metaphor. The point we wish to make is the advance itself which this association of ideas represents.

In *vv.* 19 ff., particularly *v.* 21, there is a similar advance in Ephesians: for the first time, the Church *qua* Church is referred to as *naos*.[1] However, it is particularly strange that we find in this section the use of the 2nd person plural and not the 1st person plural. One would expect that the multiple use of *syn*- underlines the unity of Jewish and Gentile Christians in Christ.[2] The reason for the 2nd person plural in these verses appears to be that it is the particular situation addressed that calls for the stronger 'you' application.

There are reasons for suggesting that one generating cause of the parts on which we have concentrated in Ephesians 1–2 is an awareness of a residue of tension between Jew and Gentile within the Church.[3] This tension originates from the Gentile side. If so, the author applies to the reported situation the cosmic insight of Colossians. This in turn is derived from his reaction against the gnosticizing heresy there; the end result is his insistence that the unity of the Church must be expressed in microcosm as well as macrocosm. It is not good enough to affirm unity with others at a distance or theoretically, it must be worked out in the local confrontation where unity so often breaks down.

In chapter 3, within a defence of Paul's apostolic office 'on behalf of you Gentiles' (3: 1), there is the same emphasis upon the Gentiles being fellow-heirs (συγκληρονόμα καὶ σύσσωμα καὶ συμμέτοχα, 3: 6). It is not said with what they are united but the implication is with God's people of old, Israel (2: 11 ff.).[4]

---

[1] The construction is parallel to 2: 15, αὔξει εἰς ναὸν ἅγιον ἐν κυρίῳ. See Gärtner, *Temple*, pp. 64 ff.

[2] Whether *hagioi* (*v.* 19) are Jewish Christians or not is irrelevant to us for the moment (cf. 3: 18).

[3] So also E. F. Scott, *MNTC*, p. 123; H. von Soden, *HNT* (1893), pp. 84 ff.: 'Die Interessen des Briefs haben zwei Pole, die völlige Verschmelzung von geborenen Juden und Heiden in der Christenheit zu einer geschlossenen Gemeinschaft und die Erfassung des großen kosmischen Ziels des Christenthums. In der Mitte steht beide verbindend der Begriff der ἐκκλησία.' He argues strongly that Eph. has a practical and not a speculative purpose. He feels that there is no antagonism between the two, rather a failure to be perfectly merged.

[4] Perhaps σὺν πᾶσιν τοῖς ἁγίοις (3: 18; cf. 2: 19; 3: 5(?)) refers to Jewish Christians? In 4: 12 *hagioi* must, however, be simply Christians; cf. Col. 1: 12, 24–9.

In this discussion of Gentile mission and the 'mystery' (3: 3, 4, 9; 6: 19 f.) of their equality through the gospel[1] there is no consideration of the counterpart mission to Jews nor of the fulfilment of that mission.[2] Chapter 4 continues the emphasis on 'oneness' (4: 3 ff.), joint ministries in the Church (4: 11 ff.) and shared strength (4: 16). Here too any consideration of the Jewish aspect of the united entity is lacking. Present, however, is a hint of possible internal difficulties and incipient dissension (cf. 4: 25; Col. 3: 9) related possibly to false teaching or to racial tension.[3] The explanation of the fact that Ephesians is concerned with Jew and Gentile relationships appears to be that this is a live issue in that Church. But it must be admitted that this is inferential, and there is nothing approaching certainty on the question.

It is clear that the 'you/we' contrast, which is one of the most important aspects of the early part of the letter, is to be explained as a contrast between all Christians generally and the specific reception of the gospel in a local situation. There is no contrast, feigned or actual, between a Jewish Christian writer and his Gentile addressees. Ephesians, therefore, does not represent the complete abandonment of Judaism in favour of Gentile Christianity, nor is it evidence for the supremacy of the latter over a diminishing Jewish Christianity. 'We' still pertains to the total Church of Jews and Gentiles made into one by the sacrifice of Christ. The situation addressed, however, does give evidence of the danger of Gentiles beginning to assert themselves too much, perhaps because Jewish Christians have by now a history of being 'weak' towards things that should be no problem. Within the Church, Gentiles in origin must always

[1] See Masson, *CNT*, excursus, pp. 177 ff.; cf. Col. 1: 21 ff.

[2] In Col. the object of Paul's ministry is variously described: it is for the Church, the Body of Christ (1: 24 f.); the mystery is made known to the 'saints', but also 'among the gentiles' (1: 26 f.); and it is directed to every man (1: 28 f.). By contrast in Rom. and Eph. the object of the ministry is Gentiles, and in Rom. there is also a concern for Israel. Col. is a purer ecclesiology.

[3] Or a combination of the two as possibly in Col., where it would seem that the difficulties are caused by gnosticizing Jewish Christians who are to be resisted in a way quite foreign to the treatment of Jewish Christians in the earlier letters, esp. Rom. 14–15 (cf. Col. 2: 16–23). Cf. S. Hanson, *Unity*, p. 122; *per contra* Percy, *Probleme*, p. 320; Dibelius–Greeven, *HNT*, p. 83.

remember that they started out with a disadvantage and had to be drawn near to participate in the ancient privileges which Israel offered. This is consistent with what we have discerned to be Paul's attitude elsewhere.[1]

The characteristic of greatest importance in Ephesians is the divergence from the expectancy of Romans.[2] This divergence appears in the absence of any hint of the future salvation of all Israel and of the interim nature of the Gentile mission. This fact needs to be emphasized as a fundamental relaxation of the tension which is present up to this time, even though Ephesians retains an awareness of the constituent parts, Jew and Gentile, from which the one Church is built. This may be accounted for in any number of ways: (*a*) Ephesians is written after the 'Gentilizing' of the Church;[3] (*b*) it is written by a disciple of Paul who is not aware of, or does not share, his attitude towards the Jewish people; (*c*) the expected conversion of Israel had been completed; (*d*) expectation of a response has been dropped because of events occurring after the writing of Romans; (*e*) response has become almost impossible because the synagogues have shut the door; (*f*) the occasion of writing is such that there is no reason to mention it; (*g*) the emphasis is so strongly upon the cosmic and universal aspect of the Church, together with the oneness of believers, that there is no room for a discussion of particular missions. A combination of the last four points might offer some satisfactory explanation of the phenomenon, if it is a Pauline letter; if it is not, there is no need to explain, only to describe.[4]

Hence we must content ourselves with the conclusion that Ephesians, together with Colossians, is another important milestone on the road toward the identification of the Church as

---

[1] Cf. M. Barth, *Interp*, XVII (1963), 5: 'When Eph.'s witness about the relation between the Church and Israel is duly heard and respected, those Pauline passages usually quoted to substantiate a conceited attitude of Christians against the Jews...may call for more careful consideration.'

[2] Cf. F. J. A. Hort, *Prolegomena to St Paul's Epistles to the Romans and the Ephesians* (London, 1895), p. 179; M. Barth, *op. cit.* p. 14.

[3] Cf. E. J. Goodspeed, *The Key to Ephesians* (Chicago, 1956), p. v; this is one of his basic propositions.

[4] 'The Dilemma of Ephesians' (H. J. Cadbury, *NTS*, v, 1958–9, 91–102) properly applies to this particular aspect of the letter also; it is 90–95% Pauline, and diverges in an important 5–10%.

Israel, to the exclusion of any continuation of historic Israel.[1] While the word 'Israel' still retains its old significance[2] and the basic contention of Romans 11 is safeguarded, the new emphasis on the Church as a separate entity over against Judaism and Gentiles, the new designation of the Church as the Temple, the new 'theoretical' basis of the Church as opposed to its earlier more empirical descriptions, all these contrive to accelerate the separation of the one from the other.

[1] Dom G. Dix, *Jew and Greek* (London, 1953), p. 1, opens his book with Eph. 2: 13 f. and claims that it is 'one of the decisive turning-points of human history' (cf. pp. 110 ff.; 58 ff.). Dix speaks too readily of a 'Gentile Church' in his otherwise careful study. To do this is to open the door to a hyper-dispensationalism. Cf. Goppelt, *Jesus, Paul and Judaism*, pp. 190 ff.

[2] In Eph. 2: 12, a fact which is increasingly important the later the letter is dated.

CHAPTER VI

POST-PAULINE DEVELOPMENTS

PASTORALS, ACTS AND LUKE[1]

The Pastoral Epistles are of marginal importance for this study, having no sections that deal with the problem.[2] They tend to be inward looking, concerned mainly with matters of Church life, practice and doctrine,[3] with little or no concern for those outside except as they are either breakaways from the Church or perverters within it.[4] These opponents are gnosticizing Jews or Jewish Christians who are subverting the Church by means of a subtle introduction of, on the one hand, an illegitimate theory of 'knowledge', and, on the other, an incorrect approach to the OT.[5] This movement is severely criticized, but the criticism does not spill over and affect the author's attitude to Judaism itself.[6] The Church neglects the Jews in the Pastorals: it is a separately structured entity focused upon itself and its Lord. It is called *oikos theou, ekklēsia theou* (1 Timothy 3: 15),[7] and has taken over the title *laos periousios*[8] (Titus 2: 14), though there is lacking that high theoretical ecclesiology of Colossians and Ephesians. The assumption lying behind 2 Timothy 3: 14 ff. is

---

[1] It should be emphasized that each of the sections in this chapter represents a very brief outline of the form that a fuller examination of post-Pauline developments might take. It is not possible within the limits of this volume to deal with these adequately.

[2] The problem of authorship is stated clearly by C. F. D. Moule, 'The Problem of the Pastoral Epistles: a Re-appraisal', *BJRL*, XLVII (1965), 430–52. He suggests that Luke had a large part in the writing of the Pastorals.

[3] See M. Dibelius, *HNT* (3rd edition, 1955), pp. 7 ff.

[4] Hahn, *Mission*, pp. 139 f.

[5] 1 Tim. 1: 3 ff.; 1: 8 ff.; 2: 8; 6: 20; Titus 1: 10 ff.; 3: 8 ff.; 2 Tim. 4: 4. For a discussion, see C. K. Barrett, *NCB* (1963), pp. 12 ff.; J. N. D. Kelly, *BNTC* (1964), pp. 10 ff.

[6] Titus 1: 10 ff. (οἱ ἐκ τῆς περιτομῆς) probably refers to Jewish Christians, on the analogy of Gal. 2: 12 and Acts 11: 2.

[7] See Dibelius, *HNT*, p. 49, for the new use here.

[8] See Preisker, *TWNT*, VI, pp. 57–8; Moulton/Howard, p. 322; Bl–D/ Funk, 113.1. See also Appendix C, below, on *laos* and cf. Dibelius, *HNT*, p. 108.

that the scriptures now belong to Christians, but this must not be pressed in view of 1 Timothy 1: 8 ff.[1]

In Acts there is something of the same atmosphere.[2] We need not describe Luke's presentation of the early Christians' adherence to Jewish institutions, of the growth of tension between Jews and Christians, nor of the development of a Christian universalism.[3] Our interest is in Luke's view of the Jew/Christian relationship, and the stage this had reached at the time of writing. We begin with the vexing question of the last chapter. If there is any significance in the conclusion of Acts, it will be summed up in 28: 28: 'let it be understood by you, then, that this salvation of God has been sent to the Gentiles; they surely will listen'. By having this follow the verbatim quotation of Isaiah 6: 9 f.,[4] Luke seems to seal Jewish rejection of the gospel.[5] Though he has quoted Paul as saying similar things elsewhere,[6] the sentiment now carries additional weight because of its finality and its emphatic location.[7] Luke is writing in a period when the missionary enterprise was making headway almost solely amongst Gentiles;[8] he demonstrates how, within

---

[1] Cf. Jeremias, *NTD* (1953), p. 11: '...es ist zu beachten, daß *v.* 9*a* eine allgemeingütige Wahrheit ausspricht!'; contrast Moule, *BJRL*, XLVII, 432.

[2] Cf. Moule, *ibid.* pp. 430–52, and *Birth*, Exc. 2, pp. 220 f. and references there.

[3] Luke's account rings true; Acts can be used as a good, though selective source for the history of the period. Cf. C. K. Barrett, *Luke the Historian in Recent Study* (A. S. Peake Memorial Lecture 6, London, 1961): 'He is the only NT writer who makes any conscious attempt to show how, when the earthly life of Jesus was over, the Church came into being, and to relate the one to the other' (p. 55; cf. pp. 57–61).

[4] Reduced, in the best Lukan fashion, to almost nothing in the gospel (8: 10). See Lindars, *Apologetic*, pp. 160–7; J. Gnilka, *Die Verstockung Israels* (*SANT*, 3, München, 1961), pp. 130 ff.

[5] R. B. Rackham, *WC* (4th edition, 1908), p. 504, notes the use of 'your' rather than 'our' fathers in 28: 25.

[6] 13: 46; 18: 6; cf. J. C. O'Neill, *The Theology of Acts in its Historical Setting* (London, 1961), p. 82, citing M. Dibelius, *Studies in the Acts of the Apostles*, ed. H. Greeven (London, 1956), p. 149.

[7] καί may add to this finality (if it is to be translated, see Haenchen, *KEK*, 13th edition, 1961, p. 108 n. 6); note the later moderating additions. See O'Neill, *Acts*, pp. 54 ff., 70, on the importance of the conclusion.

[8] See J. Dupont, 'Le salut des gentils et le livre des Actes', *NTS*, VI (1959–60), 132–55. For a protest against current opinion see J. Jervell, 'Das gespaltene Israel und die Heidenvölker: zur Motivierung der Heidenmission in der Apg.', *StudTheol* XIX (1965), 68–96.

history (and not just on theological principles),[1] this shift has taken place. In so doing, Luke lays blame at the feet of the Jews for all civil disturbances,[2] and tries to show that if either party is seditious it is they, while still maintaining that the Church is one with Judaism.[3] It has not yet separated from the parent. But his gentile *Tendenz* leads to the Church's continuity with Israel being more a matter of succession than close continuing contact.

Conzelmann rightly observes that Luke describes the Church as the 'continuity of redemptive history, and to this degree is "Israel"',[4] but such a statement must be carefully hedged.[5] *Israël* is never applied to the Church or the new people,[6] it is always used of the historic people to whom Jesus came, and who retain some 'hope'. Luke chooses to use this name for the nation in preference to *Ioudaios*. Connected with this is his use of *laos*; usually it retains its particularist connotation as a technical term for Israel. In Acts 15: 14 the ambiguous phrase ἐξ ἐθνῶν λαός could be an application to Gentiles of the favoured name,[7] but it is better taken as an allusion (cf. the following quotation)[8] to Gentiles' participating with the 'people'. A strange idea underlies the use of *laos* in 18: 10: διότι λαός ἐστί μοι πολὺς ἐν τῇ πόλει ταύτῃ. *Laos* refers to an incomplete and therefore future entity without prejudice to origin, though the likelihood is that

[1] As in the Apostolic Fathers, see H. Conzelmann, *The Theology of St Luke* (London, 1960), p. 147.   [2] *Ibid.* pp. 138 ff.

[3] In assessing this, Conzelmann is unsatisfactory; *St Luke*, pp. 145 ff., 152 ff.; e.g., πρῶτον of 13: 46 does not mean the Jews are cut off (p. 145); it is not because of John's baptism that there is a split in Judaism (146); the unity of Jews and Christians does not rest in the belief in a resurrection (148); 'Israel' is not used of the Church (162 f.). It is damaging to his case, but he is correct in admitting that there is no special Lukan use of *laos* (163 f.).   [4] *St Luke*, p. 146.

[5] See W. C. van Unnik's strictures on such an overemphasis, *NT*, IV (1960), 26–59, especially pp. 42 ff.

[6] Not in 13: 23 or 1: 6 or 28: 20; cf. Gutbrod, *TWNT*, III, 388 f. *Ioudaios* takes over exlusively from ch. 13, while *Israël* is found only in 1–13 and in 28: 20. The change corresponds to the beginning of the Gentile mission; cf. 21: 27 for the neatest distinction between the two. On Luke's use of *Ioudaios* see G. Braumann, 'Das Mittel der Zeit', *ZNW*, LIV (1963), 117–45, esp. pp. 135–40, *contra* Conzelmann.

[7] See N. A. Dahl, *NTS*, IV (1957–8), 319–27.

[8] For the importance of LXX, see Rackham, *WC*, pp. 253 f.; Lindars, *Apologetic*, p. 35 n. 3; p. 248.

Gentiles will predominate in the completion.[1] The tentative application of *laos* to Gentile Christians is almost identical to the position adopted in Titus 2: 14. Together with this should be mentioned Luke's attitude to the cult: he has not rewritten his history to eliminate all favourable references but allows for Paul's faithfulness to it (21: 17 ff.) in spite of the very heavy fire it comes under in 7: 48 ff. (cf. 6: 13 f.).[2]

Acts expresses the tension existing at the time of writing between solidarity with Israel and the understanding of the new things which God is bringing about. At the same time it represents a stage when this tension is dissolving because of the Jewish people's continuing refusal to believe.[3] Alongside an ambivalent attitude to Israel there are suggestions in Acts of growing *de facto* separation of the Church from Judaism,[4] and the accumulation of special titles to apply to it: disciples (6: 7; 9: 26), church (8: 1; 9: 31), the way (9: 2), saints (9: 13, 32), Christians (11: 26), brethren (10: 23; 14: 2), and people (15: 14(?); 18: 10(?)).[5] In this list of names are found some which have OT antecedents and Jewish overtones, but none constitutes an unequivocal claim to be the one people of God that displaces the old entity. Except for the nickname 'Christian' they are inoffensive to Judaism as designations of a special group. Most have a functional purpose,[6] which can be seen also

[1] Cf. Strathmann, *TWNT*, IV, 53; Conzelmann, following him, *St Luke*, p. 164 n. 1. His conclusion is a *non sequitur*: 'The identity of the community with Israel is therefore assumed and accepted in practice even if it is not expressed in theory.' This only shows that Gentiles can become *laos*. Note how the distinction between *laos* and *ethnē* is retained in 26: 23 (cf. D. Guthrie, *NT Introduction, The Gospels and Acts*, London, 1965, p. 311).

[2] See E. Haenchen, 'Judentum und Christentum in der Apg.', *ZNW*, LIV (1963), 155–87, esp. pp. 164 ff.; cf. Baum, *Jews*, p. 146; F. F. Bruce, *The Acts of the Apostles* (London, 2nd edition, 1952), p. 157.

[3] Cf. A. Hastings, *Prophet and Witness in Jerusalem, a Study of the Teaching of St Luke* (London, 1958), pp. 129 ff., 176 ff. Baum, *Jews*, pp. 153 ff., emphasizes that Acts deals mainly with Diaspora Jews (esp. p. 162). Haenchen, *ZNW*, LIV (1963), 155–87, also distinguishes between the manifestations in East and West of the relationship between Jews and Christians.

[4] E.g. 2: 42; 4: 23; 5: 11; 19: 9.

[5] Luke's sense of history is shown in the gradual nature of their applicability to the Church. There is in retrospect something fitting about the order.

[6] Cf. F. J. Foakes Jackson, K. Lake, *The Beginnings of Christianity* (London, 1920 ff.), part 1, 1, 300–20 (esp. pp. 304 ff.), by the editors. Cf. H. J. Cadbury, *ibid.* V, 375–92.

in Luke's presentation of Christians' relationship to other privileges. For example, the earliest disciples claim to be able to pass on to others the promise (2: 39), to dispense baptism (e.g. 2: 38; 8: 36; 10: 47), to accept all things as clean (10: 9 ff.), to do away with circumcision (15: 1, 5; 21: 20 ff.). These are not theologically conceived transpositions, even though they have a theological basis, but practical matters of the operation of the new society.

In drawing this portrait of the early history of the Church, Luke, by his structure and arrangement, goes beyond the position of his close friend Paul.[1] His purpose is not only to show the extent of the Jews' rejection of the gospel, but also to explain the growth of Church consciousness. He does not aim to establish Gentile dominance in the Church,[2] but to demonstrate that the Church can no longer remain tied to the outward forms of Judaism. It must go its own way as the group which is in historical continuity with the old Israel.

In the first volume Luke obscures the reference to Isaiah 6: 9 f. at 8: 10, so that he can use it more forcefully in Acts 28: 26 f.[3] His treatment of Mark 4: 10 ff. increases slightly the element of predestination, by making the second half of the main statement depend upon δέδοται in place of Mark's weaker πάντα γίνεται.[4] Conversely, Luke reduces the contrast between those receiving and not receiving the revelation, by resorting to a weak τοῖς λοιποῖς and by following Mark (rather than Q = Matthew?) in the placing of the 'have/have not' saying. He understands the logion less rigorously than Mark,[5] and often he is less harsh than Matthew.[6] Often Luke generalizes a

---

[1] E. Haenchen, *KEK*, pp. 91, 99 ff. (who denies that the author was Luke); Hastings, *Prophet*, pp. 182 f.; *per contra*, Baum, *Jews*, p. 167.

[2] *Contra*, E. Trocmé, *Le 'livre des Actes' et l'histoire* (Paris, 1957), pp. 67 ff., who holds it is a defence against Jewish Christian critics of Paul.

[3] Matt. uses the full LXX quotation; Luke historicizes, rather than moralizes, Jesus' words. On Luke 8: 10 see J. Gnilka, *Verstockung*, pp. 119 ff.

[4] Note Luke's preference for δεῖ; see Grundmann, *TDNT*, II, 21 ff.; Gnilka, *Verstockung*, p. 126.

[5] He also presents the disciples as more of an élite (e.g. 12: 41; 12: 48), and decreases the instances of the disciples' dullness.

[6] 11: 37–54, cf. Matt. 23; possibly Luke 7: 29 ff.; cf. Matt. 11: 12 ff. and 21: 32.

conclusion or conflates sayings tendentiously.[1] He is clearly espousing a theory in 13: 27 ff. by adding to Q a floating saying about first and last (13: 30).[2] The same stress is apparent also in the parable of the feast[3] (14: 15 ff., note 14: 24: 'not one of those invited'); less clearly in the parable of the two sons (15: 11–32);[4] and in the parable of the husbandmen (20: 9–19, esp. v. 18).[5] The healing of ten lepers, one of whom was a Samaritan, illustrates a similar reception by outsiders[6] and rejection by insiders.[7]

These features illustrate a dual lesson: there is a schism within Israel and also a hint that Gentiles begin to supersede Jews.[8] As to the first, Luke makes clear that it is the leaders who reject Jesus and the humble who receive him,[9] but essentially it is the whole generation which is evil and unwilling to hear. This fact provides Luke with the opportunity to hint at Gentile acceptance, for he knows (as his second volume demonstrates) that in the generation after 'this generation'[10] there will be a

---

[1] Jeremias, *Parables*, pp. 63 ff., 69 ff., 86 f.

[2] This continues to be the theme of the two sayings about Jerusalem (13: 31–5), but shifts over in ch. 14 to first and last in a different context.

[3] Which Matt. adds to differently; cf. the variant conclusions in Matt. (25: 30) and Luke (19: 27) to the parable of the servants.

[4] The older one becomes a second-class citizen, although the main point is the 'lostness' of the younger being overcome, as in 15: 1–10; in both 15: 7 and 15: 31 the status of the other is not called into question (cf. also 19: 9–10).

[5] Matt. (21: 43) again adds ecclesiologically (where Luke adds a christo-logical conclusion) and accumulates parables with the same point (21: 28 – 22: 14).

[6] Luke builds up the centurion in 7: 4 f. more than Matt. Where Matt. reinforces the conclusion (οὐδὲ ἐν τῷ Ἰσραήλ) by juxtaposing another ecclesiologically oriented saying, Luke adds pericopes with a christological orientation; 7: 16, 20, 23, 34, 37 ff.

[7] So also 18: 9–14. This ties together the two uses of the first/last idea found in chs. 13–14.

[8] For Luke 1–2 see H. H. Oliver, *NTS*, x (1963–4), 202–26.

[9] Cf. T. W. Manson, *Teaching*, pp. 41 ff.; Conzelmann, *St Luke*, pp. 90 ff. None the less, Luke does not multiply strictures against the leaders (cf. Matt. 23); he is not clear about the address of sayings (A. F. J. Klijn, *NT*, III, 1959, 259 ff.); they act from a variety of motives, but one is simply ignorance (16: 29; cf. Acts 3: 17); he omits μετ' ὀργῆς...πώρωσις in 6: 10, and other cases of hardness.

[10] This 'scheme' leads to Conzelmann's *heilsgeschichtlich* theory, with which he controls the evidence.

fuller acceptance by Gentiles than by Jews.[1] Thus, as to the second point, Luke goes well along the way toward a Gentile inheritance of Israel's place, though it is a different road from the one Matthew takes. At the end of the gospel (24: 21) as at the beginning of Acts (1: 6) he can refer to the hope of 'Israel' not in a transposed sense, but as something which is being lost.

In spite of this, Luke does not interpolate the idea of newness as one might expect if he really had a full theory of *Heilsgeschichte*. The one new instance is in 22: 20 concerning the 'new' covenant. However, Luke omits 'newness' at 4: 36 ('new teaching' of Mark 1: 27), and by his peculiar conclusion (5: 38 f.) modifies the point of the parable in 5: 33 ff.[2] The Lukan writings exhibit no explicit theory of a necessary rejection of the gospel by the Jewish people, and no attempt to portray things Jewish as illegitimate or outmoded on principle.[3] His attitude to the Jews is not theologically conceived (though his view of the 'times' is partly schematic); it is empirically conditioned by his knowledge of the history subsequent to events portrayed in the gospel.[4] In the light of his knowledge of later widespread Gentile acceptance and general Jewish rejection, he indicates by editorial manipulation a shift from a Jewish focus to a future Gentile (or universal) focus.

[1] Luke uses *laos* in 19: 48 as a foil to 'leaders of the people' where Matt. and Mark both use *ochlos*. He does not grasp the opportunity to introduce *ethnē* in 21: 12 ff.; though perhaps he has saved the allusion until 21: 24.

[2] Both Matt. and Luke add isolated sayings to an original pericope on the basis of similar words but without proper respect for the point; cf. Jeremias, *Parables*, p. 104. N. Geldenhuys, *NLC*, p. 197, explains this as the reason why some cannot accept, but as the original conclusion this carries little conviction.

[3] *Contra* Hastings, *Prophet and Witness*, pp. 115 f., 119 f. She thinks the contrast between the early chapters and the later ones intentionally exalts the 'new Israel' (121 f., 183 f.). See W. Manson, *MNTC* (1930) preface, where he refers to Luke as preserving 'the spirit of Judaic Christianity'; cf. B. Gerhardsson, *Memory and Manuscript* (*ASNU*, xxii, Uppsala, 1961), p. 217, esp. n. 5.

[4] See G. W. H. Lampe, 'Luke', *Peake's Commentary*, 715*d*, *f*; 716*b*, *c*; 718*a*; cf. *idem*, 'Acts', 772*b*.

MARK

Mark also is influenced by his interest in the Gentile mission.[1] His view and Luke's are distinguished by the fact that the latter's is schematic and Mark's is rather more theoretical. This is most apparent from Mark's theory of parable (4: 10 ff.),[2] and his eschatological discourse. We have already suggested reasons for Mark's carrying over or introducing into the saying (4: 12 f.) a harsher purpose than was intended;[3] this is the result of a theologically motivated translation from the Aramaic.[4] The originally isolated logion, juxtaposed with a question about the interpretation of parables, has been made into a theologically oriented statement about the hardening of Jews by means of parabolic teaching (ἐν παραβολαῖς...ἵνα...μήποτε, 4: 11 f.).[5] To account for the theory it is not necessary to claim that it owes anything to Paul's discussion in Romans 9–11,[6] only that, in Mark, it is the result of his reflection upon the problem of Jewish rejection of the Messiah.[7] The logion originates in a

[1] V. Taylor, *McM* (1953), p. 113; J. M. Robinson, *The Problem of History in Mark* (*SBT*, XXI, London, 1957), pp. 63 f.; *per contra*, G. D. Kilpatrick, 'The Gentile Mission in Mark and Mark 13: 9–11', *Studies in the Gospels, Essays in Memory of R. H. Lightfoot*, ed. D. E. Nineham (Oxford, 1955), pp. 145–58; and literature cited there (esp. Turner, Burkitt, Jeremias; see above, ch. 4).

[2] See M. Hermaniuk, *La Parabole Évangélique* (Louvain, 1947). Some would claim that ἵνα does not signify a theory: e.g. H. Windisch, 'Die Verstockungsidee in Mc 4: 12 und das kausale ἵνα der späteren Koine', *ZNW*, XXVI (1927), 203–9; A. T. Robertson, in *Studies in Early Christianity*, ed. S. J. Case (London/New York, 1928), pp. 51–7; cf. Stauffer, *TWNT*, III, 324, 328.

[3] Cf. M. Black, *An Aramaic Approach to the Gospels and Acts* (Oxford, 1946), p. 155: 'everything points to a failure in the Greek'.

[4] See Jeremias, *Parables*, pp. 13 ff.; cf. J. Gnilka, *Verstockung*, pp. 23 ff., esp. pp. 45–86; T. W. Manson, *Teaching*, pp. 75 ff.

[5] See J. Weiss, *Earliest Christianity*, II (repr. New York, 1959), 695 ff.; cf. C. E. B. Cranfield, *CGTC* (1959), pp. 145 ff.; and *SJT*, IV (1951), 398–414; V (1952), 49–66. D. Daube questions this; he explains the pericope by rabbinic parallels of public pronouncement with a private explanation, intended to create a division (*ExT*, LVII, 1945–6, 175 ff.).

[6] Though it may be true, as Taylor suggests, *McM*, p. 128; see W. Manson, *ExT*, LXVIII (1956–7), 132–5.

[7] E. Schweizer, *NTS*, x (1963–4), 421 ff., in an excellent study, under-values the importance of the Jewish address.

saying of Jesus referring not to his method but to the reception of parables by many as riddles. By inserting the saying (because of the catchword *parabolē*)[1] in the context of a question about parables (4: 10), Mark has turned it into a theory to explain Jewish obtuseness.[2]

This view is both reinforced and modified by the rest of the chapter, where Mark accumulates sayings on the same problem. The required modification is that he reports that Jesus' purpose is not to make obtuse (or even to bring this attitude into the open), but rather to reveal God (4: 22) in an intelligible manner (4: 23, 33; cf. also 4: 26 ff., 30 ff.). Confirmation of Mark's attitude is found in other closely juxtaposed sayings: 'For the man who has nothing, even what he has will be taken away' (4: 25); '...privately he explained everything to his disciples' (4: 34).

This 'privacy' motif is found only in redactional material.[3] Though these sayings are spread over the gospel (4: 34; 6: 31 f.; 7: 33; 9: 2, 28; 13: 3), the theme of secrecy is much more prominent in the first half of the gospel.[4] In the latter half the emphasis begins to shift to openness, both of meaning and of opposition. It is striking that the movement from secrecy to revelation occurs during the chapters (6–8) which bring Gentiles into special prominence.[5] Possibly all these factors have an underlying structural basis:[6] in the early chapters there is a rising crescendo of opposition to Jesus, which appears openly as Jesus himself comes more into the open. This openness is an indication of the Jews' rejection and of the turn to the Gentiles. If so, Boobyer may be correct that the cross 'is a transition point at which Jesus ceases to be king of the Jews, and begins to

[1] So also R. McL. Wilson, 'Mark', *Peake's Commentary*, para. 700a.

[2] By no stretch of the imagination is it a theory about the 'new people of God'; *contra* Schniewind, *NTD* (8th edition, 1958), p. 41.

[3] S. E. Johnson, *BNTC* (1960), p. 11; cf. E. Schweizer, 'Anmerkungen zur Theologie des Markus', *NT Sup.* VI (Leiden, 1962), 35–46.

[4] Cf. T. A. Burkill, *Mysterious Revelation, An Examination of the Philosophy of St Mark's Gospel* (Ithaca, New York, 1963).

[5] So Robinson, *Problem*, p. 64; cf. B. H. Branscomb, *MNTC* (1937), p. xxxvi; G. H. Boobyer, 'Galilee and the Galileans in St Mark's Gospel', *BJRL*, xxxv (1953), 334–48; A. Farrer, *A Study in Mark* (Westminster, 1951), chs. 6 and 13.

[6] See the statement in Hahn, *Mission*, pp. 112 ff.

be Lord of the Gentiles',[1] and that the injunction to return to Galilee represents the place from which the Gentile mission begins.[2]

For this question attention centres upon the eschatological discourse.[3] Behind Mark 13: 10 lies a saying of Jesus which envisages that the Gentiles will receive the 'good news' as a latent result of the disciples' preaching in the Diaspora—one facet of the eschatological gathering of the nations at Jerusalem. Each evangelist interprets this series of events in his own way, as the extensive differences show. Mark includes in 13: 10 the word *ethnē* which both Matthew and Luke omit,[4] and combines it with references to 'witness', 'preaching' and 'first' in a way suggestive of the same *necessary* mission to the Gentiles which is espoused in Romans 11.[5] He builds upon Jesus' expectation of eventual Gentile reception, and historicizes this in the light of the missionary theory of his day.[6] Πρῶτον may imply, but does not require, cessation of Jewish mission; it would be better to say that it is predicated upon a universal mission which is stressed again in 14: 9: 'wherever the good news is proclaimed throughout the whole world'.[7] Similar to 13: 10 is Mark's retention in 11: 17 of πᾶσιν τοῖς ἔθνεσιν, which both Luke and Matthew drop.[8] It is probably no coincidence that in Mark alone the sending of the disciples (6: 7 ff.) is sandwiched

---

[1] *BJRL*, xxxv, 342, cf. 344; cf. M. Kiddle, *JTS*, xxxv (1934), 45 ff. See also Bo Reicke, 'Jesus och Judarna enligt Markusevangeliet', *SvExArs*, xvii (1952), 68–84 (esp. pp. 83 f.); Burkill, *Mysterious Revelation*, pp. 246 ff.

[2] *BJRL*, xxxv, 341, 346 f., 338; drawing upon Lohmeyer, *Galiläa und Jerusalem* (*FRLANT*, n.F. xxxiv, Göttingen, 1936) and Lightfoot, *Locality and Doctrine in the Gospels* (London, 1938).

[3] See G. R. Beasley-Murray, *A Commentary on Mark 13* (London, 1957), pp. 40 ff.

[4] But cf. ἐν ὅλῃ τῇ οἰκουμένῃ...καὶ τότε ἥξει τὸ τέλος (Matt. 13: 14) and ἄχρι οὗ πληρωθῶσιν καιροὶ ἐθνῶν (Luke 21: 24).

[5] So W. Marxsen, *Der Evangelist Markus, Studien zur Redaktionsgeschichte des Evangeliums* (*FRLANT*, lxvii, Göttingen, 1956), pp. 119 f.; cf. Burkill, *Mysterious Revelation*, p. 122.

[6] Kilpatrick's denial of this is not convincing; cf. ch. 4 above. He also tries to 'de-universalize' Luke (*JTS* n.s. xvi, 1965, 127).

[7] Cf. 13: 20 (πᾶσα σάρξ), 13: 27; and possibly 14: 24; 10: 45.

[8] The words are taken from Isa. 56: 7; the whole of Isa. 56 is important. See R. H. Lightfoot, *The Gospel Message of St Mark* (Oxford repr. 1962), pp. 60–9; and his note on p. 69 for the differentia in Luke's version. Cf. T. W. Manson, *Jesus and the Non-Jews*, p. 12.

between the rejection in Nazareth and the feeding of the five thousand (with the account of Herod used as a time-filler, 6: 14 ff.). The rejection in his own country[1] is, in Mark's theological construction, the ideal point for the notice of the disciples' wider mission.

This same temporal transition is dealt with more fully in the parable of the husbandmen (Mark 12: 1–12 pars.). Jeremias shows that the original parable applied to the poor (πτωχοί) who were about to take over the inheritance which their leaders were rejecting.[2] While Mark is not as explicit as Matthew (nor even Luke), there is a hint that he thinks that the Gentiles inherit the vineyard because of Jewish self-condemnation (cf. Mark's own comment in *v.* 12: 'so they left him and went away'). If the hint is intended, the parable relates the Gentiles' acceptance to Jewish rejection. The same sequence may be present in 11: 17 where Mark alone refers to Gentiles, followed by an emphatic ὑμεῖς δέ, by which 'Jesus severs himself from the ὑμεῖς... who made the temple a den of robbers. This shows that, for Mark, the cleansing of the temple is actually the fundamental refusal of all the religion of the Jerusalem temple.'[3] Apart from the note of time in Mark 13: 10 (which does not actually relate the two periods), there is a reference to succession in 7: 24–30. Mark underlines that the woman in question is a Greek, a Syrophoenician by birth (7: 26);[4] he hinges her case upon a prior event that must be completed before she should legitimately be entitled to any benefit. The sequence from children to outsiders is theoretically temporal, but the theory is disregarded in this instance on the basis of her remarkable answer.[5] There is in Mark a very close relationship between Jesus' death, the rending of the veil,[6] and the centurion's con-

---

[1] Mark 6: 4 pars.; only Mark adds καὶ ἐν τοῖς συγγενεῦσιν αὐτοῦ.

[2] See Jeremias, *Parables*, pp. 70 ff., especially on the christological reorientation of Mark. Cf. M. Prager, 'Israel in the Parables', *Bridge*, IV (1961–2), 44–86.

[3] So Schweizer, *NTS*, x (1963–4), 429.

[4] Omitted by Matt., as is Mark's πρῶτον clause in 7: 27.

[5] Matt. makes the generating cause not just her 'saying' but her 'faith', and makes the possibilities of its happening more remote—οὐκ ἔξεστιν, cf. Mark's οὐ καλόν.

[6] See Lohmeyer–Sass, *KEK* (12th edition, 1953), pp. 346 ff.; G. Lindeskog, 'The Veil of the Temple', *Con. Neot. XI, in honorem A. Fridrichsen* (Lund, 1947), pp. 132–7.

fession (15: 37–9) that is consistent with the idea that a transition has occurred.[1]

The torn veil comes so close to the end of Mark's gospel, especially if 16: 8 is intended to be the end, that a turning-point may have been reached. Jewish rejection seems to be sealed.[2] However, while Mark does construct his gospel in such a way that genuine belief is theoretically difficult to attain at an early stage, he does not, even in the later stages, read in motifs of Jewish rejection and Gentile acceptance.[3] Even in Mark 11: 13 f., 20 ff. one cannot infer from editorial modifications, and there is only a hint in the context, that the withered fig-tree applies to Judaism. Moreover, while the structure and some sayings indicate that he has a particular theory lying in the back of his mind, he never inserts pointers to a new Gentile church, or to a new people of God.[4] In Mark's gospel there is no new entity or person representative of the 'new Israel'.[5] The farthest he goes is to use Jesus' 'you' in such a way that sometimes it is extended from the original disciples to the experience of the Church;[6] by its nature this is an imprecise indication of Mark's intention. The gospel reflects a stage when Gentiles are receiving the good news and Jews generally have rejected it. While Mark claims that Gentile acceptance was anticipated by Jesus, there is no corresponding hint that Mark himself anticipated a restoration of Israel.

[1] See Schweizer, *NTS*, x (1963–4), 430: 'This is the first believer in Mark's gospel. It is a Gentile.' Cf. Lightfoot, *Gospel Message*, p. 57; Hahn, *Mission*, pp. 119 f.

[2] Luke locates the rending of the veil before Jesus' death. He avoids putting the decisive event here, and instead displaces it to Acts 28: 28.

[3] See F. C. Grant, *The Earliest Gospel* (Cole Lectures for 1943, New York, 1943), pp. 207–30 ('Was Mark Anti-semitic?'), esp. his quotation from H. A. L. Fisher on p. 209.

[4] So also Baum, *Jews*, p. 36. Robinson, *Problem*, p. 65, thinks a *tertium genus* can be found by comparing rejection of Jewish custom (7: 1 ff.) with rejection of Gentile custom (10: 42). This is not apparent.

[5] *Contra* Burkill, *Mysterious Revelation*, who thinks that Peter is (pp. 119, 248); and U. W. Mauser, *Christ in the Wilderness* (*SBT*, xxxix, London, 1963), who thinks that Mark represents Jesus as the 'new Israel in his decision' in the wilderness (p. 98).

[6] As in 13: 9. This verse might appear to presuppose that Christians are outside the synagogue (so Marxsen, *Markus*, p. 118), but actually it shows the opposite: the Christians at the time of writing are still under Jewish discipline (so Lohse, *TWNT*, vii, 864 f.; Schniewind, *NTD*, p. 135; Lohmeyer, *KEK*, p. 272).

FIRST PETER

The position of 1 Peter on these matters is not unlike an amalgam of Ephesians and the Lukan writings.[1] So far as our limited study is a criterion it probably falls in the same period.[2] The apparent absence of tension between Christians and others creates a point of contact with the late Paulines and the immediately post-Pauline writings.[3] The relatively thorough transposition of attributes and titles to the Church testifies to the distance that the Church has moved away from close contact with Judaism. There is no intimation that the Church is confronted with a militant Judaism which would call for polemic,[4] nor is there any indication of a positive concern for Judaism by the Church.[5]

In 2: 11 Peter addresses his readers as 'aliens and exiles';[6] in 1: 17 there is the same term παροικία (strange land); and in 1: 1 'chosen exiles in the Diaspora'.[7] From the coincidence of these terms in combinations which exclude any geographical nuance[8] we may infer that we need not find a Jewish address behind the use of *Diaspora* and related terms.[9] These are examples of the Christian assumption of Jewish self-designations.

---

[1] For the relationship to Eph., see C. L. Mitton, *JTS*, n.s. 1 (1950), 67–73; and J. Coutts, *NTS*, III (1956–7), 115 ff.

[2] See K. H. Schelkle, *HTK* (1961), pp. 7–15, for a cautious discussion. The persecution allusions have been widely, but indecisively, discussed; see E. G. Selwyn, *SNTS Bul.* I (1950), 39–50; F. V. Filson, *Interp.* IX (1955), 400–12; John Knox, *JBL*, LXXII (1953), 187–9.

[3] E. G. Selwyn, *McM* (2nd edition, 1947), pp. 39 ff.; but cf. H. von Soden, *HNT* (1891), p. 21.

[4] Unless references to suffering require it. Note the absence of discussion of Law. See J. H. Elliott, *The Elect and the Holy* (Sup. to *NT*, XII, Leiden, 1966) on 1 Peter 2: 4–10; he states that there is no evidence for anti-Jewish polemic (pp. 34 f. n. 7).

[5] Unless 3: 15 might include Jews under the generalization. On mission in 1 Pet. see Hahn, *Mission*, pp. 141 f.; 142 n. 1.

[6] See K. L. and M. A. Schmidt, *TWNT*, v, 849 ff., on the Christian take-over of πάροικος and related terms. Cf. F. J. A. Hort, *McM* (1898), Additional Note 2, pp. 154 ff. and p. 15; Lightfoot, *Fathers*, 1.2, 5 f. (*ad 1 Cl.* 1.1).

[7] See Schmidt, *TDNT*, II, 98–104, on διασπορά; cf. Grundmann, *ibid.* pp. 64 f.

[8] Cf. H. Windisch–H. Preisker, *HNT* (3rd edition, 1951), pp. 50 f.; Hort, *McM*, p. 15; cf. Justin, *Dialogue*, § 113.

[9] So F. W. Beare, *The First Epistle of Peter* (2nd edition, Oxford, 1958), p. 48; Selwyn, *McM*, pp. 43 f., 56 ff.

Peter is addressing all Christians—Jewish or Gentile—as chosen exiles in dispersion.[1]

These transpositions reach a climax within the New Testament in 2: 1–10.[2] The thought moves rapidly in vv. 1–4 but, having introduced Jesus as 'living stone' (v. 4), concentration is fixed upon this and what stems from it. So he goes on, not altogether logically:[3] 'be built up like living stones into a spiritual house'. This picture of the Christian community as a 'house', found only in the late- or post-Paulines (Ephesians, I Timothy, and Hebrews),[4] suggests a Church-oriented, indrawn community. Further accentuating the 'churchly' atmosphere, Peter continues to describe the nature of the Church in cultic terminology: εἰς ἱεράτευμα ἅγιον, ἀνενέγκαι πνευματικὰς θυσίας εὐπροσδέκτους θεῷ (I Peter 2: 5).[5]

Having laid this groundwork in vv. 4–5, vv. 6–9 are a recapitulation of the main principle, and v. 10 rounds off the whole. The christological assertions are supported by Old Testament quotations in vv. 6–8,[6] with a primary interest in the case of those who do not believe in Jesus as the cornerstone. With v. 9 the attention shifts back to Christians (ὑμεῖς δέ),[7] leaving behind the 'stone' metaphor which has formed the basis of the discussion. Instead, Peter boldly concentrates upon the specific titles which the Christian community has taken over and fulfilled: γένος[8] ἐκλεκτόν, βασίλειον ἱεράτευμα, ἔθνος ἅγιον, λαὸς εἰς περιποίησιν (v. 9). This conjunction of communal designations,

---

[1] K. H. Schelkle's comment begs the question (HTK, 1961, pp. 19 f.).

[2] There are many theories on the origin and use of this 'hymn on the holy destiny of Christianity'; see Windisch–Preisker, HNT (3rd edition, 1951), pp. 58 and 158 ff.; F. L. Cross, I Peter, a Paschal Liturgy (London, 1954); per contra, T. C. G. Thornton, JTS, n.s. XII (1961), 14–26; C. F. D. Moule, NTS, III (1956–7), 1–11. The only full exegetical study is Elliott, Elect, passim.

[3] Cf. Eph. 2: 19 ff. with 4: 12 for a not dissimilar shift; see Gärtner, Temple, p. 75 nn. 2, 4 (and all pp. 72–88), and Elliott, Elect, ch. 1.

[4] Michel, TWNT, v, 128 ff.; but cf. Moule, 'Sanctuary and Sacrifice in the Church of the NT', JTS, n.s. 1 (1950), 29–41.

[5] See Schrenk, TWNT, III, 249 ff. on ἱεράτευμα; cf. Behm, ibid. pp. 180 ff. on θύω κτλ. Both are in the Paulines; I Pet. represents a legitimate advance on the concept dependent upon a more developed ecclesiology.

[6] See Lindars, NT Apologetic, pp. 175 ff.; cf. Dodd, Scriptures, pp. 41 ff.

[7] See Selwyn, McM, Additional Note F (pp. 277 ff.).

[8] The only application of genos to Christians in the NT, though it is common later; so Büchsel, TDNT, I, 685.

drawn from Exodus 19: 6; 23: 22, is unparalleled to this point, and represents a conscious attempt, in contrast to Paul's occasional transpositions, to appropriate the *Ehrentitel Israels* for the new people of God.

If this were a totally Jewish Christian community these titles would have always been applicable, only now in a newly pertinent way. It is more likely, however, that it is a mixed Church, preponderantly Gentile with perhaps a good number previously being God-fearers or proselytes.[1] This seems apparent from, and makes much more important, Peter's parallel to Romans 9: 25 (cf. 11: 31): οἵ ποτε οὐ λαός, νῦν δὲ λαὸς θεοῦ, οἱ οὐκ ἠλεημένοι, νῦν δὲ ἐλεηθέντες (1 Peter 2 : 10). There are important differences between Paul's and Peter's use of the reference to Hosea.[2] (1) Paul's use is in the context of equal admission rights to the 'people' (Romans 9: 24 especially), whereas Peter's is in the context solely of belief and unbelief (2: 7). (2) Paul quotes the verses almost exactly, though combining verses at a distance, while Peter only alludes to them. (3) In his exact quotation a part of Paul's purpose is to underline God's gracious extraordinary action by calling them what they were not (καλέσω, ἐρρέθη, κληθήσονται), but Peter omits this and simply transposes (ποτε...νῦν).[3] (4) Paul gives the other side of the picture concerning Israel, whereas there is no hint of interest in Israel in 1 Peter;[4] the new people of God is mainly Gentile in origin,[5] with no observable awareness of a present link with God's other people.

A further self-identification appears in 1 Peter 4: 16,[6] where

[1] Cf. von Soden, *HNT*, pp. 118 f., and van Unnik, *ExT*, LXVIII (1956–7), 79–83, both of whom emphasize the proselyte language. The latter suggests that 2: 9 (out of darkness into light), 2: 2 (newborn children), 3: 18 (προσάγω = הקריב) all allude to a proselyte background. Now they can have confidence that they belong to the People of God, even though they are sojourners in the dispersion.

[2] See Selwyn, *McM*, esp. pp. 278 ff.; *per contra*, Schelkle, *HTK*, p. 66.

[3] His καλέσαντος in *v.* 9 has a different significance from Paul's; *contra* Hort, *McM*, p. 130.

[4] Cf. Windisch–Preisker, *HNT*, p. 61: 'Durch die Übertragung der Ehrentitel Israels auf die Christengemeinde wird die Ausschließung der Juden vom Heil besiegelt.'

[5] See Selwyn, *McM*, pp. 81 ff.; Schelkle, *HTK*, p. 66.

[6] We leave aside the problem of the correspondence between this and Pliny (cf. ch. 3 above). C. F. D. Moule, *NTS*, III (1956–7), 1–11, suggests

Christianos is linked with the *oikos* idea of 4: 17 (cf. 2: 5). The present troubles, which fulfil the expected judgment of the Old Testament (e.g. Malachi 3: 1 ff.), are falling not upon the old people but upon the 'house of God', the Christians. Even the judgment theme has been baptized into Christian service to show that Christians are the continuation of the 'people', in contrast to 1 Thessalonians 2: 14 ff., where judgment falls upon the Jews.

The Church has taken over the inheritance (κληρονομία, 1: 4, cf. 3: 9) of Israel. If it is Peter, responsible for the mission to the Circumcision (Galatians 2: 7 ff.), who writes, the hints of proselyte/God-fearer audience might suggest that in his mission he had found, as Paul did, that success was to be found amongst this Gentile group rather than full Jews. If so, he indicates here that he has come, independently, to a fuller transposition than Paul ever did. Peter's full use of the Old Testament (LXX mostly) confirms this. One has an impression, and it is hardly more, that he thinks in terms of the OT having only one, and that a present, application. He is not so careful as Paul to introduce his quotations in a way that allows for the full weight of the historical context. Most often the key word is the rather abrupt διότι (1: 16; 1: 24; 2: 6), or alternatively ὅτι (3: 12; 5: 5), or γάρ (3: 10).[1] His attitude to the Old Testament would be clearer if one were more certain of the exegesis of 1: 10–12. It is possible that the three verses contrast two periods of time: before Christ's coming (προμαρτυρόμενον, *v.* 11), and the present (νῦν, *v.* 12). If so, these things which have reached the Asian Christians as a result of Christian preaching (*v.* 12) are a part of the ministry of the Old Testament prophets to 'you': οὐχ ἑαυτοῖς ὑμῖν δὲ διηκόνουν αὐτά.[2] As Selwyn rightly

two different but authentic letters for the different attitude to persecution in 1: 1 – 4: 11 and in 4: 12 ff. Cf. also van Unnik, *NTS*, 1 (1954–5), 92–110; *idem*, *NTS*, 11 (1955–6), 198 ff.

[1] Διότι never in Paul, cf. διὸ λέγει only in Eph. 4: 8; 5: 14; ὅτι and γάρ rarely in Paul.

[2] See Selwyn, *McM*, App. Note D, pp. 259–68, who claims that this is a Christian prophecy. In fact a better explanation is that 1 Peter represents a step farther towards a take-over of the scriptures than does Rom. 4: 23 f. Hort, whom Selwyn finds confusing, is better. Cf. also Beyer, *TDNT*, 11, 86: 'The searching and foretelling of the prophets was an advance service to the community'; and Windisch–Preisker, *HNT*, *ad loc.*, who cites Enoch 1: 2 (a similar, but not particularly close, parallel).

saw (though he avoided the conclusion from it), 1 Peter gives evidence of a different attitude to scripture from that held by Paul.[1] 1 Peter begins to approach the position of some early apologists who imply that the Old Testament and the prophets belong especially (only) to Christians.[2]

There are indications of the 'Gentilizing' of the Church even in the letter of the apostle to the circumcision! This must remain an inference from a hypothetical reconstruction, based on internal evidence, of the situation and the recipients. What one can be certain of is that there is a considerably greater concentration upon the Church as such, and a more consistent appropriation of Old Testament attributes and of the Old Testament itself by the new community.[3] Together with this is an absence of concern for the people who once held these things, so that in transposing them no consideration is given to the position of a Judaism without its *Ehrentitel*. The question is left hanging.

HEBREWS

Hebrews also is related to 'Paulinism'.[4] The questions of author, provenance, and *Sitz im Leben* have been opened anew by H. W. Montefiore, whose solution is a very intriguing one. He suggests that this is a letter from Apollos to Corinth, written from Ephesus shortly before Paul's first letter.[5] However attrac-

---

[1] Paul states positively that it was written 'for us' (Rom. 15: 4; 1 Cor. 10: 11; 9: 10), or that it was concerned not only with them but also with us (Rom. 4: 23 f.—a halfway position). Eph. 3: 5, if the phrase be pressed, could mean something the same as 1 Pet., where the negative is unguarded. Cf. also 3: 21 and ἀντίτυπος.

[2] Cf. Justin, *Dial.* 29.2 (above, ch. 2), who says they are not Judaism's scriptures at all; 1 Pet. says they were not serving themselves, but us. This approach, as Beare (*First Epistle*, p. 67) emphasizes, safeguards the unity of the two testaments.

[3] See Hort's statement, *McM*, p. 7.

[4] For its relationship to 1 Pet. and Paul, see C. Spicq, *EtBib* (1952), 1, 139–68.

[5] *BNTC* (1964), introduction; similarly, F. Lo Bue, *JBL*, LXXV (1956), 52–7; with this cf. T. W. Manson, *BJRL*, XXXII (1949), 1–17 (written by Apollos to Colossae, before Paul wrote his letter there); F. C. Synge, *Hebrews and the Scriptures* (London, 1959) (written before A.D. 55); W. F. Howard, *Interp.* V (1951), 80–91 (written by Apollos to Ephesus).

tive this solution is, it remains highly hypothetical and creates problems of its own. To base what follows on such a theory would unduly prejudice the results.

The harshest passage in Hebrews is found in the last chapter (13: 9 ff.).[1] The situation presupposed by the letter is that of falling back into Judaism (2: 1) from Christianity.[2] Hebrews is an *apologia* as over against Judaism and its institutions,[3] but occasional and practical—not a 'fundamental theological treatise'.[4] The coming of Jesus—Son, Heir, and Lord—has caused Jewish institutions to be superseded.[5] In 13: 10, if 'we have' is emphatic with reference to altar, sacrifice, and sanctuary,[6] there may be an example not of supersession but of transposition. Hebrews, however, rarely crosses this important dividing line.

The situation appears to be relatively early. There is a live possibility of falling back to Judaism,[7] and consequently the author advises the recipients to move forward out of Judaism.[8] The situation must be one where the participants can on no account be neutral towards the old people of God. Further, the persecution hinted at in Hebrews may be coming from Judaism[9] as an 'encouragement' to embrace again the cult which they have only recently left, and which still retains a pull upon

[1] See most recently F. V. Filson, *Yesterday: A Study of Hebrews in the Light of Chapter 13* (*SBT*, n.s. IV, 1967). Cf. E. Käsemann, *Das wandernde Gottesvolk. Eine Untersuchung zum Heb* (*FRLANT*, LV, Göttingen, 1961, 2nd edition), p. 10; B. Weiss, *Der Heb in zeitgeschichtlicher Beleuchtung* (*TU* 35/3, Leipzig, 1910), pp. 89 ff.

[2] Cf. G. A. Barton, *JBL*, LVII (1938), 195 ff.: whether the 'relationship between Jews and Christians had come to the breaking point' (p. 205) is an open question. We cannot accept the thesis of H. Kosmala, *Hebräer-Essener-Christen. Studien zur Vorgeschichte der frühchristlichen Verkündigung* (*SPB*, I, Leiden, 1959) that Heb. is addressed to non-Christian Jews.

[3] Cf. A. B. Bruce, *The Epistle to the Hebrews, the First Apology for Christianity* (Edinburgh, 1899); and C. F. D. Moule, *JTS*, n.s. I (1950), 36–9.

[4] A fact which vitiates H. Köster's argument, 'Outside the Camp: Heb 13: 9–14', *HTR* (1962), pp. 299–315 (on p. 315 n. 54).

[5] Kosmala, *Hebräer*, p. 12; Käsemann, *Gottesvolk*, pp. 32 ff.

[6] So Moule, *JTS*, n.s. I; B. F. Westcott, *McM* (1889), p. 437.

[7] So Michel, *KEK* (11th edition, 1960), p. 334. Köster contends for a Christian heresy, Kosmala and Synge (*Hebrews*) for the temptation to remain within Judaism.

[8] τοίνυν ἐξερχώμεθα, a unique exhortation in the NT.

[9] 10: 32 ff.; 12: 4 ff.; 13: 8 f.; cf. Moule, *Birth*, pp. 111 f.

them.[1] The cultic rituals of the 'first tent' are of little profit to those who, whether priests or worshippers, rely upon them for salvation. They have no right to participate in the Christians' altar (θυσιαστήριον) for they do not admit its validity; they substitute for it a superseded altar. Were they to trust in Jesus' sacrifice made outside the camp, they could participate in the new altar. In Hebrews the old sacrifice has been reinterpreted christologically: the death of Jesus corresponds to the sin offering.[2] More than this, unlike the old sacrifice, where one had to cleanse oneself before going back into the camp (Leviticus 16: 28), this new sacrifice so fully cleanses that Jesus' people[3] need not even return to the camp, but can stay outside.[4]

The desirability of separating from Judaism, under the influence of Jewish persecution, is also christologically (not ecclesiologically) grounded. Hebrews 13: 13 provides theological justification for a practical situation: having been prevented from participating in the practices of the 'old tent', Christians must not fret over any loss which this might entail.[5] The reason for the absence of anxiety is that Jesus did his most important work outside Jerusalem, fulfilling the sin offering and rendering further offerings obsolete. By being cut off, Christians are forced into a position where they can no longer equivocate.[6] They must decide for Jesus and him alone, and go to him outside the camp.[7] Far from rendering Christians unclean, they are

[1] καὶ ξέναι (13: 9) means intricate Jewish teaching foreign to the λόγος τοῦ θεοῦ of v. 7 (cf. J. Moffatt, *ICC*, 1924, p. 232). But is this pure Jewish doctrine, or is it mixed with gnostic colouring? For the former cf. Köster, *HTR* (1962); for the latter, F. F. Bruce, *NLC* (1964) *in loc.*; and cf. Montefiore, *BNTC*, pp. 243 f.

[2] *Contra* A. Snell, *RefThR*, XXIII (1964), 16 ff. esp. p. 19, who links it with execution outside the gate for blasphemy (Midr. Lev. 24; cf. Lev. 10: 1–15).

[3] *Laos*; an instance of its full application to Christians. Cf. 2: 17; possibly 4: 9; and in quotations, 8: 10; 10: 30. See Strathmann, *TWNT*, IV, 54.

[4] So Köster, *HTR* (1962), who gives this its full weight.

[5] If Montefiore is correct, the Acts evidence for being forced out of the synagogue in Corinth can be adduced. In any case the general situation holds good. See Spicq, *Con Neot* XI (Lund, 1947), 226 ff. esp. pp. 233 f.

[6] W. Manson, *The Epistle to the Hebrews* (Baird Lectures 1949, London, 1951), sees the situation in terms of Christians remaining under the cover of Judaism (e.g. p. 24). For the author, the distinction between this and falling back to Judaism must have been unreal.

[7] Cf. Strathmann, *NTD* (7th edition, 1956), p. 155; *v.* 13 can mean nothing else than that 'die Trennung von der jüdischen Kultusgemeinde,

cleansed by identification with him. By remaining *with him* outside the camp of Judaism, Christians show that the present city, to which they should have no desire to return, has been replaced as the centre of hope. The earthly materialistic expectation and confidence is replaced by a spiritualized and eschatological hope centring in Jesus himself.[1]

The passing away of the old entity and the emergence of the new, which forms the basis of the injunction of 13: 13, is one of the basic motifs of Hebrews. It is prominent in chapters 7–10 where the relationship between promise and fulfilment is considered.[2] Basic is the statement of 8: 13: 'By speaking of "new" [covenant] he treats the first as obsolete; and what is obsolete and antiquated is near disappearing' (ἀφανισμός). The author portrays a dynamic situation, where old things are going away and new things have almost attained the victory.[3] The actual situation is fluid, but the theoretical position is quite clearly settled in favour of the invalidity of the old cultic practices in the light of the new events associated with Christ.[4] In this central section where the theoretical relationship of the old cult to the new is discussed, the point is the inability of the old[5] and the infinitely better character of the true[6] and unique (ἐφάπαξ)[7] way. The old things are not transposed to have a Christian application, though the way is open for this; rather, the promise of the shadowy things[8] is fulfilled in the time now present,[9] not unlike the relationship of 'first' to 'second'.[10]

ihren Anschauungen und religiösen Lebensformen durchgeführt werden muß'.

[1] See W. Manson, *Hebrews*, pp. 149 ff.; cf. A. Feuillet, *Studia Evangelica* (*TU*, LXXXVII, Berlin, 1964), pp. 369–87.

[2] Synge (*Hebrews*, p. 12) and Käsemann (*Gottesvolk*, pp. 11 ff.) properly emphasize 'promise'.

[3] Cf. Michel, *KEK*, pp. 190 f.: 'In den beiden Gottesaussagen συντελέσω und πεπαλαίωκεν liegt die ganze theologische Spannung zwischen Altem und Neuem Bund, zwischen Vollendung und Abbruch.' This corresponds to the situation presupposed by 13: 9 ff. and also the similar statement in 10: 9: 'he takes away the first to let the second take its place'. Héring, *CNT* (1954), p. 96, makes the situation too cut and dried in 10: 9.

[4] See discussion in Käsemann, *Gottesvolk*, pp. 33 ff. esp. p. 35.

[5] 7: 11, 19, 28; cf. 7: 12, 18; see Seesemann, *TWNT*, v, 713 ff.

[6] 8: 2; 9: 24; see Bultmann, *TDNT*, I, 249 f.

[7] 7: 27; 9: 26; 10: 10; see Stählin, *TDNT*, I, 381 ff.

[8] 9: 23; 8: 5; 10: 1.   [9] Esp. 9: 8 ff.; see Michel, *KEK*, pp. 199 f.

[10] 8: 7; cf. 9: 15; see Michaelis, *TWNT*, VI, 866 f.

The absence of transposition and contemporary comparison is rectified in 10: 19 ff., which concludes the second main section of the letter. Attention focuses upon the present situation of those who are within the 'house of God'.[1] The exhortations and the recollection of persecution for the faith (10: 32 ff.) can refer only to the Church (cf. 10: 30: λαός) which is encouraged not to shrink back but to go on in faith (10: 39).[2] Attention is paid to the Church in 2: 10 – 3: 6, also in the context of exhortations to perseverance (2: 1 ff.). Those who follow Jesus are 'sons',[3] 'brethren',[4] 'children' (2: 13 f.), 'seed of Abraham' (2: 16); the group together are 'people',[5] 'the congregation',[6] 'the house'.[7] The noteworthy feature of this, apart from the language itself (clearly reminiscent of the Old Testament), is that the terms are used only casually of the Church. They fall in a passage where the main point is not concerned with the Church as such but with Jesus himself, the high priest and apostle (3: 1).

In chapter 12, again in the context of chastening and persevering, there is repeated the theme of Christians as 'sons' (12: 7 ff.). Later, in *vv.* 18–29, there is a fuller recitation of the characteristics of the two covenants, summed up in the contrast between Zion and Sinai. The new and better covenant (*v.* 24) makes access to the heavenly Jerusalem, the city of the living God, possible. The Church on earth in some way participates[8]

---

[1] Kosmala takes this term as a designation of a known group in Israel, namely Qumran (*Hebräer*, pp. 11 f., 44 ff.).

[2] *Contra* B. P. W. S. Hunt, *Studia Evangelica*, II, 408 ff. (chs. 1–12 are an anti-Judaic treatise). Synge holds a similar view, but separates the material into a Testimony Book and hortatory materials (*Hebrews*, pp. 44 ff.).

[3] As Christians, in Heb. 2: 10; 12: 5 (?); 12: 7 f.

[4] Heb. 2: 11, 12, 17; 3: 1, 12; 10: 19; 13: 22 of Christians.

[5] 2: 17; his use of *laos* is hard to pin down: mostly he thinks in terms of Israel, but often it slides over into a Christian application.

[6] 2: 12 = Ps. 21: 23; cf. Heb. 12: 23. *Ekklēsia* is not a technical term in Heb. See W. Schrage, '*Ekklēsia* und *Synagogē*', *ZTK*, LX (1963), 178 ff. esp. pp. 186 f. on Heb.

[7] 3: 2–6; cf. 8: 8, 10 (of Israel and Judah); 10: 21. See A. T. Hanson, *Studia Evangelica*, pp. 394 ff. on 3: 1–6; cf. Käsemann, *Gottesvolk*, pp. 95 ff.

[8] The passage is full of problems. The intention is to underline the surety of access into this exalted gathering of God, Jesus, angels, and righteous, and in this sense it may be said that Christians 'participate'—the eschatological community on earth with the community in heaven (cf. Gärtner, *Temple*, p. 88, cf. p. 97).

with the hosts of angels, with the assembly of the first-born (*vv.* 22 f.).[1] The use of these terms, both here and in chapters 2–3, is less a conscious attempt to displace Judaism (from which the terms are drawn) than a profound presupposition of the author. The old no longer fits these descriptive terms, they apply properly only to the new. By virtue of the fulfilment of the expectation of a new covenant, all things connected with the old covenant have passed away. In so far as the language remains applicable, it is relevant only to Christians.

Hebrews does not attempt to document a take-over, nor does it illustrate a transposition, but rather a fulfilment of promise which is christologically and not ecclesiologically grounded.[2] The exhortation to go out of the camp arises from the belief that the new situation should be recognized in fact, though this comes to a head only in response to Jewish persecution. While the concept of Christians as the 'Israel of God' underlies much in the letter it is never expressed, because as yet there is no need to demonstrate this kind of continuity with the old. Hence, while the author is clearer than Paul about the theological problem of fulfilment,[3] he is not troubled, as Paul is, by the unique problem posed by the unbelief of the old people and the need to find a place for them in understanding God's scheme. His presupposition forces him to avoid the problem.

JOHANNINE WRITINGS

The gospel of John is notable for its interest in the Jewish nation and the Diaspora,[4] an interest which comes to the surface

[1] Πρωτότοκοι is very difficult; Michaelis (*TWNT*, VI, 882) and Gärtner (*Temple*, p. 98 n. 2) take it of Christians; cf. Michel, *KEK*, pp. 315 ff.; *per contra* Spicq, *EtBib*, II, 407 f.; Montefiore, *BNTC*, pp. 230 ff.

[2] Those who stand most nearly in the tradition of Hebrews (Barnabas and the early Apologists) change his christological use of the OT to a hermeneutic centred upon the Church.

[3] See C. K. Barrett, 'The Eschatology of the Epistle to the Heb.', *The Background of the NT and its Eschatology* (in hon. C. H. Dodd, Cambridge, 1956), pp. 363–93, esp. pp. 391 f.

[4] We are here building upon the work of J. A. T. Robinson, *Twelve NT Studies* (*SBT*, XXXIV, London, 1962), esp. chs. 1, 7, 8, 9; and W. C. van Unnik, 'The Purpose of St John's Gospel' (*TU*, LXXIII, Berlin, 1959), pp. 382–411. Cf. also P. Parker, 'Two Editions of John', *JBL*, LXXV (1950), 303–14; E. R. Goodenough, 'John, a Primitive Gospel', *JBL*, LXIV (1945),

in only a few places, but is presupposed in many as a vital element in the author's universalism. He is concerned with the 'world' only in so far as it is an extension of his interest in the Diaspora; a Gentile *kosmos* does not replace Judaism as the sphere of God's activity, though it is true that in John the *kosmos* is the backdrop of redemption.[1] The prominent place of 'world' may be attributed to the fact that it is the logical ultimate concern, to the relation between the 'world' and Judaism, and to the polemic which is addressed in the first instance towards Judean Jews.

The gospel is addressed to a synagogue in the Diaspora with the purpose of winning Jews to belief in Jesus, first as Messiah and secondly as Son of God.[2] The epistles are addressed to the same situation after a lapse of time, during which some have been won.[3] This time-lag provides also for the development of protognostic influences upon the young Christians.[4] They have tried to 'go ahead' (2 John 9) and are in danger of stepping right outside both Judaism and Christianity. The attraction to Gnosticism crept into Christianity, it appears, from the Jewish Christian flank, and it may be that a loose relationship between Judaism and Gnosticism was a factor in the growing separation of the Church and Judaism in this area.[5] In 1 John any desire

145–82, 543 f. *Per contra* E. Grässer, 'Die antijüdische Polemik in Johev.', *NTS*, XI (1964–5), 74–90, esp. pp. 87, 89.

[1] So Robinson, *Studies*, pp. 108 ff.: John never makes the transition from anti-Jewish to pro-Gentile; the point of view is consistently Hebraic; the criticism of Judaism is from within; the heritage of Israel is not given to Gentiles; cf. pp. 115 f.: the basic question is who is a true Jew, not who is a true Christian. *Kosmos* is a versatile word, standing right at the centre of John's theological thought (Sasse, *TWNT*, III, 894). R. H. Lightfoot is content to find only a hostile sense (*St John's Gospel, a Commentary*, Oxford, repr. 1960, pp. 74, 76).

[2] So van Unnik, 'Purpose'. On this basis, John's is a parallel development to Paul's, not the end of a long line of development (*contra* H. W. Montefiore, *NT*, V, 1962, 157–70; M. E. Andrews, *JBL*, LXIV (1945), 183–92; C. H. Dodd, *The Interpretation of the Fourth Gospel*, Cambridge, 1953, p. 5).

[3] So Robinson, *Studies*, ch. 9. There are traces of the same formulae which van Unnik isolates in 1 John 2: 22; 5: 1; cf. 4: 15; 5: 13.

[4] Indications of incipient Gnosticism are concentrated around Ephesus and are related to Judaism or judaizing; cf. Col., Past., Rev., 2 Pet., Jude.

[5] Abandonment of Israel by the Church may be not entirely a rejection of Jews as a whole, but partly a reaction against a heretical Judaism. This may also be a factor in Heb. 13: 9 ff.

for close connections between the Church and Synagogue has had to be let go because Judaism was infected with a Gnosticism which polluted Christianity at its most susceptible points.

John uses gnostic ideas and terms as a defence; his use of *kosmos* is one example of this. However, we are more concerned with another aspect of his use of this word. There is a connection between 'Israel' and 'world' in some passages in John.[1] At 7: 4, Jesus' brothers taunt him to go to Jerusalem to reveal himself to the world.[2] At the feast there will be Jews from all over the world, so that by going up to the great gathering at Jerusalem the whole (Jewish) world will have opportunity to see and believe.[3] This is supported by 12: 19 f., where the account of the ministry has almost been completed. Jesus is at the height of popular acclaim, and the Pharisees' reaction is: 'the world has followed after him'. The context demands that *kosmos* here is the Jewish crowd in Jerusalem for the feast.[4] The association of *kosmos* and *Hellēnes* is not meant to refer to the Gentile world (this would run counter to the whole context) but to show that the gospel will eventually reach the world through hellenistic Jews.[5] In 12: 19 *kosmos* means either Jews in Palestine plus Jews in the Diaspora, or Jews of whatever origin plus proselytes, but in either case it means native Jews and visitors from overseas who will carry home the conviction that Jesus is Son of Man (12: 23, 34) and King of Israel (12: 13; cf. 11: 48 ff.).

[1] It is true that John identifies 'Judaism' with 'world' *in malam partem*, so Grässer, *NTS*, XI, 88 (referring to 1: 10; 7: 7; 15: 18 f.; 17: 25; 1 John 4: 5; cf. p. 89).

[2] Cf. 1: 31; 17: 6, and the correlative of 7: 4 in 18: 20 (both have the contrast 'secretly/boldly'). Bultmann points out (*KEK*, 13th edition, 1953, *in loc.*) that in 7: 4 Galilee is associated with secrecy and Jerusalem with boldness, but if so, Jerusalem is also related to the *kosmos*.

[3] Cf. 18: 20, where *kosmos* is paralleled by 'in the synagogue and in the temple where all the Jews gathered'. The 'world' embraces Jewish congregations in Jerusalem and in all places.

[4] 12: 9, 12, 17; particularly 12: 20, where *Hellēnes* means Diaspora Jews in Jerusalem (so Windisch, *TDNT*, II, 509; Schmidt, *ibid.* pp. 101 f.).

[5] So also in 7: 35, where *Hellēnes* could mean 'Greeks', but more likely, when coupled with Diaspora, means Jews in the dispersion (so Windisch, *TDNT*, II, 509; Schmidt, *ibid.* pp. 101 f., less surely). It is interpreted as God-fearers or proselytes by Bauer, *HNT* (2nd edition, 1925); Bultmann, *KEK*; Strathmann, *NTD* (8th edition, 1955); Barrett, *The Gospel according to St John* (London, 1955), *in loc.*; Dodd, *Interpretation*, p. 371 n. 3; J. Jocz, *Jud*, IX (1953), 127 ff. esp. p. 137.

Perhaps similar to this is 17: 6.[1] As in 15: 19, the disciples are *ek tou kosmou*, and their task is *eis ton kosmon* (17: 18), so the *kosmos* may believe (17: 21; cf. 17: 23; 3: 16 f.). The 'world' in the widest sense hears and believes through the narrower Jewish 'world', though just a small part of that world.

In 1: 9–12 *kosmos* is paired with ἴδιοι/ἴδιαι. The theological intention behind this may be similar to the above: Jesus came into the world to redeem men, but to do this he appeared in a particular place (εἰς τὰ ἴδια)[2] to a particular people (οἱ ἴδιοι) who were not disposed to receive him. The prologue sets the stage for the relationship between 'Israel' and 'world'.[3] Rejection by his own does not mean an immediate turning to the Gentile world, but rather a movement into the marginal Jewish areas (Samaria, Galilee; ch. 4). When, in the editorial introduction[4] in 13: 1, John refers to 'his own who are in the world' he means not just the twelve but all disciples everywhere. This usage is different from 1: 11 f. yet is continuous with it, for up to this point only Jews (and marginal Samaritans) have believed. Whereas in 1: 11 f. 'his own' tend to reject, in 13: 1 'his own' are those who have accepted. The transition may occur at 10: 3 ff.[5] Behind the phrase 'his own sheep' lies the idea that Jesus calls all his own people to follow, but only some do so. *Idios* moves with little difficulty from the general to the particular, although always with a Jewish nuance.[6] The hint in 1: 11 that 'his own', by their rejection, become 'the world', or conversely that the 'world' will replace 'Jews', is not carried through. The *kosmos* is the

[1] 'I have made known your name to the men you gave me out of the world.' The last phrase can be used *in malam partem* also, e.g. 17: 14, 16.

[2] Cf. 4: 44, by which we must understand Judea; contrast 7: 52.

[3] Cf. Hoskyns and Davey, *The Fourth Gospel* (London, 1939), *in loc.*: 'There is, however, no final distinction between Israel and the world, between Jew and Greek...' True, but John does not obliterate every difference.

[4] So C. H. Dodd, *Historical Tradition in the Fourth Gospel* (Cambridge, 1963), p. 26; J. H. Bernard, *ICC* (1928), *in loc.*

[5] See Robinson's reconstruction of the parable, *Studies*, pp. 67 ff. Dodd, *Tradition*, pp. 382 ff., agrees with him, see esp. p. 385 n. 1; cf. Strathmann, *NTD*, *in loc.*

[6] Cf. Barrett, *Gospel acc. John*, on 10: 3. It is consistent with this that in 10: 16 'other sheep', by implication, is contrasted with 'own sheep'.

wider backdrop against which redemption happens, on stage, amongst his own (cf. 4: 22).[1]

As redemption is played out, separation is inevitable. That a decision must be made within Judaism is a constant refrain in the first half.[2] At the end of the account of Jesus' ministry, John includes an appendix which gives a résumé of Jesus' teaching and states the prophetic background for Jewish obtuseness. Yet even here, as elsewhere, he stresses the tension between belief and unbelief.[3]

Jewish opposition to Jesus is prominent throughout the gospel.[4] John portrays the Jews, both leaders (who are especially culpable) and people, as having disowned Christ. However, so Palestinian-centred is the gospel that violent opposition is reserved for Judean Jews and does not seem to be intended to include all Jews. Criticism of Judea may have been helpful in attracting the sympathetic attention of the Diaspora, for the superiority assumed by the native Jew could not appeal to the foreign-born. Certainly during the two wars with Rome there was little or no support amongst the Diaspora for Judea. No one felt strongly enough to risk anything. When John uses ἀποσυνά-γωγος[5] (12: 42; 9: 22; 16: 2) he may be including a further implicit criticism of Jamnian Judaism's exclusiveness, when compared with the relative openness of the Diaspora synagogues.

Jesus confronts this Judaism with a number of antitheses, especially in 8: 12–59:[6] knowledge of God *versus* ignorance

[1] Contrast Grässer, *NTS*, xi, 82. 'Dieser israelitische Horizont ist für Joh versunken. Geblieben ist für ihn allein Jesu Kommen und Gehen und was das an Heil für die *Welt* bedeutet.' This is the crux of his argument, and if we are correct in modifying this contrast, his thesis falls.

[2] Σχίσμα at 7: 43; 9: 16; 10: 19, always of Jewish groups faced with the need to decide about Jesus. Cf. also 2: 23; 4: 39, 45, 50; 7: 31, 45; 8: 30; 10: 42; 11: 45; 12: 19.

[3] 12: 42: 'Notwithstanding that, even from among the leaders many believed on him.' John even excuses their hidden belief.

[4] Many commentators make it unrelieved. Grässer rightly speaks of a double aspect: capable of salvation and hostile (*NTS*, xi, 77). About half the occurrences of *Ioudaios* designate those who are opposed to Jesus; see G. Baum, *Jews*, pp. 103–12.

[5] StrBill, iv, 13 Exk., esp. pp. 329 ff.; Schrage, *TWNT*, vii, 845 ff.; K. L. Carroll, *BJRL*, xl (1951), 19–32; cf. Parkes, *Conflict*, pp. 83 f. This implies a Jewish movement towards separation, but does not demand a complete breach.

[6] See Grässer, *NTS*, xi, 84 f.

(*vv.* 12–20); this world *versus* not of this world (*vv.* 21–9); Devil *versus* God (*vv.* 30–59). Another extremely important antithesis standing over the gospel is that Law came by Moses, grace and truth by Jesus (1: 17).[1] It is noteworthy, however, that the very important term 'seed of Abraham' (8: 33 ff.) does not cease to be applied to Judaism. The normal extension of this category to anyone who believes, found elsewhere in the NT, is never expressed. This is all the more remarkable when compared with the account of John the Baptist's preaching in the Synoptics.[2] Jesus admits that Jews are *sperma* (but not *tekna*, 8: 37, 39),[3] but his main point is: Who is the true Jew? or better: Who is not a true Jew? To this the answer is given: the one in whom Jesus' word does not have free course (*v.* 37), who seeks to kill him (*vv.* 37, 40), who does not understand and love him (*vv.* 42 f.); in short, whoever does not believe (in) Jesus (*vv.* 45, 51). In all this, a universal concern for who can be reckoned a child of Abraham is lacking.[4]

John's tradition about Jesus' view of circumcision (7: 22 ff.) and the Sabbath (7: 22 ff.; 5: 10 ff.; 9: 14 ff.) is similar: the incidents themselves show the antipathy of Jews to Jesus, but Jesus' refutation of their arguments does not introduce a wider application to the Gentiles or the later Church. John demonstrates the obstinacy of Judean Judaism and polemizes against it, but his eagerness to win Jews in the Diaspora[5] makes him underplay the destruction of the Temple, the Church as the true Temple, the supersession of the Sabbath and the opening of membership in the children of Abraham.

When one assesses the relationship of the Church to Israel, one finds that there is little in the way of later conditions written in.[6] Chapters 13–17 presuppose a group of some kind

---

[1] Cf. the law is 'your' law, 8: 17; 10: 34. For the antitheses see Dahl, *Volk Gottes*, pp. 169 f.

[2] Matt. 3: 9 par.; cf. Dodd, *Tradition*, pp. 330 ff., who holds that John's tradition is closer to the original than Matthew's (cf. pp. 379 ff.).

[3] This distinction cannot be pressed (C. H. Dodd, *RHPR*, xxxvii, 1957, 5–17, esp. p. 12 n. 19; cf. Bauer, *HNT*, *in loc.*).

[4] For a different view see F.-M. Braun, *Jean, le Théologien*, ii (Paris, 1964), 175–86.

[5] The explanations of Aramaic expressions may point to the inclusion of God-fearers and their friends (cf. Robinson, *Studies*, pp. 122 f.).

[6] The most notable is probably ἀποσυνάγωγος, 16: 2.

in close relationship to Jesus, indeed dependent upon him for its very life. The characteristics of this small community are primarily functional, not essential.[1] The sheep and sheepfold of chapter 10 indicate a community which can be expanded to include 'other sheep',[2] but the emphasis is upon following the shepherd and not the fold as such.[3] Nor is there anything in the so-called prayer for the Church (chapter 17) which presupposes an organization of any kind.[4] The gospel of John is primarily concerned with what it means for a Jew to believe. John does not attempt to substantiate any particular theory of the relationship of the new community to the old, the Church to Israel.[5]

However, John does imply that Jesus, in his own person, has a special relationship to Israel. As Dahl points out,[6] the Temple is his body (2: 19–22); he, not the Manna of the Torah, is Bread of Heaven (6: 32 ff.); he, not the Torah nor Israel, is the Light of the World (8: 12; 9: 5; 12: 40); he, not the rabbinic teaching, is the Way (14: 6); he is the true Passover Lamb

---

[1] *Contra* F. J. A. Hort, *The Christian Ecclesia* (London, 1897), p. 223: chs. 13–17 are 'the weightiest and most pregnant body of teaching on the Ecclesia to be found anywhere in the Bible'. Dahl is more balanced (*Volk Gottes*, p. 174): 'Jesus organisiert keine Kirche, sammelt aber Jünger um sich, die mit ihm und dadurch mit Gott und mit einander persönlich verbunden sind...Die Gemeinschaft der Jünger bildet kein neues Israel...' These are two of the basic similarities between the Synoptics and John, according to Dahl.

[2] As in 10: 1 αὐλή refers to Israel, but whether 'others' are Diaspora Jews or Gentiles is not clear.

[3] Cf. Moule, 'The Individualism of the Fourth Gospel', *NT*, v (1962), 171–90; 'Even when Christ is the Vine it is a matter for each branch, individually, to remain or be detached. When he is the good Shepherd, it is the individual sheep who listen and respond or who are deaf to his voice...' (p. 184).

[4] So Dahl, *Volk Gottes*, p. 173; cf. p. 168.

[5] So E. Schweizer, 'The Concept of the Church in the Gospel and Epistles of St John', *NT Essays in mem. T. W. Manson* (Manchester, 1959), pp. 230–45: 'John does not describe the Church as the New Israel or as God's People or as God's "Saints": he never mentions the word "Church" at all'; and Dahl, *Volk Gottes*, pp. 173 f.: '...der Gedanke, die Kirche sei das neue, bzw. das wahre Israel, nicht ausgesprochen wird.' *Per contra*, J. Jocz, *Jud*, IX (1953), who claims that in John (as in Paul!) 'die Juden... die Ungläubigen aus dem Hause Israels sind, die Gläubigen aber, Juden wie Heiden, sind Israel im Geiste und in der Wahrheit' (p. 142).

[6] *Volk Gottes*, p. 170.

(19: 32 ff.; cf. 1: 29, 36); he is the living Water (4: 5 ff.); he alone can explain true worship (4: 19 ff.). He claims the right to teach, demand response, lead the people (chapter 10), and so he supplants false teachers. Since he is 'the Saviour of the world' (4: 42), 'the King of Israel' (1: 49; cf. 12: 13) and 'King of the Jews' (18: 33, 39; 19: 3, 19, 21), salvation is from the Jews. Therefore John says that Jesus' death is 'for (ὑπέρ) the nation, and not only for the nation, but also to gather together into one the scattered (διεσκορπισμένα) children of God' (11: 52). The plain significance is that, in the first place, Jesus dies for his nation; but, as an extension of this, salvation is available to the Diaspora and beyond, embracing eventually (but secondarily) the whole world.[1]

John also implies that Jesus is himself true Israel. This is evident from 15: 1 ff., where Jesus claims to fulfil the Old Testament vine metaphor.[2] Disciples who cling to him bear fruit, non-productive branches are pruned away.[3] By relating to him, we may infer, disciples share in Israel, though it is nowhere hinted that branches can be added. John need not be concerned with added branches (as is Paul) since the gospel is addressed to the Diaspora. Possibly related to this metaphor is the notice in 1: 47 about Nathanael being 'a true Israelite'. John may understand by this that only as one follows Jesus is one truly an Israelite, a position which would correspond to the implications of 15: 1 ff.[4]

John's purpose in writing to Diaspora Jews is to show the need to confess Jesus as the Christ, the Son of God, and to warn his fellow Jews not to reject Jesus as Judean Jews had.[5] His

[1] So also C. H. Dodd, 'The Prophecy of Caiaphas', *NT Sup*, VI, 134–43.

[2] So Barrett, *John*, p. 393: 'The vine in his handling of the material ceases to represent Israel and becomes a christological definition applied to Jesus himself.'

[3] The stress is on the negative; Who is not a true Jew?

[4] Cf. Jocz, *Jud*, IX (1953), 141: 'Die theologische Voraussetzung bei Joh scheint zu sein, daß Christusgläubige Juden nicht mehr "Juden" im gewöhnlichen Sinne des Wortes seien...Juden und Heiden, die die Messias glauben, sind Israel. Das kann man z. B. an Nathanael sehen, ἀληθῶς 'Ισραηλείτης will sagen, daß es auch andere nicht wahre Israeliten gibt.'

[5] Bo Reicke, in an open lecture given in the Divinity School, Cambridge, 16 February 1965, showed that Rev. may also fit into this situation. He claimed that under the Flavians the Jews lost their special status and

background may have predisposed him to think in terms of a nucleus in Israel, and if so, he has applied this to the separation which takes place as a result of Jesus' ministry. In presenting Jesus' ministry John is not concerned with transpositions or Christian applications, nor need he deal with how a Gentile can become a Christian. While John is conscious of the need for the gospel to spread universally, he sees this in terms of its prior spread to the Diaspora. On this matter, he has not reached the same solution which Paul reached,[1] but on the question of Jesus' identity with 'Israel', he is beyond Paul's formulation. Jesus' followers, though not the 'Church', by remaining in him are a part of Israel but not yet the 'true Israel'. The tentative solution found in John's gospel appears to be the antecedent of Justin's more exact formulation: Jesus is Israel, therefore Christians are true Israelites.

MATTHEW

Matthew's redaction of the gospel also has a distinct tendency to take over the 'Israel'-idea.[2] The Christian community is confronted by post-Jamnian Judaism,[3] and this situation informs much of the editorial comment in, and the arrangement of, the gospel. The Church is working towards an identification of itself

therefore, with no political reason to remain Jews, many became Christians. The 144,000 (7: 4–9)—a great multitude from all nations (cf. 11: 3)—were joining the Church; in fact so great was the number that John hoped many of the rest would join as well. The author of Rev., he claimed (in a paper to Prof. Moule's NT Seminar, the same day), is interested in winning Jews for the gospel before the end. It is a positive attitude.

[1] For a comparison of John and Paul on the Church and Israel, see J. Bligh, *Analecta Biblica*, 17–18, 1 (Rome, 1963), 151–6.

[2] See W. Trilling, *Das wahre Israel. Studien zur Theologie des Mtev* (3rd edition, *SANT*, x, München, 1964); R. Hummel, *Die Auseinandersetzung zwischen Kirche und Judentum im Mtev* (*BEvTh*, xxxiii, München, 1963); G. Strecker, *Der Weg der Gerechtigkeit. Untersuchung zur Theologie des Mt* (*FRLANT*, lxxxii, Göttingen, 1962); and G. Bornkamm, G. Barth, H. J. Held, *Tradition and Interpretation in Matt.* (London, 1963).

[3] See W. D. Davies, *The Setting of the Sermon on the Mount* (Cambridge, 1964); K. Stendahl, 'Matthew', *Peake's Commentary*; P. Bonnard, *CNT* (1963), introduction. *Per contra* Strecker, *Gerechtigkeit*; P. Nepper-Christensen, *Das Mtev, ein judenchristliches Ev?* (*Acta Theol. Danica*, 1, Aarhus, 1958); cf. H. B. Green, *JTS*, xv (1964), 361 ff. (a review of Strecker); E. Schweizer, *EvTh*, xxiii (1963), 611 ff.

with 'new'[1] or 'true'[2] Israel, but this identification is difficult to attain for it is still an *intra muros* struggle.[3] The Christian community is no longer tied to the institutions of Israel,[4] but it shies away from making the rupture complete by transposing titles[5] or by working through the gospel on the basis of a remnant idea. However, the tendencies represented in Matthew will soon make the breach inevitable.

The two most important titles of Israel are, in Matthew, never taken over by the Church. In many cases *laos* is the people which opposes Jesus and his message (13: 15; 15: 8 (both quotations); 27: 25, 64), or it is used genitivally with a description of the leaders who are especially opposed (2: 4; 21: 23; 26: 3, 47; 27: 1). Only in the early uses (1: 21; 2: 6) is it found in a context which expresses hope for the people (cf. 4: 16 and 4: 23). Matthew uses 'Israel' in a completely literal way to apply always to the nation; there are no marginal cases where it might apply to the Church. The harshest context is Matthew 8: 10, where a saying, taken over from Q, is tied to a saying found elsewhere in Luke. Matthew's intention is to show how the way is open for the Gentiles to come in, and to give a severe warning that Jews may find that they have changed places with the Gentiles.[6] In other places, however, Matthew uses 'Israel' in a context which permits a hopeful stance towards Israel (10: 6, 23; 15: 24, 31; 27: 42 (?)). In reporting Jesus' attitude to Israel it is possible that Matthew is himself subscribing to it and indicating that in his own day the Church is still carrying out a mission to them.[7] Consistent with

[1] So Hummel, *Auseinandersetzung*, pp. 160 f.; 156 n. 72.

[2] So Trilling, *Wahre Israel*, pp. 138 ff., 162 f., 213 (see criticism by Strecker, *Gerechtigkeit*, p. 199 n. 1; D. R. A. Hare, *The Theme of Jewish Persecution of Christians in the Gospel acc. to St Mt* (*SNTS* Mono. 6, Cambridge, 1967), pp. 156 ff.).

[3] Bornkamm, *Tradition*, p. 39; Barth, *ibid.* pp. 92, 108, 111 f., 116; *per contra*, Hare, *Persecution*, pp. 147 f.

[4] For evidence see Hummel, *Auseinandersetzung*, ch. 3.

[5] With the possible exception of *ekklēsia*.

[6] Cf. Ps. 111: 10. He does not express 'die heilsgeschichtliche Ablösung des jüdischen Volkes' (*contra* Strecker, *Gerechtigkeit*, pp. 101, 117 f. and Goppelt, *Christentum und Judentum*, p. 181). Luke is closer to this by virtue of his addition in 13: 30.

[7] Working against this is Matt.'s last sentence and Jesus' last words (28: 19). Trilling, *Wahre Israel*, thinks this is the key to the whole book

this is the fact that *Ioudaios* in the main narrative does not appear as a term of abuse, nor does Matthew distinguish between 'Israel' and 'Jew'. The only possible case is in 28: 15 where *Ioudaios* probably means Judean.

There is a gap between the Church and Synagogue,[1] and there may be an assault upon the Church by the Synagogue, as the recent book by D. R. A. Hare details.[2] There is a contemporary dispute which gives rise to many of the questions dealt with by Matthew,[3] but there are indications that he would like the two to live harmoniously. He adds an interpretative conclusion to the parable of garments and wineskins (9: 16 f.; καὶ ἀμφότεροι συντηροῦνται) which seems to have the point of minimizing the old/new contrast.[4] As a conclusion it is misleading: the main feature of the parable is the inability of the old to contain the new, not the preservation of wine and wineskins. By this change he refers to Judaism and Christianity.[5] Similarly Matthew concludes chapter 13 with a saying on discipleship in the special case of a scribe's conversion (13: 51 f.).[6] It is doubtful, though, that Matthew, with his blurring of old and new, has preserved the original intention of the saying,

(p. 21). On particularism and universalism, see Jeremias, *Jesus' Promise*, esp. p. 34; Davies, *Sermon*, pp. 326 ff.

[1] 'Their' synagogues (4: 23; 9: 35; 10: 17; 12: 9; 13: 54; cf. 6: 2, 5; 23: 34) and 'their' scribes (7: 28 f.); see Bornkamm, *Tradition*, p. 39; cf. Davies, *Sermon*, pp. 296 f.; Hare, *Persecution*, pp. 104 ff.

[2] *Persecution, passim*. The main criticism of this is that too much of the evidence is read through the perspective of Matt. 23: 29–39, though his main contentions carry conviction. It is strange that he nowhere deals with Matt. 7: 15 (see Davies, *Sermon*, pp. 199 ff.); cf. 11: 12; 12: 29; 13: 19; 23: 25.

[3] Hummel, *Auseinandersetzung*, pp. 35, 55, 99; cf. Davies, *Sermon*, pp. 256 ff., 286, 315.

[4] Luke (especially) and Mark retain this contrast more fully. Both Matt. and Luke (= Q) add an unnecessary generalization to Mark's parable—an apologetic for the new form which Christian life and worship took (cf. Schniewind, *NTD*, 9th edition, 1960, p. 120; Hare, *Persecution*, neglects this type of evidence).

[5] He alters the context in keeping with this (9: 14); cf. C. G. Montefiore, *The Synoptic Gospels*, II (London, 1927, 2nd edition), p. 138 (citing Klostermann); W. C. Allen, *ICC* (3rd edition, 1912), *in loc*.

[6] C. F. D. Moule, *Studia Evangelica*, II, 91 ff., suggests that this is a secular, not a rabbinic, scribe (pp. 98 f.). Cf. K. Stendahl, *The School of St Matthew* (*ASNU*, xx, Uppsala, 1954), p. 30.

which probably referred to the storehouse of God (cf. 13: 27; 20: 1, 11; 21: 33) where old things had been kept but from which new things are now coming. By shifting the saying to apply to the scribe Matthew has put new and old on the same footing as in the wineskins parable.

Matthew uses the first/last idea in a more clear-cut way. In 12: 43–5 he makes an explicit application to Jesus' generation (or his own?); their last condition is worse than their former because they reject the 'greater one' (12: 41 f.). A purely temporal idea gives way to a succession between two groups in 19: 30 ff., where 'many who are first will be last, and the last first' stands as an introduction to the following parable, which itself concludes with a similar saying (20: 16). By so doing, Matthew changes the point of the parable from equality in the kingdom to reversal of orders, though he has not gone so far as to introduce non-payment of the first. He applies it to a situation where Christians are held to be second class, and tries to turn the criticism by a saying of Jesus.[1]

Close to this antithesis is the comparison running through the parables of 21: 28 – 22: 14.[2] The parable of the unlike sons (21: 28 ff.) does not teach any reversal of categories but rather the opportunity of the irreligious to be obedient and hence to enter the kingdom, while leaders in Judaism will be excluded.[3] In the next parable of the husbandmen, Matthew embellishes the conclusion to make it apply to the Church.[4] All gospels agree that the vineyard will be given to others, but Matthew reinforces the conclusion by an explicit statement that 'the kingdom of God will be taken away from you, and given to a nation (ἔθνει) producing the fruits from it'. The contrast

---

[1] See Jeremias, *Parables*, pp. 33–8; originally it applied to the 'poor' (cf. Baum, *Jews*, p. 49: it 'does not in any way refer to Jews and Gentiles'). It *is* intended to refer to Christians and Jews, with the implication that Christians are every bit as good as Jews.

[2] Cf. Lohmeyer–Schmauch, *KEK*, Sonderband (1956), p. 323. K. W. Clark, *JBL*, LXVI (1947), 165 ff., uses this group of parables as the main evidence for 'the Gentile bias in Matt.'

[3] Προάγουσιν is exclusive; Jeremias, *Parables*, p. 125 n. 48; Lohmeyer–Schmauch, *KEK*, p. 308 n. 2.

[4] For other ecclesiological variations in Matt. see above, ch. 6. Cf. Trilling, *Wahre Israel*, p. 61; Strecker, *Gerechtigkeit*, p. 33; Schniewind, *NTD*, p. 219; Lohmeyer-Schmauch, *KEK*, pp. 314 f.

between the nation[1] and the chief priests and Pharisees (against whom the parable is directed according to Matthew 21:45) is for Matthew a present contrast between the Church and the leaders of contemporary Judaism.

Matthew allows himself the greatest freedom in 22: 1–14.[2] The leaders of Judaism are again found wanting and the outcasts of Palestinian society are invited to take their places. The refusal of the one group and the acceptance of the other, however, does not take on the form of a *heilsgeschichtlich* scheme.[3] The invitation in the parable is firmly addressed to Judaism, not to the Gentile world. The 'Church' exists as the group of those who have responded, but it is a mixed group (22: 11–14). This second parable[4] deals with the internal character of the Church, not the larger external question of Jew and Gentile. The gospel is written in such a predominantly Jewish milieu that interest centres in the question of the relationship of non-Christian Jews to the Christian Church.

This is the reason also for Matthew's editorial changes to Mark's theory of the purpose of parables (13: 10 ff.). The principal alteration is the starker contrast between the disciples and a hardened people,[5] apparent from the addition of the verbatim LXX quotation in contrast to the added saying (cf. Luke 10: 23 f.): 'Blessed are your eyes...'[6] This heightening occurs under the influence of the division between the Church and surrounding Judaism,[7] which has heard for forty years, but has not understood. By altering Mark's ἵνα to ὅτι Matthew changes the theoretical basis of the statement into an observable result, but it is no less harsh for that, as his retention of μήποτε in the quotation shows.

---

[1] Strecker, *Gerechtigkeit*, p. 33, and Hare, *Persecution*, pp. 156–62, try to make *ethnos* into a *tertium genus*. This is anachronistic.

[2] Bonnard, *CNT*, pp. 318 f.; G. Bornkamm, *Jesus*, p. 18. T. W. Manson, *Teaching*, Detached Note B, pp. 83 ff., thinks Matt. has conflated two parables in *vv.* 1–10 and added a third in *vv.* 11–14.

[3] Contrast Luke's conclusion in 14: 24 (οὐδεὶς τῶν ἀνδρῶν) which agrees with his schematic view.

[4] For the relationship see J. Schmid, *RNT* (3rd edition, 1956), p. 308; cf. Jeremias, *Parables*, pp. 106, 110 ff.

[5] So Gnilka, *Verstockung*, p. 89 (see all pp. 89–115); cf. G. Barth, *Tradition*, pp. 105 ff., 116.

[6] See Stendahl, *School*, pp. 129 ff., 135.

[7] See Bonnard, *CNT*, p. 193; Davies, *Sermon*, pp. 234 f.

Chapter 23, which contains a strong polemic against the leaders of Judaism,[1] need not imply that the Church is totally cut off from the Synagogue. In fact some of the sayings presuppose that all intercourse between the two is not precluded.[2] When Matthew uses 'you' in 23: 1–12 he refers to the Church, and it is just this section which is most Matthean.[3] There is still an externally observable continuity with Judaism. The difference is found in the Christian standard of action, which is marked by self-limitation in contrast to self-exaltation. The editor applies sayings of Jesus to a Christian community[4] that was living in such close contact with pharisaic Judaism that it was in danger of retaining too many of its customs.[5] In the second section (*vv.* 13–36) there is less in the way of a direct application and a stronger polemic but the purpose is the same: a demonstration that the post-Jamnian synagogue, while it thinks it does God's will, is actually falling far short.[6] The only obedient people is the Christian community, and their obedience carries with it the judgment of God upon others.

The immediate point of contact between chapter 23 and chapters 5–7 is 6: 1–8, where a similar contrast between the two communities is found, including closer adherence to some Jewish customs by Christians. Similarly 5: 17–20 requires 'doing and teaching' in place of the Pharisees' 'teaching but not doing'. Righteousness, about which the Pharisee is concerned, is impossible apart from discipleship to Christ. The

---

[1] See especially E. Haenchen, *ZTK*, XLVIII (1951), 38–63. Bonnard undervalues the polemic (*CNT*, p. 333).

[2] The context in Matt. includes 'the crowds and his disciples'. Schniewind, *NTD*, p. 225, remarks on the similarity of this to the introduction of the Sermon on the Mount (cf. Davies, *Sermon*, pp. 106, 291 f.), both blocks of material in which we see the contemporary situation most clearly. Is it possible that behind 'crowds' we are to understand the Jewish people who are still outside the Church, but with whom the Church is in contact, though it has abandoned the leaders?

[3] Cf. Schmid, *RNT*, p. 321; Filson, *BNTC* (1960), pp. 242 f.; Lohmeyer–Schmauch, *KEK*, pp. 335, 341.

[4] But not necessarily a 'narrowly Jewish Christian group', *contra* E. Schweizer, *Church Order in the NT* (*SBT*, XXXII, London, 1961), p. 51 (4*a*).

[5] Note esp. 'Rabbi', 23: 7 f.; possibly also 'teacher'. Cf. Bornkamm, *Tradition*, p. 21.

[6] But (*contra* Haenchen, *ZTK*, XLVIII, 1951, p. 59) they are not a *massa perditionis*. See Hummel, *Auseinandersetzung*, pp. 87–9.

rebuke of 5: 17, with its dialectic between 'abolish' and 'fulfil', is picked up in the antitheses of 5: 21–48, in which there is an extension, deepening, and loosening of the Law.[1] These antitheses, based upon sayings of Jesus, are partially restructured to repudiate charges brought against Christians by the Synagogue,[2] in an attempt to stave off the break between the two.[3] This is apparent also in the paragraph 7: 13–27 which reads like a dissertation on the 'two ways': pharisaic Judaism and Jewish Christianity.

This sketchy treatment of Matthew's redactional motifs suggests that, in so far as he works towards a theory of the Church as 'true Israel',[4] he does it as a Jewish Christian for a Jewish Christian community,[5] as a part of a dispute with a pharisaic Synagogue which is also claiming to be 'true Israel'. In the post-Jamnian situation where a Jewish Christian church might stand alongside a synagogue, each has a deep need to clarify its thinking about its relationship to the cultus and the Law.[6] Each is forced to move beyond the attitude before the fall of Jerusalem towards these matters, and in doing so each is tempted to claim that it fully represents 'Israel'. The pharisaic community rested its claim basically on continuous tradition; the Christian on the fulfilment of the old and better obedience through the Messiah. Since the Church in Matthew's gospel is not a Gentile Church,[7] as it works towards the take-over of the 'true Israel' idea, it is very conscious of continuity between itself and the old entity. It is not a *tertium genus*.

[1] See, *inter alia*, E. Hasler, *Gesetz und Evangelium* (Frankfurt a. M., 1953), pp. 12 f.

[2] To introduce 'antinomians' here is unnecessary and pointless; *contra* Barth, *Tradition*, pp. 71, 75, 159 ff.; Hummel, *Auseinandersetzung*, pp. 56 ff.

[3] So also Schweizer, *Church Order*, pp. 53 f. (4b) on 19: 1–12.

[4] However, none of the attempts to make Matthew's gospel a new Law, etc. are convincing (e.g. K. Thieme, 'Matt., der schriftgelehrte Evangelist', *Jud*, v (1949), 130–52, 161–82).

[5] Matt. holds a universalist position on mission, but mission has not yet altered the basic character of his community.

[6] It is the great merit of Hummel's book (*Auseinandersetzung*) that this is stressed, pp. 35 ff.; *per contra*, Hare, *Persecution*, pp. 141 ff., 158 f.

[7] For this reason, G. D. Kilpatrick's term ('the rejudaization of the Gospel') is questionable; see *The Origins of the Gospel According to St Matthew* (Oxford, 1946), p. 103, cf. a better statement on p. 108.

CHAPTER VII

CONCLUDING SUMMARY

In the analytical section we constantly found a Jewish 'problem' lying behind particular transpositions, take-overs, and tendencies to supplant the old Israel by a new or true Israel. Attack from Judaism was the original and continuing cause of the phenomena discussed in the foregoing chapters. It centred upon the Jewish wing of the young Church—precisely the segment where one finds the earliest groping towards a satisfactory formulation of the relationship between the Church and Israel. The problem was raised in a very different form by the Gentile side of the Church, for Gentile Christians did not stand in an ambivalent relationship to Israel. They could be admitted to Israel but had no specific claim upon the attributes of Israel; these they could only assume by incorporation into the People of God. There came later a period when the Church had separated from Judaism and Gentile Christianity felt that, on sufficient theological grounds, it could make the transposition on its own; but in the formative period it was Jewish mission and Jewish reaction which created the difficulties resulting in the take-overs. It is important to note that it was the failure of Jewish mission which gave rise to the only sustained treatment of the problem of the Church/Israel relationship in Romans 9–11.

The most searching difficulties, after Jesus had come and revealed himself as Son of Man and Messiah, were posed by the twin questions of the status of unbelieving pious Jews and of Jews who had followed Jesus in the new Way of salvation. The original Jewish constitution of the Church depended upon certain simple facts: Jesus was himself a Jew; all his early disciples were Jews; his whole mission was centred upon Israel. To a very large extent, the function of these early followers was to engage in a mission to Israel: to call all Israel to repentance before the Son of Man should come again. This Israelitic concern embraced an expectation for the gathering of the Gentiles as well, in fulfilment of the prophets' hope, but the mission was not Gentile-centred, becoming so only at a later date. As an initially Jewish protest movement, problems of the self-designation, life, and organization of the early community were all met by an *apologia* to the rest of the Jewish people.

Christians confronted Judaism as the group of those who believed in the Messiahship and Lordship of Jesus, and held that he had been wrongfully accused and punished by the Jewish leaders in concert with the Roman overlords. When they proclaimed this 'good' news, calling into question the pre-suppositions of centuries of tradition concerning Israel's hopes and expectations, opposition was certain to come quickly. Acts records examples of the opposition engendered by the early preaching to Jews, and numerous reflections can be seen in Paul's letters, especially Galatians and Thessalonians. Hostility made reassessment necessary. Christians had to reconsider the importance and the validity of all the institutions which Judaism considered precious. The results of this reassessment varied in the degree of thoroughness of application, but all were christologically oriented and all stemmed from the belief that in Jesus the end times—the time of promise—had arrived.

If Jesus had inaugurated the time of fulfilment, it surely would not be long before he returned to establish it fully. However, the growing chronological gap from the time of his death created a new problem. Had Jesus returned very soon, as many in the early Church expected (1 Thessalonians, Philippians, Corinthians, even as late as Romans) there would have been little need to explain the Church's self-awareness (as, e.g., in 1 and 2 Thessalonians and Galatians). As the expectation of an imminent return faded, the idea of an interim period gave way to the full-blown concept of a second period alongside the period of time before Christ. Various 'theories' can be isolated concerning the precise nature of the relationship of one period to the other; the views in Galatians, 2 Corinthians, Luke/Acts, Mark, Hebrews all must be described in somewhat different terms. Correspondingly, the Church became more self-conscious, with a deep need to explain its existence and its relationship to the Judaism from which it sprang. As time passed all the marginal problems which had been shelved, or answered hastily, in the period of enthusiasm and imminent expectation pressed for more theologically satisfying answers. Thus mission, which was originally focused on Jews, was reconsidered in the light of the new conditions.

God-fearers and proselytes raised these questions initially. Probably as a direct result of pharisaic activity, the synagogues of the Diaspora, even in areas close to Palestine, had a large percentage of non-Jewish adherents. Attracted by Jewish monotheism and high moral standards, they stood in varying degrees of closeness to the life and worship of Israel. These constituted the most fertile ground for Christian mission. When messengers were invited, or took it upon themselves, to proclaim the gospel in synagogues, God-fearers were attracted to this sect which claimed to fulfil the religion to which they were loosely attached, for it showed signs of a willingness to rethink its attitude (if it had not already done so) to some of the more difficult observances of Judaism. The readiness of proselytes and God-fearers to adhere to this new group meant in turn that the young Church had to answer such questions, and in a way that would allow for the full equality of this group.

The most offensive demand of Judaism was circumcision, and against this problem the Church came very early. Its answer provided the archetypal solution to all the other problems. Gentiles had always been able to be admitted into Israel on the fulfilment of certain proselyte regulations, chief of which was circumcision. The Church knew that Jesus himself had anticipated a gathering of Gentiles, but nothing had ever been said about the need for their being circumcised. In Jesus' lifetime the only step that had been taken was to make it clear that even members of the People of God needed to be *baptized* for admission. Logically, Gentiles should undergo the rite of circumcision for it was a matter of cleanness and uncleanness (Acts 10: 9 ff.). However, the earliest *ad hoc* answer was that baptism could be administered without circumcision (Acts 10: 44 ff.; cf. 15: 1 ff.). It became necessary to make a ruling on the matter (Acts 15: 6 ff.), based more on their doctrine of the Holy Spirit than on their doctrine of Christ (15: 8, cf. 15: 11). The earliest Pauline formulation was that there was no difference between circumcision and uncircumcision (Galatians 6: 15; 1 Corinthians 7: 19, etc.). This later gave way to the more satisfactory statement, in the face of Jewish attack, 'we are circumcision' (Philippians 3: 3), which in turn allowed for the total spiritualizing of the idea so that circumcision itself came to have no significance: it could be reckoned to be uncircumcision and *vice versa* (Romans 2: 25 ff.). Later still this was given a firm christological basis, which followed upon the earlier partially christological basis found in Galatians 2: 4, 15 ff. and 5: 4, where circumcision is one aspect of the Law, and the Law (done away with in Christ) is insufficient for justification. In Colossians 2: 8 ff. there is a retrospective appreciation of the relationship between Christ, circumcision, and baptism. From here the development is not so clear. Probably children of Jewish Christians began not to be circumcised (cf. Acts 21: 21), and this, together with the gradual attrition of Jewish Christian leadership, contributed to the identification of Christianity as a Gentile religion. The same factors help to account for the isolation of a purely hebraistic Christianity as well.

Circumcision is a clear example of the developing need to take over aspects of Judaism, and of the way these slowly became divorced from their origins and absorbed into the theology of the Church. A similar process occurred with cultic issues, though here the solution went back ultimately to a saying of Jesus about the destruction of a 'temple'. Jesus' death was the ground for the cessation of sacrifice (though this may not have ceased until A.D. 132), and he was himself the replacement of the Temple. A question about this replacement instigated the first martyrdom in the Church (Acts 6: 13 f.). Even though many early Christians might choose to continue to approach God cultically in Jerusalem, as a whole they were aware of the fact that through Jesus they had such a close relationship to God that this was not necessary: they, themselves, are temples of the Holy Spirit (1 Corinthians 3: 16; 6: 19; 2 Corinthians 6: 16). As the Church became more aware of itself this was turned into a community metaphor: Christians corporately (i.e. the Church) are the Temple of God and the House of God (Ephesians 2: 21 f.; Hebrews 3: 1 ff.; 1 Peter 2: 5; 1 Timothy 3: 15). But even in Hebrews, the most cultically oriented book, emphasis rests upon the christological implications of the old cult, rather than the explicit transposition of these into a new Christian context. Cultic language could be taken over to apply to various Christian features (Romans 12: 1 f.; 15: 5 f.; Philippians *passim*), but it was not a consistent take-over.

As the Church grew out of the Synagogue it appropriated synagogal forms for its own, almost unconsciously. A special matter, however, proved to be the relationship between Jews and Gentiles within these communities. The early Church had to resolve at an early period any inconsistency it might have been tempted to perpetuate, and admit the complete equality of Jewish and Gentile Christians. This came to a head in the matter of table fellowship (Acts 11: 3 f.; Galatians 2: 11 ff.), about which certain injunctions were given to make matters easier for Jewish Christians (Acts 15: 19 ff.). Conditions were ripe for a less than satisfactory situation; for, with the increasing success of the growing Gentile mission and with the need for special consideration to be given to Jewish Christians, Gentile Christians began to look on the others as 'weak' (1 Corinthians 8; 9: 20 ff.; Romans 14–15). 'Weak' Christians were subordinated by their attachment to Jewish custom; thus it was to their advantage that the things of Judaism should be transposed into a Christian context, and that this should be theologically justified. Such a need lies behind the letter to the Hebrews and the editorial peculiarities of Matthew's gospel.

The main problem was Law. The Christian solution was based upon Jesus' controversies with the leaders of Judaism over the Law's validity. While early Christians found it useful and good to maintain contact with the Law (Matthew 5: 17 ff.) they were able to forgo obedience to the leaders and assert obedience to God alone (Acts 4: 19 f.). The solution to the problem of Law was fully christologically grounded (Galatians 2: 15 ff.) at an early stage, though it continued to be a problem for a period (1 Timothy 1: 8 ff.; Matthew *passim*). In very simple terms, the solution was that Christ is the end and fulfilment of the Law. However, there was a constant tendency to fail to assert the freedom that there is in Jesus (e.g. 1 Corinthians 9: 19 ff.), which leads, in post-Apostolic times, to the safer but much less satisfactory assertion that Christianity embraces a new Law.

Closely related to this is the Christian's attitude to the scriptures. In the time of the new covenant the scriptures have been fulfilled, the degree of fulfilment corresponding to the degree to which one tended to appropriate the Old Testament for Christians alone. As Christianity became increasingly separated from Judaism and the link which this provided with history, the tendency to cut the Old Testament loose from its plain historical meaning increased. Allegorical interpretation was able to turn it into a Christian book. This happened at the hands of Barnabas and Justin, though the tendency was apparent earlier in Hebrews and 1 Peter and before that in the assertion by Paul that things were written not for them alone but also for Christians (Romans 4: 32 f.; cf. 1 Corinthians 9: 9 f.). Further, a hermeneutical principle was employed which applied to Gentiles or Christians statements that formerly applied to Israel, and conversely made it possible to apply to Israel statements that originally referred to Gentiles (e.g. Jesus' allusion to Psalm 111: 10 in Matthew 8: 12 par., and Paul's use of Isaiah 65: 1 f.). Moreover, Paul's hermeneutic in dealing with the Gentiles' place in the story of Abraham, and in wrestling with the meaning of the covenant (once basing it on the case of Abraham and once on Moses) probably contributed to his assessment of the relationship of Church and Israel.

This led naturally to the taking over of Israelitic terms for Christians. Mostly this was a result of the Church's awareness that it stood in a direct continuity with Israel. Nevertheless, there was a reluctance to assume these titles; often the Church preferred to use secondary titles which did not constitute such a direct claim upon the place of the whole of Israel, or else it coined new terms. The one which it unequivocally took over was 'church', together with such descriptive terms as 'elect', 'brethren', etc.; it coined or had minted for it new titles such as 'the Way' and 'Christians'. At the same time it slowly appropriated the weightier terms, so that eventually 'people' (*laos*) became applicable to the new community (Titus 2: 14; Hebrews 2: 17; 1 Peter 2: 9 f.; perhaps Acts 15: 14; 18: 10). 'Israel', the most revered name, was yet more slowly taken over, remaining for a long time applicable only to the old entity. It was in the context of a growing accumulation of titles and attributes, and the fuller acknowledgment of the Church's inheritance in the place of abandoned Judaism, that 'Israel' could become an *Ehrentitel* of the Church.

The Church did not readily abandon its interest in the People of God; Jewish mission was a constant factor in the early Church (Acts, Paul, Matthew, John) and continued into the post-Apostolic period (Justin). When Palestinian Judaism showed itself reluctant to accept the message interest was transferred to the Diaspora. This transferral can be recognized as early as Paul, who constructed a theory to relate the work in the Diaspora to Palestinian Judaism's salvation. John, on the other hand, was more nearly in line with Jesus' view that, after Judea had heard (and rejected) the gospel, the world would hear through the Diaspora. However, as long as there was any expectation of Israel's acceptance, Christianity could not pre-empt the title 'Israel' without shutting the door to Judaism.

The early Church was concerned with the problem of Jewish refusal, and considered often the Old Testament background to this, especially Isaiah 6: 9 f. The development in the use of this text corresponded to the changing form of the problem the Church faced. The gospels reflect the simple problem of outright rejection of Jesus partly overlaid with a tendency to make this into a theory (Mark, Matthew) and a counter-tendency to use it to seal the fate of Judean Jews (John) or of the Diaspora (Luke/Acts). These all appear to write off further hope for a turning of the Jews to God in Jesus. It was Paul who pressed reminiscences of Isaiah 6: 9 f. into service for a much grander theory, in which he expected Jews ultimately to be saved. He could make this hope intelligible only if he posited that it applied to godly Jews, that it had never been God's intention, discernible also by observation, to save all Jews. Thus Paul distinguished between 'Jew' and 'Israel', a distinction in line with, but a development upon, late Judaism's distinction between one's own group (the godly remnant) and the rest. This allowed Paul to account for disbelief and to hope for belief. Only after his optimism was abandoned could 'Israel' be applied to the Church. There was a relaxation of hope in the later Paulines (Colossians, Ephesians, Pastorals) and still more clearly by those who followed him (Luke/Acts, 1 Peter, Hebrews, Mark). When these were written the respective authors seem to have had not even a theoretical basis for an expectation of Israel's salvation, let alone any practical evidence of it. Thus each could move farther towards an association of the Church with 'Israel'.

The other side of Paul's theory is his reversal of the order of priority of reception in mission. His experience in his travels

was that when, in line with Jesus' intention, he went to Jews
first they refused the gospel, but when he preached to
Gentiles they received the message. This, together with his Old
Testament exegesis, led him to expect a reception largely from
Gentiles. He constructed the theory that this Gentile acceptance
would provoke Jews into belief by a rebound reaction, and with
this in mind he went to Jerusalem to test it. Instead of an
enthusiastic acclaim, he was unceremoniously imprisoned.
Whether this was the thing which made him give up his
theory of the rebound is not sure. What is clear is that his
expectation seems to have been dropped not long after fully
formulating it.

The success of the Gentile mission created new tensions
within the Christian community, and new problems concerned
with the Gentiles' relationship to Jews who were Christians
before them. The latter was answered very early; there is no
difference at all, Gentiles need not become proselytes through
circumcision. Paul answered it in terms of their ability to
participate in all the privileges, by being reckoned as if they
had them. They are grafted in, and this metaphor continued to
be used even after hope for Jews is lost (Ephesians). Jew and
Gentile co-existed in a community having a function to perform
in the end times. Within this community tensions arose, again
as a result of the success of Gentile mission. There was a
tendency for Gentiles to 'boast' (Romans 15: 7 ff.; Ephesians
2: 11 ff.) and to put Jewish Christians in an inferior place, due
partly at least to their 'weakness' in food matters.

How far this general climate of opinion affected individual
writers is uncertain. Mark, who shows an interest in Gentiles,
constructed what appears to be a theory about Jewish rejection
and expected Gentile acceptance, the result of which seems to
be the abandoning of hope for any Jewish response. Luke, on
the other hand, had a schematic view in which the facts of the
Gentile mission are read back, in part, into his gospel. While
Acts shows that there is not a total absence of concern for Jews,
the conclusion of that volume would suggest that in A.D. 62
there was little hope. The writer of the letter to the Hebrews,
on the other hand, was so interested in the fulfilment of promise
that he did not even raise the question of a contemporary
response among Jews. When he did consider Judaism, he

pleaded for a separation of the new from the old. John is rather different, for he used the Judean situation as a warning to the Diaspora. In Matthew the pressing problem was the confrontation by a Judaism which was also claiming to be the true Israel.

The noticeable feature of these is that where there is a 'scheme' it involves the theoretical or practical priority of the Gentiles in the present time (similar to Paul), and the absence of further hope for Judaism (unlike Paul up to Romans). This feature is apparent in Mark, Luke/Acts. Where there is no 'scheme', the tendency is to downgrade Judaism and to undervalue future expectation. John's partially polemic use of 'Jew', Hebrews' emphasis on 'passing away', Matthew's new concentration on the Church, 1 Peter's transference of titles to former proselytes and God-fearers—all these tend to relegate old 'Israel' to an inferior place and to replace it with a 'Church' (sometimes Gentile-oriented) which in time will claim to be the 'true Israel'.

With this development some external factors should be noted as contributory. The persecution of Stephen and the subsequent Jewish persecutions helped, from the Jewish side, to create a break between the Church and Israel. At the same time, there was a growing recognition by the State of the Church's important differences from Israel, which called into question any favoured status they might expect. These two factors coalesce during Paul's stay in Rome with the recognition and punishment of Christians by Nero. For a few years at least it is to Judaism's advantage to emphasize the differences. Whether it becomes desirable, after A.D. 70, for Christians to separate themselves from Judean (not necessarily non-Judean) Jews is not sure. In any case the recognition of the *de facto* relationship may be found in the *Birkath ha-Minim* of *c.* A.D. 85, by which post-Jamnian Judaism tried to conclude the breach. That they were unsuccessful is shown by some allusions in the Apostolic Fathers, and especially in Justin. But the war of A.D. 132–5 did what the Synagogue Ban did not: to all intents and purposes it severed the two groups, freeing later Christians from the need to assert close contact with Judaism and providing for them evidence of the full 'judgment' of God upon Israel. From this point, Christians polemize more consistently.

As the Church grew apart from Israel it began to develop its ecclesiology, replacing *ad hoc* titles and functional characteristics by more Church-conscious terms. As long as Jesus' disciples constituted a band within Israel, there was little need to take over such terms. When it no longer saw itself as a purifying element within Israel, its relationship to the whole had to be thought out again. Reconsideration was necessary whether the whole as such had any significance, or if only the part represented by the community of Christians was faithful. In its first gropings, this involved the take-over of nominal Jewish terms, and gradually became a self-conscious appropriation of the more important cultic terms.

In general terms, the further one proceeds chronologically the clearer is the picture of the Church as a thing unto itself, and the nearer one gets to a *tertium genus*. In the years when the Church was basically another group beside the Synagogue, there were only a few hints that could lead to a *tertium genus* theory (1 Corinthians 10: 32; Matthew 21: 43). In the Apostolic Fathers, where ecclesiology was developed seemingly at the expense of Christology, a full *tertium genus* began to appear; first in *Kerygma Petri* of the manner of worshipping, and then with increasing frequency, until it became the normative view of the Church's relationship to the rest of the world. The development of ecclesiology and the growth of a *tertium genus* theory were necessary stages before the name 'Israel' could be adequately and legitimately appropriated. As long as the Church was viewed as a community gathered from Gentiles and Jews, it could not readily call itself 'Israel'. But when it was sharply separated from both, and when it had a theory that Judaism no longer stood in a continuity with Israel *ante Christum*, and when Gentiles not only could take over other titles but in some cases could claim exclusive rights to them, then the Church as an organizational entity could appropriate 'Israel'.

Behind all of the factors noted above lay weighty theological factors, foremost of which was the tendency to portray Jesus in himself as 'true Israel' (e.g. John 15: 1 ff.). From the beginning his disciples knew that his unique status as Prophet, Servant of God, Son of Man, the Anointed One of God, gave him a peculiar relationship to Israel, though there was a reticence to delineate this positively. The Son of Man and Servant concepts, particularly, lent themselves to the statement that Jesus was 'Israel'. Having originally both a corporate and an individual significance applicable to the 'saints' within Israel, they could be focused upon the one person Jesus who fulfilled these functions and was, therefore, by inference 'Israel'. Such an identification is not made in the New Testament; it remains a theological deduction made by Justin though latent in John's vine metaphor. There is thus a theological validity in the statement that Jesus, especially at that moment when he hangs on the cross, is 'Israel'.

As we have said, there is no historic instance of Jesus making this claim, or of anyone making it for him at an early period. The christological problem centred in other factors, mostly connected with the supersession of the old and the bringing of new things. Jesus was seen as the New Man, related analogically to the Old Man Adam as second is to first. The most far-reaching assertion was that Jesus, in his death, had fulfilled the Old Testament expectation of a new covenant. The former covenant was 'old', and the present one—understandable only through Jesus' death and resurrection—is 'new'. This carried with it other implications, the main one being that the character of covenant had changed from being written on tables of stone, to being written by the Spirit on living and receptive hearts (2 Corinthians 3).

By being disciples of Christ, Christians become new men and members of this new covenant. They are given the Spirit as the sign of their inheritance, and participate in all the other trans-formations which Jesus prefigures. As he is a priest, they become priests; as he is a temple, they are temples. So close is the Christians' relationship to Jesus that they are members of the Body, of which he is Head. It is this analogy of the Body which especially encouraged development in the doctrine of the Church. When the Body is at one and the same time related to Jesus, who is (tentatively) 'true Israel', and to the disciples on earth, the Church, it is not a difficult step to equate the Church with 'true Israel'. At its most profound·level, the identification of the Church with the Israel of God was a step based upon a developed Christology. It was a step which could hardly be taken apart from the explicit assertion that Jesus is 'Israel'. It is very significant that it was Justin, the first to call Jesus 'Israel', who was the first to call the Church 'true Israel'. Numerous practical and theoretical factors, social and theological needs, were at work in this development, but it was especially the lively awareness that Jesus is God's own anointed Son who fulfils in himself all that Israel was meant to be that led to the Church being identified with the 'Israel of God' by c. A.D. 160.

THE 'APOLOGY' OF ARISTIDES

The *Apology* of Aristides raises complex critical and textual problems for which a convincing answer has not yet been found. Its importance to this study lies in its witness to the continuity and discontinuity of Judaism and Christianity, and in its assertion of a *tertium genus*. The following hypothesis on these matters will need to be tested by close textual work.[1]

J. R. Harris has pointed out the many reasons (based on his examination of the Syriac version) for an early date,[2] and then, because of the difficulties of the superscription, rejected the early date. Conversely, J. A. Robinson inclined towards the reliability of the Greek version, and yet accepted an early date.[3] Geffcken accepts the priority of neither text and constructs an eclectic text in which the basic structure follows the Greek with large additions from the Syriac.[4] The discovery of some Greek papyri confirms the fluidity of the textual tradition and the necessity for constructing an eclectic text such as Geffcken's, for these attest both Greek and Syriac readings, representing an intermediate point between the two but generally closer to the Syriac.[5] It seems no longer possible to decide decisively for any

---

[1] The main materials for the construction of a text are in J. R. Harris and J. A. Robinson, *Texts and Studies*, I, I, *The Apology of Aristides* (Cambridge, 1891). Attempts to reconstruct the original text have been made from time to time, the two most important being J. Geffcken, *Zwei griechische Apologeten* (Leipzig u. Berlin, 1907), and E. J. Goodspeed, *Die ältesten Apologeten* (Göttingen, 1914). The work of Harris and Robinson is used below for text and translation.

[2] *Texts and Studies*, p. 13: style, religious ideas, ethics. He goes on: 'There is no sign of the hostile tone which we find towards the Jews in the *Martyrdom of Polycarp*, and nothing like the severity of contempt which we find in the *Epistle to Diognetus*. If the Church is not in the writer's time any longer under the wing of the Synagogue, it has apparently no objection to taking the Synagogue under its own wing.'

[3] *Ibid.* p. 80: '...the Greek, as we have it, will as a rule give us the actual words of Aristides'; cf. p. 75 n. 2.   [4] *Apologeten*, pp. xxxv ff. and 44.

[5] Published by Grenfell and Hunt, *Oxyrhynchus Papyri* (London, 1922), 1778; and by H. J. M. Milne, *JTS*, xxv (1924), 73-7.

existing text.[1] These papyri are the most important materials for constructing a text, in spite of their brevity.

The facts of the structure of the work are these: (1) the Armenian and Syriac versions agree (para. 2) in dividing the world into four races; the Greek divides the world into three races (τρία γένη) one of which is subdivided into three parts (τρία διαιροῦντα γένη). (2) The Syriac and Armenian agree substantially in including in para. 2 a discussion of the origin of each race, while the Greek includes the substance of these descriptions in the pertinent sections on the individual races. (3) The Syriac (Armenian not extant) then describes the Barbarians (3–7), the Greeks (8–13) including a digression on the Egyptians (12), the Jews (14), and the Christians (15 ff.). The Greek in its doubly tripartite scheme deals with Chaldeans (3–7, replacing Barbarians), Greeks (8–11), and Egyptians (12). It then has a complex conclusion to this part in para. 13: 13.1–6 refers to all three; 13.7 ff. refers to the Greeks alone. There follows, as before, a description of Jews (14) and Christians (15 ff.). The majority of scholars, even those who accept the priority of Syriac, accept the tripartite division of the Greek.[2]

The four-part division must be unique in Christian literature. A decision to settle for the tripartite scheme must at the same time account for the development, within a Christian milieu which has generally endorsed the tripartite scheme, of two separate witnesses to the quadripartite division.[3] There is an *a priori* presumption that the four-part is original. The more sophisticated two-level system is likely to be later than the less systematic four-part arrangement. The same conclusion is indicated by the following considerations:

(*a*) In para. 2 the generalizing circumlocution of the Greek carries little conviction of originality: οἱ τῶν παρ' ὑμῖν λεγομένων θεῶν προσκυνηταί.

---

[1] R. L. Wolff, *HTR*, xxx (1937), 233–47, makes out a case for the priority of the Greek but his hypothesis founders on neglect of the papyrus fragments which had been published some years earlier.

[2] J. A. Robinson is typical (*The Apology of Aristides*, a lecture delivered in Norwich Cathedral, 5 January 1893), p. 35: the order is 'chosen so as to work up to a climax of error and absurdity'.

[3] Editors insist that the Syriac and Armenian are independent. Geffcken, *Apologeten*, p. 48 and n. 1, seems aware of this difficulty.

(*b*) Because it is more tactful, Greek worship is more likely to come after Barbarians and before Judaism in an ascending order than between Chaldeans and Egyptians in a descending order.[1]

(*c*) In the Syriac the Egyptians are treated in a digression; note the weak introduction of 12: 1 compared with 4: 1; 8: 1; and 14: 2.

(*d*) Geffcken adduces support for the view that it is possible for an author to consider Egyptians as an adjunct to Greek religion.[2] If so, the original structure was altered by elevating 'Egyptians' to separate status, 'Barbarians' was altered to 'Chaldeans' and, together with 'Greeks', the resulting three parts were subsumed in para. 2 under the circumlocution noted above.

(*e*) The structure of the Greek in para. 13 is awkward. The subject matter is more appropriate to the Greeks than to all three sub-classes; and the surprise of the author is more intelligible if (as in the Syriac) the addressee is identified with the Greeks on an ascending scale. It is best to take para. 13 as a whole as a conclusion to the discussion of the Greeks as the Syriac does.

(*f*) Concerning the introductory descriptions of each group in para. 2 (Syriac and Armenian) which are distributed to appropriate points in the Greek, a case can be made for the priority of either, for in both recensions the result reads well. One possible motive at work could be the desire to avoid, if the Syriac structure be original, the complications of describing in the introduction a two-tiered system in the Greek.

(*g*) If the Greek be original, the tendency of Syriac is to elaborate, but its failure to accept the more elaborate structure of the Greek may create a presumption that the Syriac is closer to the original. That is, the Greek editor, in attempting to shorten the work and in line with the later usual Christian custom, reduced the classifications to three though to keep the substance of the material he had to insert sub-classifications.

Contrary to the general opinion, the possibility of explaining the derivation of a three-part system and the difficulty of accounting for a four-part system suggest that the quadri-

---

[1] Rom. 1: 14 (cf. Col. 3: 11) is evidence that 'Greeks' and 'Barbarians' are not necessarily overlapping categories to a Greek-influenced Christian writer. [2] *Apologeten*, pp. 73–6.

partite is original. The probability is that this apology held Christians to be a fourth race, and only afterwards was it reworked to conform to a later view.[1]

Given the priority of Syriac, there are two possible arrangements: a simple ascending order[2] (with the Egyptians as a digression), in which the Greek position is put, for apologetic reasons, as high as possible; or a double pair—Barbarians + Greeks, Jews + Christians. In either scheme greater closeness and continuity between Jews and the Church is maintained than elsewhere in the literature, and this, as R. Harris pointed out, is the clearest evidence for an early date for the Syriac version.[3]

[1] See Aimé Puech, *Les Apologistes Grecs* (Paris, 1912), p. 38, in support of this conclusion. Cf. v. Dobschütz, *TU*, XI, 1 (1893), 50 n. 1.

[2] Note 3.1 (Syr): 'Let us then begin with the Barbarians, and by degrees we will proceed to the rest of the peoples in order that we may understand which of them hold the truth about God, and which of them error.' The Greek eliminates the idea of order.

[3] *Texts and Studies*, p. 13.

PAUL'S USE OF ΛΑΟΣ

In the New Testament *laos* is used with little unanimity:[1] Luke/Acts prefers the word, John often replaces it with either a more general or a more particular word, Hebrews tends to use it in Old Testament allusions of the people as opposed to the priests, Paul uses it only in recognizable quotations from the Old Testament.[2] For Paul's use we have no control passage where the word is not prejudiced by Old Testament connections. Absence of the word in Pauline composition raises the question of the significance *laos* had for Paul, and whether there is some reason for his holding back from using it independently.[3]

Eleven of the twelve instances in the Pauline literature fall in the major letters: six times in Romans 9–11, twice in Romans 15, twice in 1 Corinthians, once in 2 Corinthians and once in Titus.[4] In at least nine of these instances the context includes references to Gentiles and Jews. Generally we should expect *laos* to be taken over by the Church to apply to itself as the special people of God.[5] That this happened is beyond doubt,

[1] See Strathmann, *TWNT*, iv, 49 f.

[2] Always *laos* is derived from the LXX. In each case the underlying Hebrew is עַם, usually עַמִּי or עַמּוֹ, Yahweh's people (cf. Strathmann, *TWNT*, iv, 29–39; Meyer, *ibid.* pp. 39–49, on the rabbinic literature).

[3] So far as is ascertainable, there is no idiomatic contemporary usage inconsistent with Paul's theology to cause him to avoid *laos*. Paul sometimes does avoid words (e.g. 'kingdom', *logos*, 'wisdom'; see Davies, *Paul*, pp. 36, 172 f.), but on the other hand he does use words which, because of secular or cultic associations, he might be expected to avoid: e.g. παρουσία, σπέρμα, ἐκκλησία. Even an argument from the 'exclusiveness' of λαός is gainsaid by the use of words like περιτομή.

[4] It is not noteworthy that *laos* is missing from 1 and 2 Thess., Philem., and two of the three Pastorals, but one might have expected it in Gal., Col., Eph. and Phil.

[5] Bauer/A–G and Strathmann, *TWNT*, iv, cite Rom. 9: 25 f.; Tit. 2: 14 as well as Acts 15: 14; 18: 10; Heb. 4: 9; 1 Pet. 2: 9 f.; Rev. 18: 4; 21: 3; and Luke 1: 17. In addition Strathmann includes 2 Cor. 6: 16; Heb. 8: 10; 10: 30; 13: 12, though he says on Heb. (p. 54): 'Wenn er das Wort *laos* gebraucht, denkt er zuerst an das Volk Israel.'

but the point we want to raise is whether it had happened already in Paul's writings.

In Romans 10: 21; 11: 1 f., there are three instances of *laos*. In Romans 10: 20 f. Paul uses Isaiah 65: 1 f., a text referring to the Northern Kingdom in which *ethnē* and *laos* stand in synthetic parallelism, to apply to two different groups. The 'ones who do not seek' of Romans 10: 20 are likened to 'those not a nation' ('unwise nation') of *v.* 19, and these are contrasted to Israel in the introduction of *v.* 21. He drives the application of the two verses apart; under the influence of *ethnē* in Isaiah 65: 1 *b* (which he did not quote) Paul applies the ideas of that verse to Gentiles, and *laos* in Isaiah 65: 2 predisposed him to apply that verse to Israel.[1] Paul adds to this *haraz* on obedience an allusion in Romans 11: 1, 2 from Psalm 93: 14 that demonstrates, in the face of Israel's disobedience, that God 'has not rejected his people whom he knew beforehand'. In all three instances *laos* retains its primary reference to historic Israel.

Romans 15: 10 f. are drawn from Deuteronomy 32: 43 and Psalm 116: 1, substantially reproducing the LXX, although the LXX diverges from the harshness of the MT in the first case.[2] The whole of Romans 15: 9–12 is a Pauline *midrash* (quoting from Law, Prophets, and Writings) on the keyword *ethnē*, the purpose being to explain Jew/Gentile relationships. In chapter 5 we have noted how the context linked weak/strong problems with Jew/Gentile relationships, and especially how it was followed by the references to Gentiles as an offering. In this section (14: 1 – 15: 33), the purpose is to restrain Gentiles from asserting a superiority over Jewish Christians.[3] Paul gives his plea additional weight by using the verse from Deuteronomy and retaining the particularist connotation of *laos*. Although the plural *laoi* need not have the same technical sense, it is quite possible that 15: 11 also uses *laos* of Israel. If so, Paul has again taken a sentence in which the two parts are strictly parallel and

---

[1] The LXX translation of a niphal by an aorist, which is followed by Paul, also encourages this distinction.

[2] הַרְנִינוּ גוֹיִם עַמּוֹ (cf. BH, probably עַמּוֹ (אֶת) בַּגּוֹיִם). In the second case *ethnē* again translates גּוֹיִם, while *laos* translates הָאָמִּים. Rom. 15: 11 blurs the parallelism of both LXX and MT.

[3] This might also be the purpose of the difficult phrase in 15: 8: 'Christ became a servant of circumcision...'

has, under the influence of the terms used, pushed them apart to refer to two separate, but related, entities.

1 Corinthians 10: 7 (Exodus 32: 6) clearly applies to the old people (cf. *v.* 18: *Israēl kata sarka*). 1 Corinthians 14: 21, with its allusion to Isaiah 28: 11 f.[1] (and more remotely Deuteronomy 28: 49) is more difficult. In the original context the 'people' are the scoffers in Jerusalem who will be spoken to by the Assyrians with a message of judgment. The point of contact is that in like manner Jews who reject the gospel now are judged by the incomprehensible words of the Holy Spirit.[2] That is, tongues are a sign to unbelievers, not to believers; and *laos* of *v.* 21 is not equivalent to 'believers' of *v.* 22, but rather to 'unbelievers'.[3] Consequently, it is very probable that underlying the quotation is an allusion to Jewish rejection of the gospel in Corinth, so that ἄπιστοι are Jewish unbelievers. Relevant to this is the fact that Isaiah 28–9 was used in the early Church to explain Jew/Gentile relations, with particular reference to the problem of Jewish 'hardness'.[4]

Second Corinthians 6: 16 is concerned with ethical purity, and its antecedents (Leviticus 26: 12; Ezekiel 37: 27) both demonstrate that 'cleanness' and 'holiness' are integral characteristics of the true people.[5] The *midrash* is held together by the idea of 'holiness'[6] and its application (*pesher*) is found in the change of person and number[7] as well as the introductory and

---

[1] The text varies from LXX and MT, but is closer to the latter. Both MT and Paul agree that God is the author of the speaking (*contra* LXX: 'men of strange lips' is the subject).

[2] So Robertson–Plummer, *ICC*, pp. 316 f.; cf. Ellis, *Paul's Use*, p. 108 n. 6; *per contra*, C. H. Dodd, *According to the Scriptures*, p. 83, who finds no contact at all.

[3] On the other hand, ἰδιῶται of *v.* 16 (cf. Bauer/A–G, *s.v.*, 2) are contrasted to ἄπιστοι, but are not yet fully identified with the total Christian community. They are halfway between = proselytes. *Per contra*, Schlier, *TDNT*, III, 215–17.

[4] Dodd, *Scriptures*, p. 84; Lindars, *NT Apologetic*, p. 164 n. 1.

[5] The two passages are the converse of each other; in the one, *laos* is the one chosen people of God who are promised peace, etc. if they remain true, but woe if they depart; in the other, *laos* is the reformulated unity (from Israel and Judah) of the people who look back on trouble and apostasy, and are promised peace in an eschatological time of purity.

[6] Lindars, *NT Apologetic*, pp. 15–17; Ellis, *NTS*, II (1955), 127–35.

[7] Though Paul often does this it is strange that he is not consistent here. In *v.* 17 the verbs are 2nd person plural, the pronouns of 17*b* and 18 are

concluding material (6: 14–16; 7: 1). The basic contrast in 6: 14 ff. is between πιστός and ἄπιστος. We have just seen that in the Corinthian situation there is reason to think that ἄπιστος may refer to Jewish unbelief. It is a striking fact that the distinction in pronouns could agree with this, and that *laos* could be used here, consistently, of the Jews. The section is probably a fragment from an earlier letter, when Jewish opposition was at its height: *vv.* 14–16 are a polemical statement against those of God's people who do not believe, and the reference to *naos* is an application of a Jewish motif to Christians, similar to others we have examined. Verse 16*b* is a quotation which may be used to express Jewish 'advantage'[1] (an advantage which, as 7: 1 shows, is opened up to include Christians). The other quotations which follow, all with a 2nd person plural pronoun, he takes to refer to Christians who are to separate themselves from unbelieving Jews. However, if 'they' are not to be separated from 'you' of the other verses, then this is a case where Paul, under the influence of the 'temple' idea, takes *laos* and applies it to Christians.

Romans 9: 25–9 is a *haraz*, not so much on the word *laos*, as on *huios*. We are primarily interested in the Hosea references,[2] about which three points may be made. (1) Hosea 1 speaks of judgment on Israel and mercy on Judah, although in a day to come the two will be gathered together into a new unity (2: 2). Precisely this train of thought is apparent in Romans 9: 19–24. (2) Hosea 2: 20 ff. is in the context of covenant and response to a call. (3) The oracle in Hosea exalts neither Judah nor Israel at the expense of the other. The summary in Romans 9: 23 f., which is also the introduction to the quotations, emphasizes a

2nd person plural (changed from 3rd person singular) but in 16*b* and 17 the pronouns are 3rd person plural (changed from Lev. 26, but similar to Ezek. 37, though it is more remote). There seems to be an intentional distinction between 2nd person plural and 3rd person plural in Paul's alterations.

[1] ἐν αὐτοῖς...αὐτῶν...αὐτοί would then refer primarily to Jews as αὐτῶν of *v.* 17 manifestly does. If Lev. 26: 11 is the passage quoted, Paul has changed a very natural 2nd person plural to a 3rd person plural. This is difficult, admittedly, when this verse follows so closely after 'We are a temple of the living God', where one would expect a Christian application to follow.

[2] The quotations are tied together by the repetition in Hos. 2: 1 and Isa. 10: 22.

mercy which is contemporaneous with, and related to, election
and rejection. The quotations are bound (ὡς καί) to this summary, particularly to the phrase, 'not only from Jews but also
from Gentiles'.[1] They elucidate this duality in a chiastic
structure where *vv.* 25 f. prove the case about *ethnē* and
vv. 27 ff. about *Ioudaioi*.[2] Paul's use of the quotations exactly
reproduces the argument of Hosea, and though he ends with
what appears to be a strong statement about Israel's unbelief
there is a hopeful note throughout. The possibility of belief
remains open; but Israel has not yet attained the promises
inherent in the Law because it sought them the wrong way.[3]
Laos is used as a point of reference to show how Gentiles can
become incorporated into the people of God: they move from
'not my people' over into the *laos*.[4] The term is not transferred
to the Gentiles or even to the Church as such; it is used in a
universal sense, the point of the whole section being joint
inheritance, with Israel still central.[5]

Titus 2: 14, while consistent with Paul's restriction of *laos* to
quotations, apparently goes beyond his customary use by
quoting the verse in such a way that it applies to Christians
alone, with no underlying continuity with the original people.
There is, however, a slight chance that the second part might
refer to Jewish origin of some Church members, and the first
part to Gentiles, who together combine to make up 'all men'
of 2: 11.[6] However, such a notion is tenuous, and it is likelier

[1] *Contra* Lindars, *NT Apologetic*, who isolates these verses from the context
and turns them into a sectarian proof text with discontinuity as the motive
(p. 242).

[2] So Jeremias, *ZNW*, XLIX (1958), 145–56.

[3] Cf. Rendel Harris, *Testimonies*, II (Cambridge, 1920), 26: *v.* 27 is pro-
Judaic and 'is meant to modify...a current anti-Judaic doctrine'.

[4] That is, a negative condition has been abolished; 'not my people' is
paralleled by 'children of the living God' (cf. 2 Cor. 6: 16).

[5] ἐκεῖ may have a connection with the gathering of the Gentiles to
Jerusalem (so Sanday–Headlam, *ICC, in loc.*; cf. J. Munck, *Christus und Israel*,
p. 58).

[6] If the two parts in parallel combine to make a totality. Some support
for this might be given by the context of Ezek. 37: 23, which speaks of the
two (Judah and Israel) becoming one (cf. above on Paul's use of Isa. 65: 1;
Deut. 32: 43; Ps. 116: 1). In Ps. 130: 8 (the closest antecedent) the specific
'Israel' is replaced by the general ἡμᾶς (possibly a case of drawing back from
identifying the Church with Israel?). Note the suggestions of a close contact
with Judaism and a 'Jewish problem' in 1: 10; 3: 9; 2: 11–12; 3: 3–11.

that here a transposition has been effected from the old people to the new.[1]

There is a fair degree of consistency in Paul's handling of *laos*. He does not use it apart from a quotation, and in the majority of cases he calls to mind a close link with the historic people of God, so that the term is not reapplied to Christians generally or Gentiles particularly.[2] Paul undoubtedly maintained that Church members were God's people, but he has not called the Christian community God's *laos* at the expense of historic Israel. He is reluctant to apply *laos* to Christians alone,[3] although he does show how Christians participate in the standing which being one of the *laos* gives. The associations attached to *laos/Israēl* cannot be sloughed off. If there is a fundamental hermeneutical principle with respect to *laos*, it would seem to be incorporation, and gathering into a unity what was separated and diverse (cf. the olive tree metaphor). In Jesus Christ there is a new universalism, not a bare transposition from Israel to the Church. Where there is a greater tendency to apply *laos* to the Church alone (2 Corinthians 6: 16; Titus 2: 14) it arises out of a polemical situation.

[1] Cf. 1 Pet. 2: 9 f. Strathmann rightly says: 'Abermals einen Schritt weiter geht der 1 Pet., indem er mit dem Titel λαὸς περιούσιος auch die anderen an diesen Stellen genannten Würdebezeichnungen Israels auf die urchristliche Urgemeinde überträgt (2: 9 f.)...' We note also that καινὸς λαός (Barnabas 5.7; 7.5) appears nowhere in the NT.

[2] *Contra* W. Holsten, 'Judenmission und Heidenmission', *Jud*, XIX (1963), 113–26: 'Gott hat aus den ἔθνη einen λαός angenommen. Auf diesen λαός, das neutestamentliche Gottesvolk, werden die Prädikate übertragen, die dem alttestamentlichen λαός eigen sind [citing Tit. 2: 14; 1 Pet. 2: 9 f.]... Neben das alte Israel tritt ein neuer λαός, der nicht auf Abrahams Samen beschränkt ist...In diesem Gottesvolk ist kein Unterschied...'

[3] *Contra* Strathmann, *TWNT*, IV, 53; cf. pp. 56 f.

APPENDIX C

THE SECTS OF JUDAISM AND
'TRUE ISRAEL'

The writings of Palestinian Judaism from the mid-second century B.C. to the late first century A.D. often reflect party points of view.[1] An exclusivist tendency within Judaism nearly always involves the implication that the particular group represented 'Israel'.[2] Redefinition of the term 'Israel', however, goes back at least to the time of the return from exile and probably beyond.[3] As time went on, and under the impulse of the Maccabean struggle, these divisions become sharper, so that, whereas before the majority of Jews were probably agreed upon the constitution of 'Israel', later each party tends to call the other outcast, and to identify itself with the purified remnant.

There is great uncertainty in basic matters of milieu, date, purpose, composition of the writings mentioned below.[4] Entangling the necessarily brief discussion with matters such as these must be avoided in favour of simply assessing how a sect or party thought of itself in terms of the whole in relation to others.

First Maccabees is concerned with the general separation between nationalists and hellenists.[5] The attitude found here is passed on with increasing bitterness to all the successor parties. For our purposes the most important feature of 1 Maccabees is its demonstration of the way a segment of Judaism can be

[1] On the factors giving rise to sects see Marcel Simon, *Les sectes juives au temps de Jésus* (*Mythes et Religions*, XL, Paris, 1960), pp. 18 ff.; R. T. Herford, *Judaism in the NT Period* (London, 1928), ch. 2.

[2] See, e.g., Simon, *Sectes*, p. 8; Mlle Annie Jaubert, *La notion d'alliance dans le judaïsme aux abords de l'ère chrétienne* (*Patristica Sorbonensia*, VI, Paris, 1963), p. 119: 'Qu'un mouvement d'une vitalité religieuse puissante se détachât de la masse du peuple et des chefs de la nation...cette rupture mettait en cause la définition d'Israël...'

[3] So J. Bright, *A History of Israel* (London, 1960), p. 416; cf. pp. 430, 441.

[4] Note with what ease Mlle Jaubert tries to overthrow the usual position on many documents. The opinions expressed in *The Apocrypha and Pseudepigrapha of the OT*, 2 vols. ed. R. H. Charles (Oxford, 1913), still carry weight.

[5] *Jubilees* also falls in this formative period.

sloughed off as no longer belonging to Israel. The association of *ex Israēl* with a term of abuse in many phrases underlines the exclusion which adherence to a wrong point of view brings.[1] By failing to circumcise their children (1: 48; 1: 15) the hellenists completed their own separation from Israel,[2] becoming in the process identified with the Gentiles (chapter 1, especially 1: 15).

A great difference between 1 Maccabees and 2 Maccabees is the individualism of the latter.[3] Opposition is a matter of important individuals only (Simon, Jason, Menelaus, Rhodocus); any following or party is ignored, hence there is no sense of tension between groups in Judaism. The concern in 2, 3 and 4 Maccabees is to present a good face to the world, or to encourage the Jewish community.

The *Psalms of Solomon* have an obviously polemical purpose. The group with whom the author(s) is identified is 'righteous' and 'holy',[4] and his opponents have applied to them terms applicable without distinction to Pompey or to foreign nations. Peculiarly, all the references to Jerusalem (except in Psalm 11) are used *in malam partem* so that there is a contrast between Jerusalem (Sadducee)[5] and Israel (pious sectarians).[6] The exclusive party is called *laos*, 'seed of Abraham', 'house of Israel' (9: 8–11); 'the people of Israel...the house of Jacob' (7: 8–10; cf. also 10: 5–8; ch. 11). In two places the writer slips into the 1st person plural (17: 45; 18: 4) where it becomes clearer

[1] As, e.g., in ἄνομοι καὶ ἀσεβεῖς ἐξ 'Ισραήλ (7: 5); ἐξ 'Ισραήλ υἱοὶ παράνομοι (1: 11); λοιμοὶ ἐξ 'Ισραήλ (10: 61). *Ek* here implies both origin and separation, with more emphasis on the latter.

[2] The use of *Israēl* and *Ioudaios* does not help in this matter. S. Zeitlin's observations are based on an incorrect assumption about the use of the terms in OT (*The First Book of the Maccabees*, New York, 1950, pp. 28 ff.).

[3] Neglected by A. Neuman, *The Second Book of the Maccabees* (New York, 1954), p. viii; and later by S. Zeitlin, *ibid.* pp. 56, 59.

[4] The older unanimity on their identity is being questioned today; see J. O'Dell, 'The Religious Background of the Ps. of Sol.', *RQ*, III (1961–2), 241–58, and literature cited there. On the 'righteous' see D. Hill, 'Δίκαιοι as a Quasi-technical term', *NTS*, XI (1965), 296–302, curiously without reference to *Ps. Sol.*

[5] They are accused of cultic crimes: e.g. 4: 1, 6; 7: 2; 8: 11–13 (cf. 8: 22); 17: 6, 20. The judgments upon such are described in 17: 21–5; 4: 14–22; 2: 4, 16; 5: 8–12.

[6] Some whole psalms are structured to show the antithesis: e.g. 1, 14; cf. 2: 32–7; 3: 9–12; 13: 11–12; 12: 5–6.

than ever that 'we', the party in question, are the first-born only son, the gathered congregation of Israel (συναγωγή 'Ισραήλ, οἶκος 'Ισραήλ, ἐκκλησία λαοῦ). Others have no share in it.

First Enoch 37–71 and 91–104 are the most important sections of that work for our purposes.[1] There is a party, the congregation of the righteous (38: 1), whose appearance as the party of the saints (38: 3; 39: 6 f.; 53: 6; 62: 8) brings with it the judgment of the party of all the sinners (e.g. 41: 7 ff.). This latter group is the party of authority which persecutes the righteous.[2] The polemic of chapters 91–104 is directed against these same people,[3] suggesting a period when separation from them was becoming a reality (e.g. 91: 4; 94: 1–5; 97: 4). In the Apocalypse of Weeks (chapters 93, 91) the seventh week is a transition between the first six (the past) and the clearly future: it represents the present period.[4] The 'apostate generation' is, therefore, the hellenizing Sadducaic party, while the righteous (93: 10) represents the party of the author which shall, in a near Messianic period (the eighth week; 91: 12), be predominant and be vindicated. The exact relationship of each party to Israel is not stated explicitly.

The Testaments of the Twelve Patriarchs[5] contains material that must belong to the first century B.C.[6] In this material polemic leads to judgment and a break with Israel. Some Testaments,

---

[1] Cf. also 1: 1, probably by the same author (final editor?); and also 5: 4 ff., a part of the same introduction.

[2] 'Kings and mighty' often, but not always, alludes to rulers and Sadducees, 46: 4; 48: 8; 53: 5; 54: 2; 55: 4; 62: 3, 6; 63: 1.

[3] Note 98: 15; 104: 10; and especially 99: 2: 'transform themselves into what they were not', i.e. the removal of circumcision (cf. 1 Macc. 1: 15, 48; *Assumption of Moses*, 8: 3; Josephus, *Ant.* 12.5.1.

[4] *Contra* Charles, *in loc.*; and Miss J. P. Thorndike, 'The Apocalypse of Weeks and the Qumran Sect', *RQ*, III (1961), 163–84, who tries to make the 7 weeks = 49 years in the history of the sect.

[5] Among more recent literature see M. de Jonge, *Testaments of the Twelve Patriarchs* (Assen, 1953); the review by H. F. D. Sparks, *JTS*, n.s. VI (1955), 287–90; M. de Jonge, *NT*, IV (1960), 182–235; *NT*, V (1962), 311–19; Bickerman, *JBL*, LXIX (1950), 245–60; J. T. Milik, *Ten Years of Discovery in the Wilderness of Judaea* (*SBT*, XXVI, London, 1959), pp. 34 f.; Braun, *RB*, LXVII (1960), 516–49.

[6] This can be isolated by polemical content, allusions, and also by the introductory formula. The material so isolated corresponds closely to the type found in the *Ps. Sol.* (i.e. *TReub* 6; *TLev* 4: 1; 10; 14–16; 18: 9; *TJud* 17; 21–3; *TZeb* 9; *TDan* 5; 7; *TNaph* 4; *TGad* 8; *TAsh* 7).

however, in spite of the polemizing, end on a very hopeful note (e.g. *TLev* 16: 1; *TJud* 23: 5; *TNaph* 4; *TAsh* 7) and it seems that the tribe, or part of it, will be included in Israel again. Others preclude any return (e.g. *TZeb* 9: 9, cf. 9: 7; *TDan* 7: 3, cf. 5: 9; *TGad* 8) and the tribe seems to be left outside Israel. There is some distinction, apparently, between one group of tribes and another, but the important principle is that the persons against whom the polemic is addressed in some cases retain the possibility of returning to the fold of Israel.[1]

The *Assumption of Moses* includes an 'historical' section, part of which (chapters 6–8) is of interest. Chapter 5 includes references to Jason and Menelaus and the hellenizers; 6: 1 to the later Maccabean period; 6: 2 ff. to Herod; and 6: 8 f. carries the reader to 4 B.C. The author's own days are introduced (7: 1) with a polemic against those who do not think as he does. Chapters 8–9 may properly follow after chapter 7.[2] The judgment of chapter 9 will fall upon those opponents, while the faithful who withdraw (9: 6) will be blessed greatly and avenged (10). It is these who appear to be called Israel in 10: 8.

In each case where one party's opinion is set over against the rest of Judaism it tends to claim that it is Israel, though there are many variations in the measure of exclusiveness and of the hope for others' salvation.

QUMRAN

In the Qumran literature we stand on much the same ground, but the fullness of the evidence allows greater precision. As both A. Jaubert[3] and K. Baltzer[4] make clear, the covenant is

---

[1] We might also mention the curious *Joseph and Asenath* which, though probably a hellenistic Jewish writing from Leontopolis, is concerned with inter-tribal relationships. As with *Test. XII*, it exalts Levi (for a different purpose) and it distinguishes between one group of tribes and another, though not the same ones.

[2] *Contra* Charles, who places them before ch. 6 to refer to Antiochus Epiphanes. The 'second visitation' and the 'second course' (7: 1, 2; 8: 1; 9: 2) may refer to the present problems, which are similar to the earlier ones under Antiochus, on the principle that the former events are normative for the description of later ones.   [3] *Notion d'Alliance*, pp. 116 ff.

[4] *Das Bundesformular* (*WMANT*, iv, Neukirchen, 1960). He shows the relationship between the covenant and treaty forms of the Near East and those of the OT, Qumran, and the Jewish Christian literature (Barnabas, *Didache*, *2 Clement*, *Jubilees*).

basic to the self-understanding of these Palestinian sectaries. In presenting the meaning of the covenant the community comes to identify itself with 'true' Israel.[1] However, since these writings are disseminated internally only, the question of how Qumran relates to the rest of Judaism is not often dealt with openly. The relationship is usually assumed.

Its exclusiveness needs little documentation.[2] The writings show a sectarian preoccupation which can be interpreted only in terms of a self-contained group. The constant demand to separate (mostly בדל), is in terms not just of foreign nations (כתיים and גוים) but of all fellow Jews who do not follow the rule (סרך) of the community, and especially from any who have abandoned the community.[3] Everyone must choose to join this exclusive body (e.g. 1QS 1: 7 ff., CD 15: 5 f.), even members' children, though anyone who wants to enter the fellowship may do so. Voluntary adhesion to the sect raises the question of their attitude to proselytizing. There is little evidence for 'proclamation'; probably it saw its 'mission' as long-range;[4] that is, to act as leaven for the whole of Israel and to be the nucleus around which Israel would be reconstituted in the last days. This gives rise to a separation different from that of the Christian community. For the Qumranite everything outside his fellowship was 'leprous'; for the Christian, nothing was unclean and nobody needed to be avoided, whether prostitutes, *goyim*, or Samaritans; all came in contact with the gospel at an early stage.

In Qumran, polemic is widespread as a result of its different

---

[1] The distinction between themselves and the rest has eschatological significance; see K. Stendahl, *The Scrolls and the NT* (London, 1958), pp. 6 ff.; L. Mowry, *The DSS and the Early Church* (Chicago, 1962), p. 37.

[2] The most readily available pointed text, with German translation, is *Die Texte aus Qumran*, hrsg. E. Lohse (Darmstadt, 1964).

[3] Cf. J. Jeremias, *ExT*, LXX (1958–9), 68 f. The separation is predicated upon the issue of uncleanness (1QS 3: 1–6; 5: 13; 1QM 7: 4 ff.), a metaphorical leprosy.

[4] Note atoning for the sin of the earth (1QS 8: 6, 10; 9: 4; 5: 6) and the open call to procure pardon for transgressions, obtain atonement, and abandon uncleanness (1QS 3: 6–12). There is some hope that this will happen (e.g. 1QH 6: 5 ff.), but the greatest hope is that the time of wickedness is temporary only (CD 6: 10; 13: 20; cf. 4QpNah 3: 5; 1QSa 1: 1 ff.).

kind of exclusiveness;[1] quite violent passages are found in pious thanksgiving hymns, in sectarian documents of practice and teaching, and in biblical commentaries. The impetus towards a harsh attitude is, at the periods represented by most of the documents, pervasive and uncompromising. Polemic is ingrained into the Qumran community.[2] It is addressed in the first instance towards those who do not choose to follow the Way (1QS 9: 17; 10: 19–21), but special vituperation is reserved for those who knew the Way and then forsook it.[3] Some passages in 1QH involve more personal polemic, addressed towards a particular group or an individual well known to the sect, quite possibly responsible for the original persecution of the Teacher. There is presupposed a group of related historical events in which there is a community of interest against the Teacher and his group (e.g. CD 20: 22; 4QpIsa[b,c]; 4QpHos[a]; CD 5: 6 ff.; 6: 1). Within the vocabulary of polemic there are three basic ideas; the falseness of the opponents, their deviation, and their control by Belial.[4]

Nevertheless, in spite of the fact that its opponents were within Judaism, Qumran was at pains to emphasize its continuity with Israel. When compared with early Christianity there is not the same emphasis on 'newness', rather a heavy emphasis on the continuing aspects of the old 'eternal' covenant which only Qumran properly keeps. Its attitude to the rank and file of Israel appears to be moderate; anyone may join the

[1] Contrast the NT's few real polemical passages; second century A.D. Christianity is more similar (e.g. Barnabas). There is some evidence that at some stage (or in some types of literature) there is little sectarian bias in Qumran, and little polemic; e.g. 1QM (see M. H. Segal, *Scripta Hierosolymitana*, IV, Jerusalem, 1958, 140, 141; O. Betz, *Interpreter's Dictionary of the Bible*, I, 799 b) and 4QDibHam (cf. M. Baillet, *RB*, LXVIII, 1961, 195–250).

[2] E. F. Sutcliffe, 'Hatred at Qumran', *RQ*, II (1960), 345–56, attempts to minimize this.

[3] It is not always clear when 'forsaking' refers to abandonment of the Mosaic law (e.g. 4QpHos[b]) and when to deviation from the sect's rule by initiated members (cf. CD 1: 13 ff.). See M. Mansoor, *The Thanksgiving Hymns* (Leiden, 1961), pp. 136 n. 2; 137 n. 1; Holm-Nielsen, *Hodayoth* (Aarhus, 1960), p. 106 n. 17.

[4] On this in 1QH see Mansoor, *Hymns*, p. 51; Holm-Nielsen, *Hodayoth*, p. 292; and in 1QM see Y. Yadin, *The Scroll of War* (Oxford, 1962), pp. 232 ff.

community from out of Israel.[1] Conversely, Qumran accepts responsibility for the sin of the children of Israel (1QSa 1: 3 ff.) and confesses that sin (1QS 1: 21 – 2: 1; cf. CD 1: 3–8).[2] In CD 16: 1 ff. the covenant, made with all Israel, is related to the idea that Israel's apostasy is only for a time, after which Israel will return to the Law of Moses. During the period of Belial's reign there remains a remnant of God's people who maintain the one eternal covenant (e.g. 1QM 14: 4 ff.; 13: 7 ff.). Later, God will raise up more survivors, and show his mercy by including many within his inheritance.[3]

One aspect of the question of continuity with Judaism is Qumran's relationship to the temple sacrifices in Jerusalem.[4] There are two passages in the Qumran literature: 1QS 9: 3–5 and 1QM 2: 5–6, the latter passage being dependent upon the former. The sect wants to abrogate sacrifices on the one hand but affirms the validity of sacrifice under proper conditions of ritual purity on the other. This could not obtain at the time, but Qumran's continuity with Israel is sufficiently strong that these cultic rites must be re-established later as a part of the eternal and unbreakable covenant established by God.[5]

'Newness' is another important indication of the relationship of Qumran to the remainder of Israel. There are two varieties:

[1] Note, 1QSa 1: 6; 1QS 6: 13 f.; 8: 5 f., omitting those ritually unclean such as lepers; cf. Wernberg-Møller, *The Manual of Discipline* (Leiden, 1957), p. 106 n. 40; p. 122 n. 1; and pp. 124 f. nn. 12, 14, 15.

[2] See M. Weise, *Kultzeiten und kultischer Bundesschluß in der Ordensregel vom toten Meer* (Leiden, 1961), pp. 61–112 on 1QS 1: 18*b* – 2: 18; particularly pp. 77–9 on the confession of sin.

[3] 1QH 6: 5–13; cf. 1Q 34 *bis*; 1Q 28b; and, especially important, 4QDibHam, for which see M. Baillet, *RB*, LXVIII (1961), 195–250.

[4] See, with reference to Josephus and Philo, D. H. Wallace, *TZ*, XIII (1957), 335–8, who accepts the negative in Josephus' text, so that it agrees with Philo. H. H. Rowley, *BJRL*, XLIV (1961), 119–56 (esp. pp. 131 f.), agrees that 'the Jerusalem priesthood was not recognized by the sectaries as legitimate, and on this account they had nothing to do with the Temple or its sacrifices'. M. Black, *The Scrolls and Christian Origins* (London, 1961), p. 40, rejects the negative in Josephus and claims that they offered their own sacrifices in a separate part of the Temple 'without contaminating contact with others' (cf. Josephus, *BJ*, 5.4.2).

[5] So Carmignac, *RB*, LXIII (1956), 524–32. Milik adds in a postscript that further evidence (4QS^d) confirms the view that sacrifices are effective, and he takes Carmignac's view to be certain. Cf. also F. F. Bruce, *NTS*, II (1955–6), 176–90.

'new covenant' and 'new creation', and possibly 'new Jerusalem'.[1] Erik Sjöberg has treated the question of 'new creation'
in two articles, in the second of which, on Qumran proper (re
1QH 11: 13 and 13: 12) he says: 'Es handelt sich also um die
Neuschöpfung beim Eintritt in die Sekte, nicht um die ursprüng-
liche Schöpfung des Menschen...Aus dieser schwachen und
sündigen Existenz wird der Mensch durch den Eintritt in die
Sekte und die dadurch geschehene Neuschöpfung erlöst...Ihr
[i.e. 1QH] eigentliches Thema ist die Schwachheit des natür-
lichen Menschen und die Erneuerung durch die Gnade
Gottes.'[2] It is not certain that such a personal and individual
interpretation of both passages as Sjöberg calls for can be
pressed.[3] It is possible that 1QH 13: 12 refers to the rabbinic
creatio continua,[4] or to the 'new world which God is on the point
of creating'.[5] 1QH 11: 13 may speak of the 'new creation' on
entry into the sect, but even here the clause is ambiguous, for
the conjectured נהיה, if it be correct,[6] implies a wider event
than individual admission. It is better to interpret both passages
eschatologically, of God's act in creating the 'new Jerusalem'
when pure sacrifices will again be offered.[7] The phrase in
1QH 13: 12 is quite consistent with this, as is the 'new Jerusalem' concept with its futurist connotations.

The two 'new creation' passages were both in the *Hymns*; the
'new covenant' passages fall in other writings.[8] In 1Q 28[b] the
faithful members of Qumran are called an eternal covenant.[9]
God's blessing is sought upon the priests of the community, that

[1] In none of the fragments of the work given that name (1Q 32; 2Q 24;
5Q 15; unpublished fragments from 4Q and 11Q) does חדש appear. Cf. also
1QM 12: 12–13 = 19: 5–8: the eschatological praise to Zion, Jerusalem and
the cities of Judah. We may omit 1QS 10: 4.

[2] *StTh*, IV (1950), 44–85 and *StTh*, IX (1956), 131–6. The quotation is
from p. 135.

[3] T. Gaster, *The Scriptures of the Dead Sea Sect* (London, 1957), p. 214 n. 4,
takes one in this way.   [4] *Ibid.* p. 215 n. 3.

[5] So Holm-Nielsen, *Hodayoth*, p. 213, cf. p. 187.

[6] See Holm-Nielsen and Mansoor, *in loc.*

[7] Cf. Black, *Scrolls*, pp. 136, 139, on 1QS 4: 21; K. H. Schelkle, *Die
Gemeinde von Qumran und die Kirche des NT* (Düsseldorf, 1960), pp. 65 f.

[8] 1Q 28[b] (at 3: 26; 5: 21; 5: 5); 1Q 34³ (2: 6); 1QpHab 2: 3 (though the
noun is uncertain); CD 6: 19; 8: 21 = 19: 34 (B); 20: 12. The first two
documents use only the verb 'renew', the second two only the adjective.

[9] לברית עולם, 1: 2–3; cf. 2: 2–5, apparently of the High Priest.

he may renew for them the covenant of the everlasting priest-hood (וברית כהונת עולם יחדש, 3: 26), and also upon the Prince of the Congregation, that God may renew for him the covenant of the community so that his people's kingdom may be established for ever (וברית ה[י]חד יחדש לו להקים מלכות עמו לעול[ם], 5: 21). The sect is in a direct line with the old, now impure, priesthood; in the Messianic age to come the priesthood and kingdom of God will be established for ever in the Holy City through the congregation of the faithful. 1QS 4 corresponds to this looking ahead for the establishing of the 'new'. God has chosen the sect for an eternal covenant (4: 22) though there is an interval in the present until the making of the New (4: 25). Different is the verbal form in 1Q 34, fragment 3, 2: 5–6. The context recalls the sect's (new) covenant on becoming a separate entity. It is an historical and not an eschatological reference, intermediate between the concern with the 'renewal' of the old covenant and other passages which emphasize the 'newness' of the sect's covenant. This 'new covenant in Damascus' implies a fresh start, a new event in God's plan for Israel,[1] the name of the place itself emphasizing the discontinuity with the old covenant. The importance of the new covenant is seen most clearly in the fact that to forsake the new covenant is tantamount to abandoning one's place in Israel.[2] It is striking that there is a shift of emphasis from one document to the other. There is no single view concerning the place of Qumran's covenant vis-à-vis the Mosaic covenant. All agree that there is a new element to the covenant, but some understand the 'newness' to have been ushered in from the time of the Teacher, and others think of the 'newness' as not operating until the victory over the sons of darkness.

There are many proper names having a special significance in Israel which might be reapplied profitably by the new Sect.[3] The most relevant is of course 'Israel', which is used exten-sively.[4] Its simplest usage is historical or nominal or geographical, usually quite easily discerned. It is also apparent that 'Israel'

---

[1] הברית החדשה בארץ דמשק, CD 6: 19; 8: 21 = 19: 34; cf. 20: 12. The text is from Rabin, *The Zadokite Document* (Oxford, 1954), *in loc.*

[2] CD 19: 34–5 B; cf. also 1QpHab 2: 3 (on Hab. 1: 5); CD 20: 10 B; 20: 13 B.

[3] See J. Amoussine, *RQ*, IV (1963), 389–96, on Ephraim and Manasseh.

[4] Kuhn, *Konkordanz zu den Qumrantexten* (Göttingen, 1960), for references.

applies to the sect generally, mostly in CD and 1QS.[1] There is a yet more specific application of 'Israel' to the laity, as distinct from the priestly class.[2] 'Israel' can also carry eschatological weight, but it is difficult to determine whether it refers to the full Israel to be regathered at the end, or the extension of the sect itself in the Messianic age.[3]

The uses of 'Judah' cover the same range as 'Israel'. It is used historically, geographically and with eschatological overtones. On the one hand the *Damascus Document* uses 'Judah' with a polemic force,[4] while on the other hand 1QpHab (8: 1); 1QM (1: 2); 4QPB (1) refer 'Judah' to the sect itself. 'Benjamin' also appears to be a self-designation of the sect (1QM 1: 2), although structurally the Hebrew is ambiguous.[5]

By contrast 'Levi' and 'Levites' nearly always refer to one class within Qumran. The words can have an historical significance but never, in spite of Levi's identification with the Temple, a polemical force. Like 'Levi', 'Aaron' is used almost exclusively of the sect. 'Israel' and 'Aaron' are often closely linked,[6] sometimes drawing a distinction between priests and laity. It is used of the priests of the sect alone (CD 10: 5; 1QSa 1: 16, 23; 2: 13) or generally of the sect (CD 12: 23; 14: 19; 1QS 5: 21; 9: 7); but always it emphasizes either the priestly caste within Qumran or the priestly character of the community.

'Damascus', used only in CD,[7] is always used *in bonam partem*: it is the place, metaphorical or literal,[8] to which the

---

[1] 1QS 2: 22; 5: 5; 5: 22 (?) (cf. Mansoor, *Hymns*, p. 56 n. 54; p. 93 n. 25); 1QSa 1: 14, 20 (cf. 1: 1); 2: 12; 4QpIsa^a c. 3 (?); 4QpIsa^d 1: 1; 4QPB 1: 3 (?); CD 1: 5, 7; 3: 13; 6: 2; 10: 5 (?); 12: 8, 19, 22; 13: 1; 15: 5.

[2] This is clear from 1QS 5: 6; 8: 4–13; 9: 6–11 (cf. Mansoor, *Hymns*, pp. 94, 124, 133 f.); CD 10: 5 (?); 14: 4, 5, 19; 16: 14; 20: 1. Cf. Milik, *Ten Years*, pp. 99 f., particularly n. 2.

[3] Cf. 1QM 2: 9; 3: 12, 13; 5: 1; 10: 3, 9; 11: 6, 7; 12: 15; 15: 1; 17: 7, 8; 19: 8; 1QSa 1: 1 (?); 2: 12, 14, 20 (?); 1Q29 3: 2; 4QpIsa^d 1: 1, 7; 4QpPs37 2: 1, 11, 12; 4QF 1: 4; CD 4: 4.

[4] CD 4: 11 (4: 3?); 8: 3; 20: 27; *contra* Rabin, *Zadokite Document*, p. 15.

[5] For a discussion see J. van der Ploeg, *Le Rouleau de la Guerre* (Leiden, 1959), pp. 57 f.

[6] CD 1: 7; 6: 2; 19: 11; 20: 1; 1QS 5: 6; 8: 6, 9; 9: 6, 11.

[7] Geographically in 6: 5; 7: 15; 7: 19; connected with the new covenant in 6: 19; 8: 21 = 19: 34; 20: 12.

[8] Cf. H. H. Rowley, *The Zadokite Fragments and the DSS* (Oxford, 1952), pp. 75 ff.

Qumran community once went. In contrast to this, 'Jerusalem', as the place from which they came, is used *in malam partem* in many instances,[1] in others geographically. To leave behind 'Jerusalem' and embrace the hated name 'Damascus' is an unexpected reversal. This radical contrast however is never explicit in any writing; it represents two strains of thought within Qumran which are not worked out consistently. Two other place names, 'Ephraim' and 'Manasseh', are used cryptically. Some instances are important.[2] In 4QpNah 1:12 only the last four letters of Ephraim are visible, but the reconstruction is convincing. The context is that God is going to destroy the Lion of Wrath (1:5 f.) and those who follow him: the seekers-after-smooth-things (1:2, 7) and the priests of Jerusalem (1:11). Ephraim is related to this group of evil-doers. In 4QpPs37 E.3, both Manasseh and Ephraim are mentioned as lying behind the quotation of Psalm 37:14, and both carry a heavy weight of ill favour. This is reinforced by the publication of more pieces of 4QpNah (cols. 2–4)[3] where both Ephraim and Manasseh reappear a number of times. The evil deeds of seekers-after-smooth things will be revealed to all Israel and they will recognize that they have ruined Judah's glory (3:3 f.). The result will be that the 'simple ones of Ephraim will flee from the midst of their assembly and forsake those who misled them and join themselves to Israel' (3:5). The concern then shifts to Manasseh (3:9) to whom the House of Peleg[4] has joined itself (4:1). The identification of Ephraim with the Pharisees makes sense of the treatment in 4QpNah and 4QpPs37 (and possibly for 4QpHos[a]) and the identification of Manasseh with the Sadducees is not too far-fetched for 4QpNah.[5]

The lessons to be learned from this material, in connection with 'true Israel', are the following: (*a*) increased exclusiveness, with a corresponding measure of polemic, leads, by the nature

---

[1] 1QpHab 9:4; 12:7; 4QpIsa[b] 2:7, 10; 4QpIsa[c] 11; 4QpNah 1:11; these are all *pesharim*, which have a tendency to increased polemic.

[2] See J. M. Allegro, *JBL*, LXXV (1956), 89–95.

[3] J. M. Allegro, *JSS*, VII (1962), 304–8.

[4] Allegro, *ibid.* p. 308: 'being those who "went out from the Holy City" but later caused dissension among the people...'.

[5] So Amoussine, *RQ*, IV (1963), 389–96; he thinks the sect distinguishes within the Jewish people Judah, Ephraim, Manasseh, and Israel. This is only partially true, for both 'Judah' and 'Israel' are equivocal.

of polemic, to a denial of others' right to a status which both claim. This can be seen most clearly in the *pesharim* and their use of Israel's special nomenclature to apply to both themselves and their opponents. However, there is no complete consistency in the application of special names to the sect.

(*b*) The use of abusive epithets leads to an identification of Jewish opponents with non-Jewish opponents, effectively barring them from a share in Israel.

(*c*) Polemic is not solely a function of growing time-gap from the point of separation, important as that may be. It is possible for a more moderate approach to be expressed either in the early stages or because of later changed conditions.

(*d*) Positively, the exclusion of opponents encourages the identification of the particular sect as alone 'holy'; the growing awareness of separateness, and *ipso facto* of holiness, is a factor in the fuller application of all the special titles to the sect.

(*e*) There is, therefore, a clear tendency to name themselves 'Israel' and to deny that name to others, on the remnant principle grounded in the covenant. Within Qumran, particularly in the literature connected with the 'Rule' (1QS, 1QSa, CD), there is a still more restrictive principle at work limiting particular titles ('Levi', 'Aaron', 'Israel') to parts of the structure of the sect. This move appears never to have been considered in Christianity.

(*f*) In none of this literature is there the additional problem created by Christianity's drawing in Gentiles to all the privileges and responsibilities of the People of God. No assistance in assessing this facet of the Church's apologetic can be found in any of the Palestinian Jewish writings.

I. INDEX OF PASSAGES QUOTED

A. THE OLD TESTAMENT

229

B. NEW TESTAMENT

D. APOCRYPHA AND PSEUDEPIGRAPHA

F. OTHER ANCIENT AUTHORS

II. INDEX OF GREEK WORDS
(SELECTED)

III. INDEX OF AUTHORS

IV. INDEX OF SUBJECTS